Local Government: Management and Corporate Planning

Local Government: Management and Corporate Planning

TONY EDDISON
Institute of Local Government Studies
University of Birmingham

LEONARD HILL BOOKS AN INTERTEXT PUBLISHER

Published by
Leonard Hill Books
a division of
International Textbook Company Limited
24 Market Square, Aylesbury, Bucks.

First published 1973

ISBN 0 249 44113 6

Jacket design based on an idea by Tony Eddison, showing a plan of Nagarjunakonda, *circa* 300 B.C.

Printed in Great Britain by
Clarke, Doble & Brendon Ltd
Plymouth

TO MARGARET

Contents

Acknowledgements

To the institution, INLOGOV, I owe a great debt to Henry Maddick for his part in setting it up in the first place, to my colleagues for their commitment and dedication to the development of its work, to the local government officers and other students who have formed the vital part to an exciting interface between practice and teaching. I also owe thanks to the many students of other institutions, especially the many planning schools I have visited, for their part in stimulating the development of my thoughts.

For permission to use material I want to thank all the local authorities and the officers concerned, of which there are many. It is a measure mostly of the degree of commitment to change which now resides in local government.

For typing the various drafts and struggling with my writing I owe a debt to Miss Heather Mears and Mrs Joan Jones. I am equally grateful to Mrs. Gael Heller for proof reading and indexing.

Thanks are *not* extended to my colleague John Stewart because they would be a totally inadequate expression for a truly great inspiration. Those words do not spring from a feeling of final relief because the book is finished but from a sure knowledge that the book is simply a by-product from John's continuing inspiration to me. Local government is very fortunate in having captured his undying interest.

My wife Margaret and our two children Simon and Jane, have made it possible by missing holidays, days out and many other things. They regard me as the "Billy Liar" of the family especially when I set out to design a dust-jacket before writing a word of the text! I am convinced they will be shocked to discover that the book actually exists anywhere but in my imagination. To have them I am a very lucky man.

Acknowledgements

[illegible]

Introduction

This book is intended for all those concerned or interested in the shaping, implementation, control and effects of the policies of local governments. This means not only those people who are professionally and politically involved but, equally important, the consumer as well. Most of the examples and cases are from British sources, but they serve largely to sharpen up underlying principles which are of much wider application.

Over the last few years, it has slowly, but ever so slowly, been borne in on me that whilst the boundary to my professional field has been a strength in many ways, it represents at the same time a great weakness. Town planning has, until recently, been seen in isolation from other kinds of planning whereas it can only really begin to take on a purposeful meaning when seen in relation to the other parts of a much more complex system. It is the inter-connectedness of things or rather the understanding of the inter-connectedness of things that holds out exciting prospects. I have been working over recent years with approaching seven hundred people from a wide variety of professions; accountants, engineers, solicitors, social workers, doctors, architects, educationalists and others. They were everyone of them concerned with planning and they were the people who shook me into realising that planning, as discussed in this book, cannot be the province of just one profession or discipline. We are concerned here with the boundaries of professions not their central parts. The concern is perhaps for what they all lack—a realisation and then an understanding of their inter-connectedness in a common cause.

This then is not an instruction manual nor yet is it divorced from practice. The object has been to relate theory to practice, to discuss ideas in their practical context. For those with a concern for the real purposes of local government, for those keen to steer rather than control, I hope it will be a stimulus to new approaches, an agent for change, not for change's sake but as a means of improving local government's contribution to the way society operates.

I frankly don't like compartmentalising and dividing a book up into chapters for me is difficult because almost all the parts are inter-dependent. Again it is the inter-connectedness of things. Nevertheless I have succumbed to the convention (despite a strong yearning to abolish even the paragraph!). There is a rationale behind the ordering of the subject matter and lest it escapes the reader I had better establish it at the outset.

The approach has been firstly to set a working context for local government, to advance a view of its role in society. Granted that role the case for corporate planning in local government has been made. It is against that background that the nature of the planning process has been discussed as a means of laying a base for the consideration of different approaches to that process and the relationships between them. It is at this point that the problems at the interface between community and authority are raised—the issue of public involvement in public policymaking.

Problems of organisational design have been treated only after an analysis and discussion of the processes the new structures are expected to sustain and to adapt to. There follows some speculation about emerging characteristics of new planning processes and organisations and a consideration of general and more specific ways in which change may be approached and introduced.

If the book has a ring of optimism that is because I am an optimist. If the optimism seems at points, if not throughout, to have pushed out the nuts and bolts, the rules and the instructions, then the reader should take a deep gulp of the optimism and turn to the Epilogue.

1
Local Government – A Working Context

One of the express purposes of this book is to stimulate change in the way local government operates, in the approaches it brings to bear on carrying out its task. The intention is to bring together a series of ideas and developments, not so that a solution may be prescribed for local government's problems, but so that those people in practice who are aware of the possibilities may build on, may adapt or draw on the ideas here presented to improve local government's effectiveness.

AN 'AGENCY' OR 'INITIATIVE' ROLE?

Underlying this purpose is an assumption (or maybe a philosophy) which is possibly unpalatable to many but which needs elaborating at the outset. It concerns the role of local government in society. There can be no dispute that the *effect* of local government (and other levels and scales of government also) is intervention, intervention in the sense that it causes things to happen which may not otherwise happen or, on the other hand, prevents things happening which may otherwise happen. Thus we compel people to send their children to school, we prevent smoke emissions, we exercise influence on what a man may do on his own land. Almost everything a local authority does impinges in some way on the 'freedom' of the individual or groups of individuals. The great philosophical and political debate centres on the extent of intervention. It only rarely throws up the complete non-interventionist argument. The very moment we accept local government as an institution we accept the fact that its *effect* will be intervention in the 'natural' order of things. The issue, then, is not whether or not local government should intervene—its very existence ensures that, but the degree to which it should intervene.

Its development in Britain, at least in the last 150 years, has derived substantially from a societal concern to remedy certain public health 'evils'. Indeed, many of the early developments in modern British local government can be traced to the public health field—the 1835 powers to pave and clean streets, the subsequent 'sanitary' powers through the second half of the last century, which were bestowed on both urban and rural authorities. Many of the present housing and National Health provisions have their origins in the public health concern of the last century and the housing function is still heavily influenced by public health legislation.

The interesting feature of this tremendous stream of legislation is that it, perhaps fortuitously, determined the role of local government in society. It was a role which can best be described as an 'agency' role, that is to say, local government had imposed upon it certain obligations which Parliament prescribed. In other words, local authorities were seen substantially as convenient instruments for implementing the will of national government.

"The local administration of public services is essential; that the local organs of administration should be democratically elected bodies is not. Nevertheless our view is that although certain services may be provided locally by outposts of central government, or by *ad hoc* bodies appointed by it, democratic local self-government is an essential institution and that where functions, present or future, can be performed by local authorities, they should be performed by them. Although local authorities are elected bodies they have to operate within the framework of the constitution in which sovereignty lies in Parliament. In this respect English local authorities are in the same position as those in other countries whose practices we have examined. But our review of local government administration at home and abroad in Chapter 2 shows that, despite the sovereignty of the legislatures and the overall responsibility of central government, local authorities in those countries with the exception of Eire enjoy wider discretion than our own.

"Local authorities occupy a wide range of subsidiary or dependent positions in relation to Parliament and the central government. Even where a local authority has legal independence of action, it owes it to statute, and in any case is likely to be dependent on the central government for finance. It would be wrong to say that local authorities have no life other than that which Parliament breathes into them; but they have no purpose other than that which Parliament allows." (1.1)

This view of the role of local government does not admit of a great deal of initiative. Granted that local government exists, its role can be seen anywhere along the scale extending from 'agency' to 'initiating'. History has put the emphasis on the 'agency' function. Since the second world war, there has been a shift, however, and nowhere is it better seen perhaps than in the Education Act 1944, but even more especially in the several Town and Country Planning Acts from 1947 onwards. These Acts were not the *first* to to give scope for initiative to local government but they had the distinction of almost encouraging initiative and moreover, in two areas of major concern, education and town planning. It is true that central government has often reacted nervously to some of the initiatives taken, especially in the Education field and has on many occasions gone to great lengths to crush initiatives, even when they were being exercised by a local authority of the same political persuasion. The initiatives taken by Hertfordshire County Council to ensure the provision of nursery education in Hertfordshire despite the wishes of the government of the day are well documented (1.2) (as well as being an object lesson in initiative). The more recent initiatives being taken to circumvent the provisions of the Education (Milk) Act, 1971, are another example even though they were perhaps more politically motivated.

In the Town Planning field the County Boroughs and County Councils were specifically charged with the task of preparing a plan 'indicating the manner in which the local planning authority propose that land in their area should be used' (1.3). Here was an opportunity for local authorities to prescribe the future physical shape of their areas, to control the use of land and to plan for as far as twenty years ahead. Admittedly, the plans were subject to central government approval but in essence it presented an opportunity for local government to exercise initiative itself and subsequently to defend it.

This is not the place to debate the advantages and disadvantages of varying degrees of local autonomy. From a planning point of view the significant feature is that in practice there is no *fixed* degree of autonomy. It is neither free nor rigidly controlled. Where the emphasis actually lies is difficult to say and it probably varies over quite short periods of time, it depends very much on the attitude (not just political) of the local authority of the day but the Local Government Bill, 1971, seems to have about it a shift towards bestowing scope for greater initiative on local government. A liberal and unvarnished expression of this kind of emphasis was given in his Memorandum of Dissent by Derek Senior :

"Local government has a general responsibility for the well-being of the communities it represents : its concern is not confined to the discharge of the duties imposed on it by Parliament. It must seek to promote community well-being in all its aspects—economic as well as social, cultural as well as physical—whether or not it has a statutory duty in relation to any particular aspect. And in discharging its statutory duties it must put the general well-being of the local community before the sectional interest of the central government department that is nationally responsible for the function concerned." (1.4)

The underlying assumption in what follows is that what Derek Senior says should be a working basis for local government's operation, largely because it represents a purposeful orientation, an optimistic outlook, which is what local government can be said to have lacked in the past.

LOCAL GOVERNMENT AND THE URBAN SYSTEM

One's view of local government, at least for those inside it, both professionally and politically, will vary according to the profession, department, committee or political party to which one belongs. An engineer is daily confronted with the problems arising from the highway network, the sewerage system, maybe street lighting or flood prevention. Similarly the education officer is concerned with problems and issues specific to his field and so one could go on right through all departments. Even the Accountant, the Architect, and Solicitor, who have direct responsibilities centring on all or certainly more than one department have a 'specialist, professional' view of local government reflecting a worthy concern for directing their own specific skills at the job in hand. The same, to a lesser extent, can be said of the politician. Rarely is local government seen by people inside it as an integral part of a wider scheme of things. The town planning tradition has perhaps been the only one concerned with a system wider than local government, but if anything, it has paid a higher price for its sins of omission. The town planners have failed quite seriously to pay attention to implementation and action. They have been guilty of giving expression in their plans to pious hopes and aspirations with insufficient concern for whether the resources and powers were available either to carry them out by local government or for them to be carried out by some other agency. One result has been that until recently town planners have not been taken very seriously by the other professions, by the other 'political' forces in the local government system.

Local government operates within the urban system. It comprises a vast range of other systems and sub-systems—some closely related, others inextricably linked. They all interact to a greater or lesser degree so that a change in one either directly or indirectly affects another or alters the climate for change in another. We can describe many of these systems—a transportation system—an education system—an employment system, and so on. Very few begin to take on any meaning unless seen in the context of their *relationships* with other systems. Thus a transportation system only springs to life when seen in terms of its *relationships*, its *interactions* with other systems, i.e. the systems it serves. Some systems have a much heavier bearing on human behaviour or concern human behaviour much more than others and these are the ones in which local government is most interested. They are also the most dynamic because human activities are involved. They are always changing. They are difficult to understand. The concern is with patterns of human activity—journeys to work, manufacture and distribution of goods and raw materials, journeys to shops, to cinemas, to other recreation and leisure pursuits, their locations and consequent impact—with the effects of the education process on children and their development—with the effects of the economy, with a very wide range of human activity. The urban system is dynamic. Its momentum derives from the pattern of decisions and subsequent actions, both large and minute, taken by the people in it (1.5).

Local government is part of this complex political, social and economic system. It does not stand apart from it, nor does it control it. It simply affects the way it operates, indeed, that is its responsibility. It follows, therefore, that it should develop an understanding of its relationship with this system. It needs to trace out the relationships and linkages. The responsibility, within this system, is to secure that the social, economic and physical conditions which the public desire actually exist, given the resources the public is politically prepared to devote to the achievement of this state. This raises the vexed issues of what is 'desired' and 'by whom'? but these issues are raised later (Chapter 6). At this stage it is important to stress that this view of local government does *not* necessarily imply a widening of its functions. It does not mean a giant bureaucratic control machinery. Its role is essentially one of seeing that the conditions are there, whether provided by local government, private agency, central government or some other body, under which people can exploit their potential and at the same time allow others to do the same. It is a role concerned with creating opportunities, for enabling people to develop their skills and interests, to improve their lives themselves. It is concerned with making sure that the total system does not harm, does not inhibit opportunity. This is a service different from the one we know. It implies a different approach (*a*) to the way it organises itself for this task and (*b*) to the kinds of policies, solutions and actions it adopts. This is a case for unhitching our minds from the stereotype solutions, formulas and controls with which we are familiar. We must free up areas for choice—think in terms of creating opportunities rather than controls.

THREE DIMENSIONS FOR CONSIDERATION

There are three dimensions in which the case for approaching corporate planning can be considered—they are *impact*, *interaction*, and *learning*.

(*a*) *Impact*

Local government has taken on through time, on an *ad hoc* basis, bits and pieces of responsibility to remedy isolated weaknesses in the natural system. If we trace the history of the massive volume of legislation this is clearly the pattern. Specific issues have been identified, legislation passed and local government has found itself with another responsibility to add to its present catalogue. This has resulted in a failure on local government's part to see its task in perspective. This is understandable. It has not appreciated the tremendous potential impact it could have on the way the urban system works—the impact it does indeed have. The quality and quantity of action a local authority takes (or does not take as the case may be) has a great influence on the way the total system works. What a local authority does sets certain cues—it creates or stifles opportunities for people—it sparks off or stultifies actions and interactions. Even when one looks at local government through the operation of the *separate* services one can find evidence of how different authorities have interpreted their powers by contrasting the services which they provide in terms of impact on the community. In some places the education service is just 'ticking over', in others really exciting things are happening—primary school children are 'finding' themselves at school—the school is playing a major role in some communities. Contrast local authority housing and one soon begins to see the opposing impacts this is making in different places. Compare what some towns do to pedestrians with the consideration there is in others. These are isolated examples. If one thinks in terms of the vast sums of capital invested by local government the impact (or its potential when viewed in these terms) can perhaps be imagined.

That is viewing impact in a forward-looking, positive way. It can be seen in other forms i.e. in the way local government identifies and responds to specific problems and needs in its area. It is impossible to avoid all problems in the preventative sense and inevitably a large part of local government's work will be remedial in nature. This presupposes a recognition on local government's part that it has these remedial responsibilities in general rather than merely specific ways. Again it depends whether local government has an 'agency' or an 'initiative' role. Impact, then, is a shorthand way of expressing the need for a local authority to be conscious of its environment, to be outward looking because that is where the root of its tasks lies. It is an ever-changing environment where problems form and reform, grow and decline. The enormous variety of links between a local authority and its environment, needless to say, are of critical importance. Introversion breeds irrelevance—impact has to be relevant. A consciousness of impact is an important pre-requisite of policy making in local government.

(*b*) *Interaction*

We have failed on the whole adequately to recognise the inter-connections, the interactions between one service and another. To some, the connections between the police service and the education service may seem 'rare and philosophical' but on closer analysis there are quite strong links between these apparently disparate fields. What happens to our children in schools may well be a major factor in determining the future clientele of the courts, detention centres and prisons. Plowden (1.6), Seebohm (1.7), Buchanan (1.8) and Sharp (1.9) have all emphasised the links between objectives of services, services within and outside the local government system. But, even these reports did not go far enough. They were all, in their way, too restricted.

What has happened in the development of local government is that we have created a whole series of arbitrary compartments, some we call professions, others departments and still others committees, we even have different compartments in the forms of units of government. The effect of the creation of all these has been twofold. Either problems in society are totally ignored because they neither fall in one compartment nor another or those problems are distorted to fit our arbitrary compartments. One only has to scan a list of current problems for which local government has varying degrees of concern to realise how true this is—poverty, leisure, labour shortages, unemployment, vandalism, racial conflict, gypsies, problem families, educational deprivation. Again, that is partly what Plowden, Seebohm, Buchanan and Sharp were saying. Clearly the links *between* the objectives of services are too significant to be isolated in one compartment whether it be a profession, department, committee, or tier of government. The policies of one affect the climate for change, the scope for action in another. Problems are mercurial in their origins and the movement towards their remedies is equally complex and elusive.

(*c*) *Learning*

When any plan or policy is adopted or implemented there is only one thing about which we can be certain and that is that it will be wrong. Wrong in the sense that it will not achieve precisely the effects expected of it, always assuming that in adopting a policy or implementing a plan we had certain expectations in mind. Too often policies are pursued because they are fashionable. They are somebody's 'pet scheme' or cherished idea. Given the charitable view that we *do* have expectations, some policies or plans will exceed them, some will fall far short, others will have unexpected side effects, good or bad. What we need to do is to learn, to measure or assess the progress and effects of policies. The richest vein of information as a basis for any policy is the progress of *previous* policies (or someone else's previous attempts).

The 'wrongness' of plans and policies is something we should begin learning about. One of the most glaring examples of omission in this respect is the British New Towns. Each town has been started with no systematic learning from its predecessors—there was no learning.

Monitoring the environment tracing out effects and side effects, analysing the environment could present us with a much firmer base for policy formulation than we have now—it is the business of learning.

A BASIS FOR PLANNING

Planning cannot be a clean slate operation. The need to prepare plans and policies derives from many sources, of which the following are a few:

"(*a*) pressure groups (e.g. amenity societies);
(*b*) individual initiative of officers and/or members;
(*c*) legislation (e.g. Social Services Act 1970);
(*d*) in response to emergence of specific needs;
(*e*) by strong pressure external to the authority (e.g. directives or codes of practice issued by government departments);
(*f*) by competitive situations (e.g. an attempt to keep up with other authorities);
(*g*) as by-products or spin-off from other policies;
(*h*) as incremental variations of existing policies;
(*i*) by a combination of any of the above." (1.10)

The unpredictable nature of policy origins does not invalidate the view that policies, when formulated, should reflect the needs existing in the environment in which a local authority operates, the environment which it is trying to influence. Sensitivity to, and hence information about, these needs is a fundamental pre-requisite of any planning effort in local government. This is the very basis of planning. How this information might be collected, what information involved and similar issues will be discussed later. It is important at this juncture to stress that if local government is adequately to fulfil the role described here, its ability to do so must lie substantially in its basis of knowledge and understanding of its environment. This does not *necessarily* imply more information but it does imply the availability of information across the whole range of local authority services. Data available and indeed quite common to public health inspectors has significance in other fields. Similarly, housing departments will have data important to the effective running of the social services. Other departments will have information of common interest to all departments. The way this information is framed, the degree to which it is regarded as important, reflects the extent to which a local authority recognises its purpose as responding to the needs of its environment and the people in it.

CORPORATE PLANNING AND THE CONTEXT

This is the case for establishing a process of corporate planning in a local authority. The nature of problems, the range of remedial and preventative actions and policies are complex. They demand not 'one professional' approaches, but a 'multi professional', a 'multi skill' attack—an attack which draws together political, professional and other skills to develop a system of planning, which learns and adapts, which does not delude itself about the complexities of the task. We have explored the case for corporate planning. The emphasis will be on the *process* of corporate planning within this working context. It is a process which will fail or succeed depending on the degree of commitment and understanding largely of the professional man and the politician in local government.

"Stress is laid . . . on the absence of unity in the internal organisation of a local authority which is the result of the close association of a particular service, the service committee, the department concerned and the hierarchy of professional officers. The separateness of the committees contributes to the separateness of the departments, and the professionalism of departmental staff feeds on this separateness." (1.11)

Professionalism in local government represents at one and the same time a great strength and a great weakness. The professions themselves extol their own strengths, which often cannot be denied. They are seldom alive to their weaknesses and, when they are, cannot rationalise them.

Perhaps the educationists are the most rigid, although it is the one profession which has possibly the least claim to that name for there is no professional training. In most local authorities with responsibilities for education, the education function is regarded as almost completely separate and in many cases even boasts a separate name. Corporate planning involves the drawing together of professional and other skills to attack problems facing local government. It is a movement which is gathering momentum slowly. Talking about corporate planning, proclaiming its implementation or adopting the label do not add up to achieving the process. Many 'new' approaches on techniques come and go without making any significant impact in the management processes, indeed many of them remain isolated from them altogether. Corporate planning runs the danger of becoming the thing no self-respecting local authority should admit to being without. The concept is inherently attractive. The great temptation is to leap into the mechanics and organisational structure for corporate planning. The intention is not to prevent anyone from doing that (in which case they should now turn to Chapter 4 onwards) but to sound a note of warning. Our policy-making institutions have not yet displayed any great understanding of the nature of planning itself. It is only on the basis of understanding the nature and limitations of plans that any kind of plan is likely to be successful. Perhaps one of the great weaknesses of planning within the East European countries is not a lack of commitment to planning but a singular lack of appreciation of its nature. Hence the next two chapters which explore, in the local government context, some of these problems.

REFERENCES

1.1 Maud Committee on Management in Local Government, 1967, Report Vol. 1, p. 68, HMSO, 1967.

1.2 T. BLACKSTONE, *A Fair Start—the provision of pre-school education*, Chapter 7, Allen Lane, 1971.

1.3 Town and Country Planning Act, 1947, HMSO, 1947.

1.4 Royal Commission on Local Government in England 1966–69, Vol. 2, Memorandum of Dissent, Derek Senior, p. 39, HMSO, 1970.

1.5 For a much fuller, but simpler, exposition of the urban systems view see J. B. MCLOGHLIN, *Urban and Regional Planning—a systems approach*, Faber, 1969.

1.6 Children and their Primary Schools—a report of the Central Advisory Council for Education (England) (Plowden Report), Vol. 1 : Report, Vol. 2 : Research and Surveys, HMSO, 1967.

1.7 Report of the Committee on Local Authority and Allied Personal Social Services (Seebohm Report), cmnd 3703, HMSO, 1968.

1.8 Traffic in Towns—a study of the long-term problems of traffic in urban areas (Buchanan Report), HMSO, 1963.

1.9 Transport Planning—the men for the job, HMSO, 1970.

1.10 Policy Formation Analysis, INLOGOV—Advanced Course Group Report, University of Birmingham, Autumn, 1971.

1.11 Maud Committee on Management in Local Government, 1967, Vol. 1, p. 57, HMSO, 1967.

2
About Planning

The case for planning the affairs of a local government authority as a whole is a strong one. This case has been presented as the working context for local government. Establishing it in principle, however, leaves untouched the problems of creating the reality. There are both conceptual and operational problems. The principle is something to which we may readily subscribe (although some do not) but the bridge between principle and reality requires a probing of the nature of planning itself. The object is to create frameworks for thinking about planning, for developing it; but especially it is to help those involved in the business of public planning to establish more effective ways of shaping and implementing plans and policies. The threads in this chapter are the base for the rest of this book and will be referred to, extended and adapted as some of the operational designs for planning are treated later.

Planning has many dimensions. The word itself conjures up many different meanings to different groups, different professions, different organisations. The word has different connotations in the public and private sector. In local government 'planning' has taken on a specific formal meaning. Most authorities have 'planning' committees. They employ 'planners'. This is town and country planning and the profession with that name. It has caused confusion and no doubt will continue to do so, for as local government increasingly strives to improve its 'planning' processes, the field of operation is clearly much wider than town and country planning and the traditional areas of interest of a 'planning committee'. Confusion is not confined to the public sector. In industry the term planning is sometimes applied to the setting of future actions. It is a process seen *separately* from the actual implementation of those plans.

A catalogue of different meanings, of confusions and contradictions, is of little help in understanding the *idea* of planning. But that they exist needs to be recognised before any attempt is made to investigate, improve or reshape the planning process. Any definition of planning needs to be robust enough to stand a variety of tests. Not surprisingly there are hundreds of definitions. The differences derive from some of the factors already mentioned. The following definition, which is adapted from Dror (2.1) is offered here as a base from which it is possible to analyse the nature of planning:

"Planning is the process of preparing a set of decisions for action in the future directed at achieving goals by optimal means and of learning from the outcome about possible new sets of decisions and new goals to be achieved."

THE PROCESS

The notion of planning as a *process* is probably the most important aspect of this definition. It is not new but the full significance of pursuing planning as a process does not yet seem to have penetrated many of our organisations. The process comes very much second to the plan itself, whether it is a plan in the map sense or a project or policy. A plan represents an 'end-state', which assumes a major importance. This is especially so in local government. It is an importance which very often militates against the planning process itself. Notwithstanding the advances in thinking in the physical planning field, the plan is still regarded as a pinnacle, as the end-product. Manifestations of this view of plans are not difficult to find and the lessons to be drawn from them are important in our consideration of planning.

The Planning Advisory Group which reported in 1965 (2.2) recommended a system of development planning (substantially adopted since) which, it was thought, would reduce the long gestation period of urban plans. The preparation, submission, examination and final approval by central government more often than not took nine or ten years. The recommendation did not involve any fundamental questioning of the validity of the idea of a plan itself. This was taken for granted. All that was suggested was that the degree of detail should be radically curtailed so that the length of time involved in the formal planning process would be reduced. In fact the evidence seems to suggest that there will be little reduction in this time. But, this is not the main weakness. The weakness derives from the fact that attention is all the while focussed on the plan rather than on the process itself. Even McLoughlin, whose work (2.3) has greatly influenced thinking in the town planning field, stresses the need to treat planning as a cyclic process but in doing so seems still to subordinate the process to the plan.

"Reviews must take account of both specific proposals which are different from those expected, of changes in the political, social and economic context in which the plan operates and which generate new needs, desires and aspirations in the community and its members." (2.3)

The whole system of physical planning in England and Wales is based on the supremacy of the plan. Even the structure of local government in this area is conditioned by the idea that the 'plan' is supreme. The County Councils are planning authorities, they are the plan makers but have very few powers of implementation either direct or indirect.

"Sometimes of course, it is possible to lose sight of the connection between a long-range planning activity and the more immediate operations of the governmental system; the process of visualising possible designs for the long-term future of a community can easily acquire its own internal momentum, and the danger may then arise that it ceases to exert due influence on the solution of current problems." (2.4)

Our legislation, our professional town planners, our structure of government, the internal organisations of local authorities, are all geared to producing plans. Moreover, these plans are expected to be right. They are more often than not prepared in the belief that they will work and even if they do not work 100%, no effort will be spared to make them come as close as possible to this state. But plans do *not* work. Any planning system is likely to be much improved by building into it this well established truth. Plans have three sources of obsolescence:

1. They are based on faulty forecasts.
2. They do not take into account changing aspirations.
3. They do not take into account the unexpected.

These are not faults in a plan. They are realities of life. We do not have 'complete' information about the present, let alone the future. A plan prepared today will be inferior to one prepared tomorrow because our information will be more complete by then. The lesson is obvious. We have a plan today based on today's data. Tomorrow we have a different plan, based on tomorrow's data and so on. We cannot ignore new information. If our plan is thereby shown to be weak, it must be changed. The practical man will immediately raise obvious difficulties in taking such a weather-vane approach. The situation is perplexing. At one end of the scale there is the 'prepare a plan and implement it, come what may' approach and at the other, the hand-to-mouth existence. But the realities remain. What is required is a *process* of planning which seeks to set in motion a decision-making machinery affecting the future based on changing information about both present *and* future. Time is crucial. Information is crucial. Decisions in time are crucial. But the plan is not inherently crucial. A plan should be conceived at the outset as something which *will* change, which *should* change. It is about adaptation. It is a continuing process during which events will take place, objectives will be realised, projects will be completed but the process continues. The rest are by-products from this process.

Focussing attention on the *process* of planning has been stressed. It has been stressed because it is important, and the evidence that it is recognised as such is fairly thin on the ground. For whatever reason, whether it is political or professional, or through some other cause, our investment is currently in plans, not planning. This is at least so in the physical planning field and it is quite probable that planning in other fields, perhaps even corporate planning, will develop a similarly unhealthy preoccupation with plans. The commitment needs to be to the process—in terms of approach, of thinking as well as in the variety of modes of expression for policies and plans.

SYSTEMS APPROACH

The distinction needs to be drawn between planning and decision making in general (2.5). Planning is concerned with 'sets' of decisions. In Chapter 1 stress was laid on the interdependence, on the inter-related nature of problems and issues. Comprehensiveness is concerned with mapping out the effects of an improvement in one part of the system on the overall way the system operates. Not that this will be completely possible for all circumstances and over all time periods, indeed it is likely to be impossible more often than not. However, by recognising the nature of the systems approach it immediately presents a frame of thinking which makes the mapping and tracing out of effects easier to perceive and thereby presents alternative solutions or perhaps even more important, different perspectives, new insights into the nature of the problem. We may not be close to a method of finding optimal solutions to complex problems. Clearly our capacity to predict system-wide effects over time is still severely limited. But, the road to optimality is paved with *improved* solutions and it is probable that the systems frame of thinking will open up some of these improvements.

THE FUTURE

The definition of planning (*ante*) specifies action 'in the future'. This is unremarkable, since it is difficult to imagine planning for action at any other time. But the implication is that doing so will involve predictions, predictions of a number of variables. As we have seen, plans have built-in sources of obsolescence, all of which derive from the fact that the future is uncertain and no matter how sophisticated our forecasting systems are, or become, this obsolescence will always be present to a greater or lesser degree. Friend and Jessop (2.6) divide uncertainty into three classes :

"1. Uncertainties in knowledge of the external planning *environment* including all uncertainties relating to the structure of the world external to the decision-making system and also all uncertainties relating to expected patterns of future change in this environment, and to its expected responses to any possible future intervention by the decision-making system.

2. Uncertainties as to future intentions in *related fields of choice* including all uncertainties relating to the choices which might in future be taken, within the decision-making system itself, in respect of other fields of discretion beyond the limited problem which is currently under consideration.

3. Uncertainties as to appropriate *value judgments* including all uncertainties relating to the relative degrees of importance the decision-makers ought to attach to any expected consequences of their choice which cannot be related to each other through an unambiguous common scale—either because the consequences are of a fundamentally different nature, or because they affect different sections of the community, or because they concern different periods of future time."

Uncertainty can be reduced, it cannot be eliminated. There will often be a price attached to a reduction—usually time and manpower. Clearly the importance of reducing uncertainty in a particular respect needs to be set against the costs. Uncertainty is a reality and it needs to be confronted and managed within the planning process. It serves yet again to stress the significance of treating planning as a continuous process. It focusses once more on adaptation. As time passes decisions *have* to be taken but planning needs to move to a situation where those decisions are taken which are likely to achieve as closely as possible our *present* objectives but which, at the same time, leave as many options open for the future as possible. As time passes new information, new insights, new perspectives on the problems, different problems will emerge. Planning needs to avoid queering its own pitch for the future.

Dror sees uncertainty in these terms (2.7);

"But future values are very difficult to predict, adding a serious primary uncertainty to the primary and secondary uncertainties of predicting the results of different policy alternatives. In such cases, parts of the overall goals should often be to increase options (that is, leave to the future choice between defined goals) and build up resources for goal setting in the future (that is prepare resources which permit choice of as yet undefined and unknown goals in the future). The more we expect the future to be different from the present, and the more we would like the future to be different from the present, the more we should be doubtful of present efforts to establish substantive goals for the future. Taking into consideration the rate of social transformation in the contemporary world, the conclusion seems justified that preparation of resources for goal choice in the future should constitute an important component of the overall goals for preferable policy making".

GOALS AND OPTIMAL MEANS

Two other elements of the definition need to be mentioned. They are dealt with in more detail in later chapters. Goals and goal setting are fraught with conceptual as well as operational difficulties. At this definition stage it is sufficient to stress the goal *orientation* aspect rather than the problems of goal setting. The simple assumption is that decisions for future action are likely to be better reached if they are set against an understanding of what objective or goal the action is designed to achieve or to move towards. The fact is that this *is* simple but it is *not* common practice, at least, not in any systematic way. The evidence is to be found in almost every organisation and certainly in local government. The planning process needs to be goal orientated.

The other element is optimisation. The effective use of resources, whether they are financial, manpower, land or any other kind, is an area of crucial concern in the planning process. Resources are rarely abundant. The scarcer they are the more important it is that they are used effectively.

LEARNING SYSTEM

In Chapter 1 the case for policy planning in local government was considered along three dimensions, one of which was the learning dimension. It is about feedback and review, but there is more to it than that.

In this chapter so far, a definition of planning has served as a basis for thinking about planning. Two important points emerge :

1. The separate consideration of each element serves to highlight its interdependence with other elements and that learning and feedback are not fashionable glosses to planning but the crucial links which give the dynamic to the process. Feedback is information, information about the changing environment, old information revised, new information, information about the state of the process. Information is produced and required at all points in the process and so changes the process itself. The whole essence of planning is that it is dynamic and that the approach to it should be likewise. An explicit statement of objectives itself creates a framework for the consideration of alternatives and possibly sets yardsticks for evaluation. But evaluation needs to be carried out *post hoc*. Objectives need to be challenged through the flow of information in the process itself.

2. That planning, in many respects, has up to now deceived itself by evading the realities of uncertainty about the future, of change through the passage of time, of natural errors in forecasting. There has been, both professionally and perhaps politically a 'faith' of planning, a faith in the 'omnipotence' almost of plans. The case has been made for those involved in planning to take as their starting point that the plans they produce will be wrong, that

they will not 'work'. This is the beginning of the learning system. A planner, of whatever sort, is not in business to produce plans. His task is to understand the planning system so that he can help to enable it to produce the effects society wants of it.

The definition holds good conceptually at a number of levels. It could be applied equally to national economic planning as to the planning of a particular project or even an element within a project. The principles of the process are relevant at both extremes. The definition is also valid along both the short and long-term scales and it stands the tests of a variety of subjects. It is perhaps useful at this stage to distinguish between different levels.

PLANNING AND CONTROL

Very often a distinction is drawn between planning and control. They are sometimes advanced as constituting different levels or distinct stages. In the physical planning field, for example, most local authority planning departments have separate sections for 'control' and 'plan-making' and indeed, in the White Paper on Local Government Reform these two functions were to be put at different levels of government. The definition used here does not accept control as separate from planning.

R. N. Anthony provides a framework for analysis at different levels, closely relating the actual processes which go on inside organisations rather than as definable abstractions. His (2.8) is a three-way distinction defined as follows:

"*Strategic planning* is the process of deciding on objectives of the organisation, on changes in these objectives, on the resources used to attain these objectives, and on the policies that are to govern the acquisition, use and disposition of these resources;

Management control is the process by which managers assure that resources are obtained and used effectively and efficiently in the accomplishment of the organisation's objectives;

Operational control is the process of assuring that specific tasks are carried out effectively and efficiently."

The distinction is not between planning and control. Strategy connotes big plans, important plans, plans with major consequences. Management control involves planning too but it is concerned much more with the ongoing administration of the organisation within a context of objectives and policies that have been arrived at in the strategic planning process. Control in Anthony's terms involves a check on this. "Conformance to plans is not the standard against which performance should be measured. 'The closer the better' is not necessarily the best rule. That is why our definition of management control is worded in terms of the effective and efficient utilisation of resources, rather than conformance to plans. Of course, the plans do provide a starting point for the appraisal of performance, and there can be a presumption that plans should be followed in the absence of contrary evidence. But this presumption should be rebuttable, and the rebuttal process should not be made too difficult. To do otherwise is to run the great risk of stifling initiative and encouraging unthinking mediocrity."

Operational control is focussed on tasks, on execution.

The significance of the Anthony framework is that planning as defined here takes place at all his levels. The requirements, particularly for information but also for expertise, organisation etc. will be different at each level but the planning process operates at all three. This framework is raised here to underline the point that the inherent nature of planning does not change but that it is useful to see it operating at different levels. There will be other levels in the public sector, but the process of planning is the same.

MODELS OF THE PROCESS

It is not the purpose of this book to advance a 'new' model of the planning process. New processes will develop but they will develop because people working them think in different and changing ways. Many models of the planning process have been advanced, often given expression in some variant of Figure 2.1.

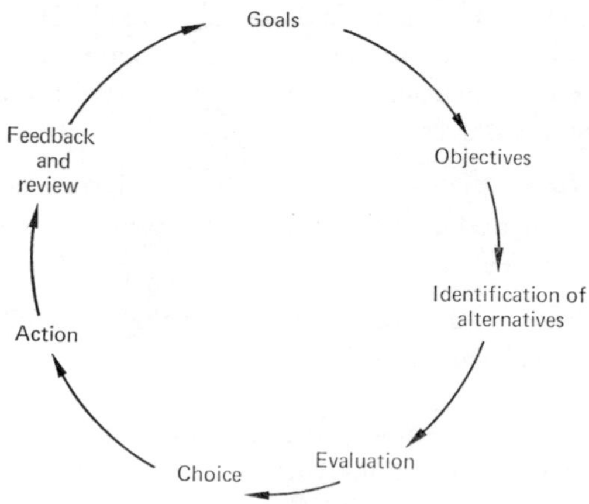

Figure 2.1

Dror has produced a summary (2.9) of six normative models of public policy making. They are (1) the pure-rationality model; (2) the 'economically rational' model; (3) the sequential-decision model; (4) the incremental-change model; (5) the satisfying model; and (6) the extra-rational-processes model. (What follows under the six headings is adapted and, in part, taken from Dror (2.9)).

The pure-rationality model

Most models rely to a greater or lesser degree on rationality. It includes six phases:

1. Establishing a complete set of operational goals, with relative weights allocated to the different degrees to which each may be achieved.

2. Establishing a complete inventory of other values and of resources with relative weights.

3. Preparing a complete set of the alternative policies open to the policy maker.

4. Preparing a complete set of valid predictions of the costs and benefits of each alternative, including the extent to which each will achieve the various operational goals, consume resources, and realise or impair other values.

5. Calculating the net expectation for each alternative by multiplying the probability of each benefit and cost for each alternative by the utility of each, and calculating the net benefit (or cost) in utility units.

6. Comparing the net expectations and identifying the alternative (or alternatives, if two or more are equally good) with the highest net expectation.

Many of the shortcomings of this model in terms of its usefulness in the real situation will be obvious. For example, in almost every situation, in local government at least, the establishment of a complete set of operational goals will be impossible and assigning exact weights or even reliable indices will be almost equally impossible, especially if it is intended to arrive at trade-offs between one goal and another.

The business of throwing up alternatives is improving but 'a complete set' is impossible simply because there will be too many. However, a more important obstacle is simply the limits to our creativity and the drawbacks in the process of throwing up alternatives which, put crudely, is simply a mental process of successively cutting down options, if only to make the task manageable. But very often the narrowing down is unconscious.

Tackling the obstacles to arrive at a complete set of alternatives (or even a wide-range), predicting their costs and benefits relative to operational goals, presents problems. In fact the more complete the set of alternatives (especially the inclusion of novel alternatives) the less likely is it that predictions of costs and benefits will be possible. Data tends to grow out of what we do already, not out of what seems like a good, new idea.

Economically Rational Model

Dror writes: "Recognising how hard it is to achieve pure rationality in real policy making, some authors who are interested in improving decision-making recommend that the various phases of pure-rationality policy making should be developed in practice only insofar as it is economical to do so, that is, insofar as the cost of the input (in terms of what else could be done with the resources) into making policy making more rational is less than the benefit of the output (in terms of the marginal improvement of the policy's quality). Since the idea of this model is to be only as rational as is economical, I will call this the 'economically rational' model.

In the general terms stated above, the economically rational model seems beyond reproach to me, insofar as one accepts its basic assumption that rational processes are the highest form of problem solving. But insofar as one accepts extrarational processes, not as an unavoidable evil, but as a sometimes optimal way to solve problems, the economically rational model needs some important modifications." (2.10)

Sequential-Decision Model

This model puts the notion of alternatives and their evaluation into a new perspective. Any evaluation of an alternative approach to a particular problem is surrounded by a good deal of uncertainty. "Its basic idea is that if some of the information needed to succeed in an activity can be learned only during the early stages of carrying out that activity, the more promising alternative ways to carry it out should be undertaken simultaneously, and the decision as to which is the best alternative should be delayed until the information has been learned." (2.11) The interpretation of this approach in the local government setting makes the mind boggle at first and in many instances (or maybe even most instances) we would need an entirely new breed of politician or a much more sophisticated electorate before risking it. It cannot be dismissed entirely. "When initial uncertainty is high, when different paths can be tried out at the same time in order to learn important information from their first stages, and when time is at a premium, then the sequential-decision model can be an important guide on how to time experimental policies and delay decision on one definite policy so as to reduce both uncertainty and wasted time as much as possible." (2.12) There are those who have argued this approach in the context of local government reform and certainly it has attractions in this respect. Where it is least attractive, that is to say in political terms, is probably where major capital works are involved, such as trunk roads or urban motorways, but there are many other 'policy' areas where as an approach it has everything to commend it. One way of resolving uncertainty about effects of a range of policies is to try them all and find out. Public transport subsidies, park and ride schemes, bus lanes—indeed, many aspects of urban transportation—could be approached nationally in this systematic way. There are other possibilities in many spheres of local and central government operation. Within each local authority area there will be scope for trying *different* policies in different parts of the area with a view to comparison and testing out of policies. Uniformity and consistency have their uses. They also run the risk of securing mediocrity everywhere. In fields where policy choices are inherently difficult because of uncertainties about effects this model has much to offer.

The Incremental Change Model

Writers like Lindblom seem to dismiss the rational approach simply because it does not happen in practice. What happens, they say, when they observe decision-making processes, is 'disjointed-incrementalism'. Braybrooke and Lindblom hold that decision making is (1) incremental or tending towards relatively small changes; (2) remedial, in that decisions are made to move away from ills rather than towards goals; (3) serial, in that problems are not solved at one stroke but rather successively attacked; (4) exploratory, in that goals are continually being redefined or newly discovered; (5) fragmented or limited, in that problems are attacked by considering a limited number of alternatives rather than all possible alternatives; and (6) disjointed, in that there are many dispersed 'decision-points'. (2.13)

Because it happens this way they end up in the position of recommending it as *the* way. Attacking rationality does not, however, demolish its attraction as a basis for other approaches and certainly the other extreme is positively harmful to advance in policy making. It is the easiest thing in the world for complacency to set in. Writers in public administration and political science who describe what actually happens in decision making and whose interest stops there are knowingly or unwittingly buttressing complacency. We know that the world is full of people expending vast energies to stay the same—the dynamic conservatives described by Donald Schon (2.14). What Braybrooke and Lindblom observe is probably accurate and insofar as it assists us to improve things, it is a valid and helpful position statement. The concern, however, is to improve.

The Satisfying Model

"The central argument for this model says that a search for alternatives must in fact go through the following stages. First, policymakers identify obvious alternatives based on recent policymaking experience, and evaluate their expected payoffs in terms of the satisfactory quality. If they consider an expected payoff to be satisfactory, they carry out that alternative without trying to find additional alternatives that would have higher payoffs. Only when all the expected payoffs from the obvious alternatives fall below the satisfactory quality do policymakers try to find more alternatives, taking somewhat innovative alternatives and their expected payoffs into consideration. Alternatives are searched for in this manner until one with a satisfactory payoff is found, or until the policymakers despair of doing so and lower their standards for what they consider satisfactory. In either case, the end result is that policymaking tends to achieve satisfactory quality but not, in most cases, optimal quality." (2.15)

It is the ring of reality behind this model which makes it attractive. The great danger is that what is satisfactory can become determined by the product of the inertia and conservatism of the machine itself.

The extrarational model

All the models described so far derive from the basis of rationality. This last model attempts to wrestle with intuition and judgment. It states that extrarational processes play an essential, often major role in policy making. The problem is that our knowledge about these extrarational processes is very limited. Dror says

"If we knew the characteristics of the extrarational processes, which perhaps include many different and separate processes with different, specific features, we could allocate them defined roles in optimal policy making, depending on whether their net output in a certain case is higher than that of 'more rational' methods. Since we don't know even that much about extrarational processes, we have no way, even in theory, to decide what their optimal role in policymaking might be. But we should not, on that account, underestimate their importance in either actual or optimal decision making and policy making, which the decision-sciences literature often does. Instead, I think the evidence about extrarational processes, unclear as it is, forces us to accept in part (after careful screening) the policymakers' introspective and observational impressions about the importance of extrarational processes in policy making, and leave the burden of proof on those who argue that such impressions have no validity at all.

There are perhaps enough indications so far to make some sort of *prima facie* case for the claim that extrarational processes are sometimes a better method for policy making (and have a higher net output) than pure rationality, even if the latter is feasible.

Whether policy makers regard extrarational processes as being sometimes ideal or not, they have little choice but to rely greatly on them. The question thus becomes the less 'sensitive' one of what is the best possible mix of rationality, extrarationality, and their various subtypes; and of how to create conditions that will allow these two different components of policy making to work together." (2.16)

Dror describes this model as the opposite to rationality. It probably does not really stand examination as a model itself. When we talk of extrarationality we are essentially talking about sophisticated use of information or the improvisation of information based on a knowledge of the world. The information used is not made explicit and could probably never be made so, but intuition is merely the process of drawing on the vast storage of information to the mind to aid choice. Looked at in this light, it becomes more helpful to regard this approach as a variant of rationality, and like some of the others, with attractions because it comes close to the picture we have of reality.

POSITION STATEMENT

We have defined planning thus :

Planning is the process of preparing a set of decisions for action in the future directed at achieving goals by optimal means and of learning from the outcome about possible new sets of decisions and new goals to be achieved.

This is not a law, it has served as a base for thinking about planning. At this stage it is perhaps worth thinking about the relationship between what has been said and the planning situation in local government. Local government is not short of techniques, or at least that is not where it is most deprived. Where it is deficient is in ways of thinking about its planning activities, whether they are in separate departments, city or county wide, whether they are comprehensive in the sense of covering a wide range of subjects or whether they are fairly specific. The *idea* of planning, thinking of planning as a *process* is at different stages of development in different professions. The town planning profession has probably gone furthest and maybe the social workers have the most to learn. These two professions are chosen because they seem to have much to offer each other. The casework orientation of many social workers diverts the attention and skills away from the development of social policy. The town planners are too much concerned with planning and not enough with the effects of planning. In *all* professions the recognition of planning as a process has still to mature. The planning activities in local government tend to be lists of projects, lists of plans at various stages of some cumbersome formal machinery. In this chapter we have explored a variety of ways of thinking about planning but the most important has been to see it as a process, to see it as continuous, to accept the realities of uncertainty and the obsolescence of plans. Our planning needs to be robust enough to cope with all these as well as to produce decisions and action on our current problems. The models discussed are not to be slavishly copied or rejected. They are aids to thinking about the realities of planning in practice.

REFERENCES

2.1 D. YEHEZKEL DROR, 'The Planning Process: A Facet Design', in *Planning Programme Budgeting: A Systems Approach to Management*, edited by FREMONT J. LYDEN and ERNEST G. MILLER, Markham Publishing Company, April, 1968.

2.2 The Future of Development Plans, Report, HMSO, 1965.

2.3 J. B. MCLOUGHLIN, *Urban and Regional Planning—a systems approach*, Faber, 1969.

2.4 J. K. FRIEND and W. N. JESSOP, *Local Government and Strategic Choice*, Tavistock, 1969.

2.5 D. YEHEZKEL DROR, 'The Planning Process: a facet design'; p. 93 in *A Systems Approach to Management*, edited by FREMONT J. LYDEN and ERNEST G. MILLER, Markham Publishing Company, April, 1968.

2.6 J. K. FRIEND and W. N. JESSOP, *Local Government and Strategic Choice*, Tavistock, 1969.

2.7 J. YEHEZKEL DROR, *Design for Policy Sciences*, p. 64, Elsevier, 1971.

2.8 R. N. ANTHONY, *Planning and Control Systems: a framework for analysis*, Harvard University Press, 1965.

2.9 J. YEHEZKEL DROR, *Public Policymaking Re-examined*, Chandler Publishing Company, 1968.

2.10 *op. cit.*, p. 141.

2.11 *op. cit.*, p. 142.

2.12 *op. cit.*, p. 143.

2.13 D. BRAYBROOKE and C. LINDBLOM, *Strategy of Decision*, Free Press, 1963.

2.14 D. SCHON, *Beyond the Stable State*, Temple Smith, 1971.

2.15 *op. cit.*, p. 147.

2.16 *op. cit.*, pp. 152–3.

3
Goals and Objectives

During the exploration of the planning process in Chapter 2 the specific question of goals and objectives was set on one side but the point was established that there is a need for the planning process to be *goal orientated.* It is a theme developed here and in Chapter 4 also.

MASTER PLAN IDEOLOGY

Public planning, although existing in a limited form in the last century and long before, has taken on a new image, received a new impetus in the second half of that century and through this one. Nowhere has this manifested itself more than in the urban planning field, i.e. that part of the public policy making arena concerned with physical hardware, engineering works, locational and spatial planning. It has been a movement not much concerned with explicit goals and objectives, but rather a missionary fervour for change in the physical fabric leading unquestioningly in the minds of the planners to changes in the social environment (3.1) : the emphasis was on 'wholesomeness', the city beautiful, on the achievement of standards in the provision of a whole range of facilities.

"For generations it had been generally understood that the physical environment was a major determinant of social behaviour and a direct contributor to individual's welfare. Having accepted professional responsibility for the physical environment, the city planner was thus accorded a key role as agent of human welfare; the clearly prescribed therapy for the various social pathologies was improvement of the physical setting. If only well-designed, and well-sited houses, playgrounds and community facilities could be substituted for the crowded and dilapidated housing and neighbourhoods of the city's slums, then the incidence of crime, delinquency, narcotics addiction, alcoholism, broken homes, and mental illness would tumble. Acculturation of ethnic, racial and other minority groups to the American, middle-class urban ways-of-life but awaited their introduction to the American middle-class, physical environment." (3.2)

The comprehensive master-plan, the blueprint approach has pervaded our public planning systems in the physical field for many years and has by no means died, indeed, it is very healthy in some quarters despite (*a*) the coming of the Town and Country Planning Act 1968 and (*b*) the obvious redundancy of almost every master-plan and blueprint ever produced. Even the plan for Milton Keynes, Britain's latest new town is specifically referred to as a Master Plan (3.3) although in detail it departs dramatically from the more traditional master-plans for new towns. The image of the comprehensive panacea is understandably attractive to the ardent technocrat. The dangers of a passionate belief in what this approach has to offer cannot be overstressed. The weakness of the philosophy has been, to some extent, exposed within the physical planning field (3.4) but the exposure is only making slight impact in practice. It needs to be exposed in other areas too and alternative approaches developed.

It is easy to see why the master-plan has had such a following from professional planners. The master-plan carries authority, it represents an ordering of action in conformity with a 'comprehensive' view of the physical problems at the time. Physical development and redevelopment have such a major impact both on the ground and in terms of capital expenditure that it almost asserts its own importance on the scheme of things. The major road schemes for the City of Birmingham conjured up by a far-seeing engineer in the early part of this century are fundamentally still the ones being implemented over fifty years later.

GOAL-ORIENTATED APPROACH

A distinction needs to be drawn between a goal and an objective.

"Goals are statements of directions in which planning or action is aimed. They derive from human values and as such are ethical, that is empirically untestable. They are fundamental in that they stem from the apparently insatiable wishes of the human species for greater self-fulfilment. As such they would not be suddenly changed or abandoned. They are ideals over a horizon which will never be attained, since progress towards them over time implies their reformulation in yet higher ideals.

Objectives on the other hand, are seen as specific steps toward the attainment of a goal, and thus although an end in itself, also as the means of achieving a more distant goal. They are attainable, and thus factual as opposed to ethical in that the degree of attainment can be specified, measured and tested."

Although expressed slightly differently, the essence of these definitions coincides with the Greater London Council's use of the terms in, *A general introduction to the GLC's Planning-Programme Budgeting System.*

The emphasis on goals and objectives marks a move away from rigid plans, standards and regulations towards a commitment to the idea of planning, to the process itself.

". . . the test of a governmental planning effort's effectiveness can be applied only on the *output* side of an activity, never on the input side . . . One of the long-standing habits of traditional city planning, like other social professions, has been to measure worth in the input side. Standards are input criteria. So are land-use regulations. So are new towns. To be sure, all of these imposed constraints and new facilities are intended to accomplish certain purposes. And yet, because goals are not made explicit and because these means have become the stock of the trade, it is difficult to avoid the inference that the aim of the profession has been to apply the professional instruments." (3.5)

Notwithstanding the operational problems surrounding the adoption of the planning approach to decision making and action, its attractive characteristics are its goal/objectives orientation, its evaluation of future courses of action and indeed alternative futures, and its dependence on feedback—the rational model. Whether or not rationality, complete or partial, is possible there can be no questioning the desirability of a constant orientation towards goals and objectives. To adopt policies or plans without having given thought as to why they are being adopted, to what is expected to happen as a result, is plainly to be discouraged. This is not to say that before taking any action we must be *certain* of effects or that we should never take an inspired guess. The future is shrouded in uncertainty. But it is only when the policy maker (either as a group or as an individual) probes the ends-means relationship then creativity can truly begin, that policy planning can begin to reflect the dynamism of reality. (3.6)

Problems of setting goals in general terms but particularly the expression of objective in operational terms and writing has been for the 'technocrats' (i.e. the professional people involved in improving planning and policy formulation processes) to take goals and objectives rather for granted. There are several examples (*post*) which illustrate the dangers either of goals and objectives being the goals and objectives of those professionally involved in the planning process perhaps in a rather paternalistic way or for the stating of goals and objectives to become a ritual with little later connection with the planning process. (3.7)

". . . perceptions, interests, and values are to a large extent formed by location of the observer in a given social matrix. The resulting multiplicity of societal perspectives cannot by sheer force of logic be integrated into a single normative scheme or, as planners like to put it, a hierarchy of values. Differing perspectives lead to clashes of social interests that are usually capable of being resolved only through processes of negotiation, bargaining and political pressure. The comprehensive plan which expresses but a single perspective and a single hierarchy of values cannot, therefore, obtain the commitment of all the parties whose interests may be affected, except where a clear-cut overriding sense of crisis prevails." (3.8)

The notion that policy makers can have grasp and understanding of the overall public interest is untenable. The problems the policy-making machine chooses to focus on, those it ignores or those it remains ignorant of altogether, are a reflection of its values and preferences. So too are the solutions and priorities it chooses to adopt relative to those problems.

It is not possible to devise a value-free approach to policy making. All groups in the community cannot be satisfied. Public policy making is essentially a conflict situation and the conflict centres on values. It is often argued that democracy is the carrying out of the will of the people and our interest in values, etc. should stop there if we are ever to get anything done. In other words, it is strongly felt that 'values' are adequately represented through the democratic processes, that Councillor X, if elected, is capable of reflecting the values of the majority in the decision-making and policy formulation processes. Would it were so simple. The unfortunate feature of democracy is that it is too coarsely grained—that an awful lot of harm can be done to a whole range of interests before 'popular disapproval' takes a hand. In fact, of course, there are many things which one might regard as undesirable but which would never give rise to 'popular disapproval' sufficient to change a government, local or national. In this respect politicians are not blameless—they too often steer just within the safe political limits and care little about those lost on the way. It is impossible at an election to vote on separate issues—one opts for a package of policies (or non-policies, as the case may be). Elections represent a sieving out of values and preferences. They form part of the policy-making process but it is crude and there is a need for other devices to secure more useful and relevant inputs into the process. Whose goals, whose objectives should a local authority set for itself? Is it the rich, the poor, the private property owners, the public tenants, the inner areas, the suburbs, the skilled, the unskilled, the blacks, the whites, the catholics, the protestants? Whose goals shall be met and whose shall be ignored? Conflict and controversy arise from these and similar questions and there is evidence of it in the world's press every single day.

On the whole, goals themselves are relatively uncontroversial. Most people would agree with the sentiments behind 'Freedom from personal harm and property loss' or 'A wide range of job opportunity' or yet still, 'easy, safe accessibility' and 'satisfactory housing/shelter in relation to needs and income'. Most of us say 'yes' to these and many more.

The difficulty arises because we can't have them all in the same proportion and some of us see one goal as more important, as having greater priority over another and that some ways of achieving these goals are infinitely better than others.

More than likely, our view of what is better or what is more important is dictated by our values. Traditional local government operates within the democratic framework where goal setting and the establishment of objectives has to be performed within the cut and thrust of local and national politics.

The rationality of goals, objectives and the planning process has to be robust enough to withstand—better still to assist a meaningful dialogue in this cut and thrust of the political arena.

AN APOLITICAL EXAMPLE

In idealised form the goal orientated approach is under trial at Milton Keynes. The significant feature here is the apolitical nature of the process. The Development Corporation of course operates outside the formal democratic system and could well be said to be the latest technocratic view of what is 'good for you', the general public. The implications of this situation would make an interesting subject for study but the significant feature is the expression of goals and objectives in this particular context. The following is an extract from Walter Bor (3.9);

"Before any physical proposals were developed the members of the Milton Keynes Board under the chairmanship of Lord Campbell, their officers and the consultants discussed and identified a series of goals which would guide the development of the new city. Amongst these were all-embracing ones like flexibility and keeping options open, particularly with regard to transport, and building a socially balanced city.

In terms of subject matters, they included goals with regard to the urban society of the future, transportation and employment, housing and social development, health and education, leisure and agriculture, and special working parties concentrated their attention on these. After a three-month discussion period, altogether some 70 specific goals were identified and agreed upon which were then brought together under six main headings, as follows:

1. Opportunity and freedom of choice.
2. Easy movement and access.
3. Balance and variety.
4. An attractive city.

5. Public awareness and participation.
6. Efficient and imaginative use of resources.

1. A city of opportunities would provide a variety of choices for all its residents—and for those living outside it. Opportunities for a large variety of jobs and for changing jobs, for education and choice of education, for a wide range of housing and change of housing, for genuinely competitive shopping, for diversity of leisure opportunities.

2. Easy movement and access means that there must be a high degree of accessibility between all activities and places making up the city: homes, jobs, education, health, shopping, recreation. There should be freedom of choice between high-quality public and private methods of transport not only for those who need it but also for those who might choose it instead of private transport. Provision should be made for the use of the car unconstrained by congestion and for free and safe movement as a pedestrian or cyclist.

3. By balance is meant the concept of avoiding undue bias towards any one group by creating a wide range of jobs requiring different skills and levels of education. It also means ensuring the provision, simultaneously with housing and places of employment, of all the necessary services, educational, social, shopping, cultural and leisure facilities. Variety will be provided by creating a large number of different places within the city all with their own character and identity as well as building a wide range of housing to choose from in terms of types, design and tenure.

4. An attractive city would be lively socially and visually—it would offer variety and diversity, in terms of social provisions and the built environment, in short an attractive way of life. There would be a full recognition of the two different but complementary scales which will characterise future cities—the large scale of the fast moving vehicle on generously landscaped main roads, of vast shopping halls stadia, some high-rise buildings where they take advantage of favourable considerations and emphasise important features—and the small and intimate scale of the local environment, historic villages and new housing groups, greens and paved spaces to experience at walking pace as distinct places with their own identity.

5. A city aware of its problems and able to deal with them would diminish the difficulties which have been experienced in earlier towns. It would be continually informed of its own performance and ready to take action whenever appropriate. Its residents, business-men and interest groups would themselves be informed and thereby be enabled to participate effectively in the conduct of the city.

6. A city that made efficient and imaginative use of the resources put into it would ensure the multiple use of these resources. It would ensure that the physical contribution of these resources allowed for their efficient operation. It would devise the appropriate management of administrative techniques to achieve high utilisation of the resources. It would act as a catalyst to the use of private social resources—both to the benefit of the individual and of community."

As an example of specific objectives, those for housing in Milton Keynes were stated in the plan as being :

> 50% home ownership; at least 50% of households in Milton Keynes should own their own houses, and this ration should be achieved as soon as possible.
>
> Quality : housing in the new city should be built to a quality which can stand the test of the future.
>
> Variety : housing, whether for rent or sale, should be available in a wide variety of sizes and types.
>
> Attraction to all income groups : housing must be available over a wide price range to allow the relatively poor as well as the relatively wealthy to move to the city.
>
> Mix of houses : no large areas of the city should be developed with houses of a similar type, size or tenure.
>
> Mobility : provision must be made for people to change their houses or tenure arrangements as their needs, resources, or preferences change (3.10).

Here is an interesting example of a statement of fairly generalised goals, elaborated at a second stage but still expressed in fairly general terms, but more so in some respects than others. For example, 'the attractive city would be lively socially and visually . . . in short an attractive way of life' is very vague indeed and rings very much of 'aesthetic spiritualism'. On the other hand, the concepts of 'accessibility' and 'balance' are approached much more closely and confidently. Again, some of the housing objectives are more operational than others.

An objective becomes operational when it is expressed in terms which point to criteria for evaluation after the event. Objectives expressed in 'as much as possible' terms (3.11) or in the form 'visually exciting' do not lead to the establishment of indicators of performance. There is no way of telling whether the objective has been met. This is the point at which the setting of goals and objectives runs in danger of becoming simply a ritual—a fashionable thing to do. It would be unfair to level this criticism at Milton Keynes, where a unit exists specifically to monitor events against the objectives and standards set. But in general, it is a valid test to apply. Does the objective lead the way to criteria for evaluation? This need not necessarily be in quantitative terms, although this is clearly preferable, but objective setting is helpful only if it makes explicit what is being attempted and if it gives focus to the learning process stressed earlier (Chapters 1 and 2). Of course it is not easy to make objectives operational. Some will remain vague, and we need generalised goals to help us to arrive at more operational objectives, but there is a strong case for a shift in the direction of making objectives *more* explicit instead of hiding behind professional instruments.

In a sense these are technical obstacles. With the exception of instances such as Milton Keynes, most planning operations take place within a democratic framework, more often than not in a local authority. Here it is a question of not imposing technocratic goals and objectives on a community. It has already been said that the formal democratic machinery is coarsely grained and that we need new devices to under-pin this system, e.g. Community Development Projects, a variety of participation measures, the spontaneous creation of interest and pressure groups, demonstrations of one kind and another. Very often it is argued that 'participation' in all its forms usurps the function and responsibility of the elected member (3.12). The truth is that some politicians dislike participation and community involvement as much as some officers but there will be no choice, save in deciding which are the most helpful ways of striking up new relationships between these three elements. One thing is sure, it will not happen overnight but there can be no doubt that it *will* happen. None of the new devices will resolve conflict, rather they are likely to heighten it and this is where a new breed of politician and officer will be needed. The distinction drawn here is between a situation where public views, objections, comments, etc are treated merely as a piece of data, leaving policy formulation little changed, and a situation where there is continued informal and formal sounding of community reaction through political and pseudo-political activities as a positive influence on policy formulation. One thing we should be perfectly clear about —the public policy-making system will always fail to accommodate conflict. Outside it, spontaneous expression of differences will arise and so they should. The problem, then, is not to arrive at a set of goals and related objectives which reflect consensus but to create a framework which :

(*a*) is aspiration and purpose orientated;

(*b*) reflects the values of the political masters at any point in time;

(*c*) can be readily adapted to change, whether it be change in the environment or change in political control.

"For the authority to set its objectives, is to determine the relative rate of progress in achieving its various goals. Objectives can be set for differing periods. The specific objectives are unlikely to be achieved in the defined time-span. That barely matters. A standard is being set. Time is being used to measure relative speed.

The objectives set are a function of the resources that the authority is willing to devote to meeting the needs and problems delineated by its goals. To set objectives is to indicate priorities in the use of resources. It is a political decision.

Objectives must be set by councillors. This should perhaps be recognised as their central task. For to set objectives implies a review of policies. To set objectives is to confirm policies or to modify them. Objectives should not be set in the abstract. The objectives must be based both on an understanding of the present position of the authority, of the environment in which it is placed and of the constraints upon it. The analytical process and the political process combine in the setting of objectives." (3.13)

The important relationships here are between the politicians, the professionals and the clients. Handled constructively a framework of goals and objectives provides at once a basis for choice and debate.

Thus, goals and objectives are not simply terms which appear at the early stages of a theoretical rational model—they are not static. They give point to both the political and technical planning processes, *if* these processes are approached in certain ways.

REFERENCES

3.1 HERBERT J. GANS, 'The Goal Orientated Approach to Plans', p. 78 in *People and Plans*, Basic Books, 1968.

3.2 M. M. WEBBER, 'Comprehensive Planning and Social Responsibility', *Journal of American Institute of Planners*, November, 1963.

3.3 LLEWELYN-DAVIES, WEEKS, FORESTIER-WALKER and BOR, *Milton Keynes: Interim Report*, p. 6, 1968.

3.4 N. LICHFIELD, 'Goals in Planning' paper to Town and Country Planning Summer School, 1968.

3.5 M. M. WEBBER, 'Permissive Planning', *Town Planning Review*, January, 1969.

3.6 N. LICHFIELD, 'Goals in Planning', paper to Town and Country Planning Summer School, 1968.

3.7 The GLC, for example, takes as an identification of its objectives the statutory duties laid on the Council by the London Government Act, as they have been interpreted in the discussions of the members of the planning committees and their officers, incorporated into the earlier draft stages of the Development Plan and discussed by the Council, as a whole. 'GLC—Tomorrow's London', *RTPI Journal*, July/August, 1971.

3.8 JOHN FRIEDMAN, 'The Future of Comprehensive Urban Planning: a critique', *Public Administration Review*, May/June, 1971.

3.9 WALTER BOR, *The Making of Cities*, p. 224, Leonard Hill Books, 1972.

3.10 JONATHAN WELFARE, 'Programme Budgeting: the experience of Milton Keynes', *RTPI Journal*, Sept./Oct., 1972.

3.11 See for example (among many others) Mosbrough Master Plan Clifford Culpin and Partners (1968) where the following statements appear: "The main aim behind our proposals is to enable the City of Sheffield to expand at Mosbrough in the best possible way.
At Mosbrough our basic objectives will be to promote the best possible conditions for living, working, education, recreation and communications. Individual freedom of choice over as wide a range as possible of these activities will be an additional key objective."

3.12 Public Participation and policy planning are treated in Chapter 6.

3.13 J. D. STEWART, *Management in Local Government*, Charles Knight and Co. Ltd., 1971.

4
Corporate Planning and PPBS

In Chapter I a working context was advanced for local government, laying particular stress on the interrelated nature of problems and possible solutions to those problems. Chapter 2 explored the nature of planning and here it is proposed to explore Planning, Programming, Budgeting Systems, in the context of the problems of urban management and corporate planning. Emphasis will be laid on how the programme budgeting system may, with adaptation, provide a much improved framework within which corporate decisions of a local authority may be taken. The intention is to develop a framework which is robust enough to accommodate the many difficulties and constraints found in local government.

FOUR MAJOR ASSUMPTIONS BEHIND IMPROVED DECISION MAKING

It is appropriate here to set out and elaborate the four basic assumptions with which PPBS is under-pinned. In a sense these assumptions seem facile and perhaps too obvious to deserve mention. It is only when the current approaches to decision making in local government (or perhaps even in any sphere) are probed that no matter how obvious these assumptions are, they seem not to have penetrated or influenced things very much in practice.

1. *Decisions are likely to be better if we know what it is we are trying to achieve*

Perhaps the most useful way of probing this assumption is to take a series of common examples which expose how prevailing decision-making systems either fail to take it into account or pay only superficial attention to it. The essential point is that many decisions to implement certain projects or policies simply reflect the existence and responsibilities of a unit within an organisation which over time has perhaps developed an interest in perpetuating itself rather than meeting specific needs in the community. Once a Baths department, or a Parks department, even an Education department is set up, each develops an interest in promoting baths, parks and perhaps schools. Interest focusses on inputs rather than outputs. The performance of a unit or of a local authority department is judged by what it produces rather than the *effects* on the community of what it produces. Thus we cannot rest on having built *x* miles of urban motorway, on having adopted a no-parking policy, on having opened *y* community centres or acquired so many acres of public open space. These can be judged in terms of their impact, in terms of whether they are achieving whatever it is the local authority wanted to achieve by investing its resources in these particular inputs. All local authority expenditure can only be judged by the dividends it produces in terms of its impact, its effects. There are limits to how much probing can be done. It is always possible to go on asking the question, 'Why are we doing this—what is its purpose?' The sceptics would say and often *do* say that it is better to do something than to do nothing. Plainly the argument is to attempt to extend the area of questioning to produce more *relevant* action. Needless to say there are occasions when doing nothing *is* the best answer. When that answer is arrived at through the process of analysis and probing we can be satisfied.

To 'enable old people to lead as full and independent a life as possible' (4.1) is an objective. Planning decisions in this area are likely to be better if this objective is explicitly stated. It is the starting point for identifying alternative ways of securing its achievement. It is not a justification for carrying on providing the same facilities that have always been provided for old people. A perpetual consciousness of the objective serves as a base for new ideas and a challenge to old ones.

Whilst the point should not be laboured unduly it is helpful at this stage to reflect on the pervasiveness of 'standards', to reflect how slavish subservience to standards very often dulls any sense of purpose in the decision-making arena other than the one of achieving a particular standard. Whether self-imposed or, as is more often the case, imposed by central government or by a profession on itself, there are many examples which illustrate the dangers. For instance, the public open space standards (drawn up in 1925 by the National Playing Fields Association) recommend a provision of open space of 10 acres per thousand population divided up into various categories including some attached to schools. What these standards totally obscure is the *distribution* of open space, the needs of different age-groups, the possibility that leisure outlets may take a variety of forms of which open space is only one, that leisure demands change and that it is the *combination* of possibilities which is important. The achievement of such a standard is almost meaningless in general and in London, for example, totally impracticable. The Greater London Development Plan sets a lower standard which in places like Lambeth is still too high and of course is ignored. What London and similar places have to focus on is the entirely different objective of ensuring the accessibility of a range of outlets for leisure pursuits given the constraints of the situation and changing leisure patterns. They are *not* trying to achieve an arbitrary standard but rather to provide a satisfactory provision and distribution of leisure facilities according to the needs of the area.

There are many standards or professional sacred-cows (e.g. the concept of 'density') which obscure rather than illuminate the purpose behind them. Some in the public health field, in the fire service, deserve probing. The argument is not against standards but against their tendency to be arbitrary, to remain unquestioned and to block the exploration of a wider range of solutions to achieving what is desired. Decision making benefits if during the process there is an explicit objective to be achieved.

2. *Decisions are likely to be better if information is available as to how resources are being deployed as between objectives rather than as between a department or committee responsible for implementation*

"The present federal budget design is largely the product of a historical response to the need to safeguard the integrity of appropriations against careless, ill-informed, maleficent administrators in the executive departments. It is an instrument for the control of spending. It was not designed to assist analysis, planning, and decision-making, and it does not work well for that purpose. It is a conventional comptroller's budget, not a manager's budget." (4.2)

Therein lies the obstacle. The traditional budget in local government provides information for control purposes, it is not intended to aid decision making.

Figures 4.1 and 4.2 show typical local government committee budgets. They reflect the activities carried out or overseen in these cases by the Highways and Health Committees and implemented largely by the Borough Engineer and Medical Officer of Health respectively. What these budgets fail to provide is information which will expose choice, which will show what resources are being deployed as between different ways of achieving certain objectives. Almost all local government budgets take a similar form.

Traditionally the 'planning process' which lies behind such budgets, is for the engineer or whoever is responsible for the service concerned to come up with a list of projects, policies and schemes for developing his service. He takes for granted, almost, that what was spent in his area in the previous year will be forthcoming in the following year plus an increase which will vary according to a variety of factors, the economic and political climate, the strength of competing claims, the rate of inflation and a good deal more. The main focus of the engineer's energies will be on securing that he is successful in getting agreement, and hence the resources, for the develop-

HEALTH COMMITTEE

1968–1969 Gross Expenditure £	1968–1969 Income £		1969–1970 Gross Expenditure £	1969–1970 Income £
		Local health:		
147,000	13,000	Administration	—	—
6,000	1,000	Health centre	16,000	3,000
74,000	2,000	Clinics	88,000	8,000
75,000	17,000	Day nurseries	94,000	19,000
96,000	—	Midwifery and training	96,000	—
85,000	—	Health visiting and training	100,000	—
35,000	32,000	Welfare foods	20,000	3,000
6,000	—	Family planning	9,000	—
132,000	7,000	Domestic help	150,000	7,000
101,000	—	Home nursing	124,000	—
11,000	—	Chiropody	26,000	—
8,000	—	Tuberculosis	8,000	—
6,000	1,000	Vaccination and immunisation	25,000	1,000
234,000	3,000	Ambulance	268,000	2,000
108,000	4,000	Training centres	125,000	4,000
18,000	7,000	Hostels	19,000	6,000
37,000	1,000	Other services	62,000	1,000
1,179,000	88,000		1,230,000	54,000

		Public health:		
105,000	10,000	Administration	124,000	13,000
105,000	—	Clean Air Act	59,000	—
22,000	1,000	Other statutory functions	26,000	1,000
50,000	—	Northumbrian River Authority	47,000	—
6,000	—	Tees Port Health Authority	6,000	—
288,000	11,000		262,000	14,000
		Government grants:		
—	50,000	Clean Air Act	—	29,000
288,000	61,000		262,000	43,000
		Cemeteries:		
11,000	—	Administration	12,000	—
97,000	29,000	Cemeteries	110,000	34,000
21,000	26,000	Crematorium	25,000	29,000
129,000	55,000		147,000	63,000
£1,596,000	£204,000		£1,639,000	£160,000

Figure 4.1

HIGHWAYS COMMITTEE

1968–1969 Gross Expenditure £	1968–1969 Income £		1969–1970 Gross Expenditure £	1969–1970 Income £
		Highways:		
309,000	—	Administration	381,000	—
902,000	10,000	Roads	1,122,000	7,000
313,000	—	Public lighting	348,000	—
14,000	—	Car parks	42,000	—
273,000	—	Sewers	302,000	9,000
8,000	—	Coast protection	11,000	—
54,000	19,000	Properties	47,000	19,000
2,000	1,000	Accident prevention	3,000	2,000
60,000	—	Contribution towards purchase of vehicles	—	—
1,935,000	30,000		2,256,000	37,000
		Government grants:		
—	210,000	Roads and lighting	—	—
1,935,000	240,000		2,256,000	240,000
		Cleansing:		
33,000	—	Administration	48,000	—
430,000	15,000	Refuse collection	527,000	20,000
125,000	31,000	Refuse disposal	135,000	30,000
70,000	4,000	Conveniences	84,000	4,000
235,000	10,000	Street cleaning	275,000	4,000
72,000	1,000	Snow clearance	78,000	1,000
27,000	28,000	Markets	29,000	28,000
992,000	89,000		1,176,000	87,000
		Government grants:		
—	14,000	Street cleansing and snow clearance ...	—	9,000
992,000	103,000		1,176,000	96,000
£2,927,000	£343,000		£3,432,000	£336,000

Figure 4.2

ment of his service. It is true that in very tight economic circumstances he may be forced into a consideration of which of his existing activities he should curtail to enable him to develop other aspects of the service, but the search for cut-backs is *ad hoc* and normally hits so-called 'peripheral' activities. This is incremental budgeting. The converse is zero-base budgeting which implies starting from scratch each year or for each budget cycle. The object is to expose to challenge *all* the activities of the local authority each year. There are obvious criticisms of this approach, indeed it has been sharply attacked in its application at the Department of Agriculture in the United States (4.3). This attack however can be substantiated only partly in terms of zero-base budgeting. There were many other reasons why the system collapsed, the most obvious being that it was *imposed* on the organisation which was unprepared for it. Personnel felt threatened and inadequate to deal with it. The surprising feature was not that the attempt at zero-base budgeting collapsed but that it was ever attemped in that way.

Obviously it would be of questionable value to go right through a department's budget every year with a view to having to justify afresh each item of expenditure against the organisation's objectives. The exercise is enormous and denies the reality that many items of expenditure derive from past commitments and cannot be switched on and off at frequent intervals. The kernel of zero-based budgeting however is a valid need to expose much more of a local authority's expenditure to systematic scrutiny, some of it annually but perhaps more usefully on a continuing basis. The approach should be through an arrangement of information in such a way that systematic scrutiny is possible. What is required is information on the extent to which objectives are being met, information on costs related to effectiveness in achieving those objectives. With the traditional budget it is not.

Exploring Figure 4.2 further, items such as roads (£1,122,000), sewers (£302,000) and coast protection (£11,000) appear. All these three items are disparate in the sense that they represent expenditure designed to achieve differing objectives. They do not contribute towards the same objectives. The decision makers need to be presented with the information on coast protection in an entirely different framework. Resources expended on coast protection can be seen as an investment in protection of people and property from hazards, in this case due to weak sea defences. The resources so expended have to be judged against other investments in public safety measures. The judgements will not be easy and at the end of the road may be subjective, but even a subjective judgement can be sharpened up given information cast in a relevant framework. Decisions are likely to be improved if information is presented in this way.

3. *Decisions are likely to be better if the effectiveness of current programmes, policies and projects are evaluated*

The learning process has been stressed already. Given an *orientation* towards goals and objectives one of the most important pieces of information is the effectiveness of current programmes at achieving those objectives. The most obvious point is that the mere fact of launching a project, of adopting a policy, of sanctioning a building programme does not automatically secure that it is effective. Effectiveness itself needs to be monitored.

It is important, in addition to straightforward monitoring of effectiveness, to be conscious of the range of activities which are contributing towards the achievement of objectives. Very often they will lie in unexpected quarters. Indeed, there will be many activities of *outside* agencies contributing towards our objectives or maybe negating our efforts. But even within the one local authority there is likely to be a range of activities making an impact on a variety of objectives. Sometimes the impact will only be a by-product from another activity, not its main impact. Thus the expenditure of finance on rent collectors, whilst having its main impact perhaps as a general support service to the overall housing objectives of the local authority, can be seen also as an investment in at least two other aspects. Firstly as fulfilling a welfare function through weekly visits to old people's dwellings. It is a point of contact for old people and before a local authority abandons this system of collecting rents in favour, say of central collecting points, it should not ignore the consequential side-effects. The second respect in which a rent collector can be seen as an investment is simply as an effective reporting device for housing maintenance.

The evaluation of effectiveness and measurement of outputs presents its own problems. These problems however do not invalidate the general principle and even if the evaluation never raises itself above the completely subjective this at least secures that the decision-making machinery is focussed on collecting information about effectiveness. It is not simply carrying on activities for the sake of it or to perpetuate the existing units of administration.

4. *Decisions are likely to be better if alternative ways of achieving an objective are considered and analysed*

An awareness of goals and objectives needs to be extended to a consideration and analysis of a variety of ways of their achievement. Indeed, the identification of fundamental objectives makes this easier and aids the generation of alternatives. The setting of objectives provides a yardstick against which to judge alternative approaches and policies. There are two opposite dangers in generating alternatives. The first is that of exposing too many. The second is of constraining the alternatives within traditional ways of thinking, within the framework of our present organisational structures. Of the two the second is more likely to prevail. The alleviation of many urban problems will very often lie outside the organisational unit which first considers them or outside the confined range of options which spring to the mind of one professional group. We need to develop ways of extending the range of alternatives considered and having done so there remains the problem of evaluating them, not just in present terms but in terms of their future impact.

THE NATURE OF PPBS

The danger of *describing* PPBS is that of making it appear as a technique, as a set of mechanisms, even magic mechanisms for better if not perfect decision making. Thus at the outset it should be understood that PPBS is *not* a technique. It is *not* helpful to regard it as a mechanism for decision making although it is possible to put this interpretation on it. It is appropriate to draw attention to the words Programming, Planning, Budgeting Systems themselves. Substitutes are often used. In Great Britain, 'programme budgeting' is the most common name. The danger is that the name itself will convey a meaning or even induce an approach to the subject which denies or distorts the fundamental nature of PPBS itself. PPBS is essentially an *approach* to decision making. It is not a technique but a way of presenting information in a systematic way so as to expose policy choices, making as explicit as possible the costs and consequences of these choices. As will be seen there is no set of rules which can be laid down describing how to do it. Indeed, this would destroy the concept altogether. There are many approaches some of which will be explored. But, the philosophy behind PPBS is contained in the four assumptions set out above and expressed in a shorthand way in the very words Programming, Planning, Budgeting Systems. They express a concern for Planning, for Programming (in the sense of both time and sets of decisions for action), for Budgeting of resources of various kinds and for the systems approach, the learning approach. Any abbreviation is permissible only to the extent that it does not destroy these fundamental processes underlying PPBS.

THE PROCEDURES OF PPBS

A note of caution first, again underlining what has been stated. In any description of procedures there is the danger that it can be interpreted as a sequential set of instructions. This is not the intention. Perhaps even the word 'procedures' should be avoided. The procedures will be set out in a critical way, exposing various ways of approaching them none of which can be judged as 'correct'. The very nature of situations in which PPBS has to operate renders it necessary to conceive of several rather than one approach. On the other hand some approaches will be advanced as more helpful than others in terms of what PPBS can contribute. Realities of practice may present reasons for modifying the approaches. This is accepted.

There are four main components of PPBS :

1. programme structures;
2. programme analysis;
3. the corporate plan;
4. review and feedback.

Programme Structures

Stress was laid in Chapter 3 on the need for the planning process to be orientated towards goals and objectives. Goals are less specific than objectives, giving expression more to general hopes and aspirations rather than to expectations. A programme structure is an hierarchical way of arranging goals, objectives, sub-objectives and activities, which gives expression to what a local authority as a whole sees as its current needs and problems and the variety of choices open to it to meet those needs. It is a way of relating activities to goals and objectives regardless of the pattern of departmental and committee responsibilities within the authority. Thus it becomes possible for activities with common objectives or outputs to be considered together along with the cost of each. The fact that operationally they may be administered or implemented by different departments or sections or even by different authorities altogether, does not prevent the activities being compared relative to the objective to which they are contributing.

Rather than describe the programme structure in any more detail it is more helpful to examine specific examples. The examples are from British Local Government.

The Institute of Municipal Treasurers and Accountants (4.4) suggests five tests for a programme structure.

"(i) clear statements of objectives, free from ambiguity;
(ii) opportunities for choice between alternative means whereby the purposes of an immediately superior level may be served;
(iii) the avoidance where possible of gaps or overlaps between and within objectives/programmes;
(iv) the expression of programmes and activities in terms of assessable outputs and impacts wherever possible, in order to monitor the efficiency and effectiveness of each alternative, and
(v) the lowest level in a structure being that below which output, effectiveness or cost ceases to be significant to the authority."

These tests are useful for considering the programme structure illustrated here in Figures 4.3 and 4.4.

Figure 4.3 *PROGRAMME STRUCTURE EXAMPLES: London Borough of Islington**

The following is a list of the major objectives.

PLANNING AND DEVELOPMENT

Overall Objective:

To shape and co-ordinate the land-uses and the physical redevelopment of the Borough to provide a satisfactory urban environment sustained by adequate economic activity.

HOUSING

Overall Objective:

To provide an opportunity for residents of the Borough to live in satisfactory homes in pleasant surroundings by promoting private, and where necessary, public development of a mixture of dwellings whose size, type, tenure and price will meet the continually changing demands of the local community.

SOCIAL SERVICES

Overall Objective:

To assist members of society who are in any way handicapped or deprived, to lead and/or re-establish as full and satisfactory lives as possible within the community.

HEALTH, SAFETY AND PROTECTION

Overall Objective:

To maintain and, where possible, improve the physical and mental health of the population of the Borough, and reduce the number of accidents involving physical injury.

LEISURE

Overall Objective:

To provide accessible, year-around opportunities for the varied enjoyment of leisure time by the inhabitants of the Borough.

TRANSPORTATION

Overall Objective:

To assist in the provision of facilities for safe, speedy and efficient travel by the inhabitants and workers of Islington (co-operating with the Greater London Council, and acting as its agent) through the maintenance of the established road system, the improvement of principal non-metropolitan roads and distributor roads, the applica-

* Extracts from the Borough's position in summer 1970. Since then there has been a change of political control but this has not involved *fundamental* changes in the PPBS. The system is developing.

tion of traffic management techniques, and any other appropriate means. In all traffic measures to have full regard for the environment and amenities of the Borough.

GENERAL SERVICES

Because the individual programmes have such different aims and functions there is no overall objective for this basic programme.

The housing and social services objectives are now broken down in detail:

HOUSING

1. Research and Planning

To review the condition of housing in the Borough, to identify existing and future housing need, and develop programmes leading towards the overall objective within the framework for urban renewal as a whole.

2. New Housing

To reduce the number of unsatisfactory dwellings in the Borough.

(*a*) *Non Municipal*

To encourage the private sector, Housing Associations, Housing Societies and other bodies to replace sub-standard dwellings with new housing where this is the most economic and suitable method of urban renewal.

(*b*) *Municipal*

(i) Where necessary, to replace sub-standard dwellings with new Council housing where this is the most economic and suitable method of urban renewal.

(ii) Where possible all houses and flats should be designed and built in such a way that at a later date it will be possible to offer them, should it be necessary, for sale.

(iii) To minimise the disruption of existing neighbourhoods.

3. Rehabilitation and Modernisation of Housing

(*a*) *Non Municipal*

To encourage the private sector, Housing Associations and other bodies to renew unsatisfactory housing where this is the most suitable method of urban renewal.

(*b*) *Municipal*

Where necessary, to increase the number of satisfactory dwellings in the Borough by use of the Council's powers to rehabilitate or modernise properties or areas of unsatisfactory housing (including Council property not up to modern standards).

(*c*) *Housing Improvement Grants*

To investigate and exploit opportunities for the improvement of individual houses or areas of housing through the provision of improvement grants and the declaration of general improvement areas.

(*d*) *Unfit Dwellings*

To use the Council's statutory powers to require repairs or improvements to dwellings in an unsatisfactory state, or to close or demolish dwellings unfit for habitation where these are not covered by other programmes.

(*e*) *Baths and Laundries*

To provide public warm baths or showers for persons living in dwellings without them. To maintain existing laundry facilities on an economic basis where there is a need for them.

4. *Home Ownership*

The Council wishes to encourage home ownership in order to give stability and security to the family.

(*a*) The Council will build, when necessary, flats and houses for sale to existing Council tenants, owner occupiers and tenants displaced in Housing Development Areas, tenants of slum houses and those on the housing waiting list.

(*b*) The Council will offer for sale, within the limits imposed by the Ministry of Housing and Local Government, Council flats to those Council tenants able and willing to purchase them.

(*c*) To grant housing loans to inhabitants of the Borough otherwise unable to purchase a house.

5. *Assistance to Individuals*

(*a*) *Lettings and nominations*

To ensure that accommodation available to the Council is occupied as quickly as possible in accordance with priorities aimed at obtaining the maximum relief of the social pressures caused by unsatisfactory housing throughout the Borough.

(*b*) *Out-county development*

To reduce the number of persons in unsatisfactory accommodation in Islington, both directly and by making the Council accommodation available, by the provision of housing outside the Borough for persons wishing to move (particularly the elderly) and by seeking new more flexible means of direct co-operation with New Town Authorities.

(*c*) *Housing advisory service*

To assist residents of the Borough in solving their housing problems other than by way of an offer of Council accommodation.

6. Housing Management

To maintain satisfactory housing conditions for tenants of the Council through application of the principles of good housing management, including the maintenance of balanced communities, the encouragement of the advantages of the typical urban social environment and the establishment of good landlord/tenant relationships. To assist in the elimination of housing need by keeping under or over occupation of Council dwellings to the minimum.

(*a*) *General Management*
(*b*) *Buildings and estate maintenance*
(*c*) *Estate improvements*

7. Rents

(*a*) *Municipal*

To charge tenants of Council flats at least 'fair rents' with a generous rent rebate for those in need.

(*b*) *Non-Municipal*

To encourage the Minister of Housing and Local Government to progressively decontrol properties so that all rents of all controlled dwellings shall be on the basis of at least 'fair rents'.

8. Unassigned Administration

SOCIAL SERVICES

1. Families and Children

(*a*) *Family advice*

To prevent family distress and breakdown and/or the need for children to be received into care or appear before a court, by the provision of readily accessible advice, guidance and assistance from social workers, the establishment of family advice centres, and any other suitable arrangements (including facilities for adoption, child protection, and the supervision of children in their own home).

To maintain contact between children in care and their families and to encourage forms of intermediate care which can lead to the re-establishment of the family.

(*b*) *Family planning service*

To promote the physical and mental health and social well-being of families (particularly mothers) through the availability of family planning advice and equipment and the collection and examination of cervical smears.

(*c*) *Day Nurseries*

To assist single parents, working or unwell mothers, their family and children by the provision of day nurseries for children under five, with priority for those cases where this may prevent family breakdown (where there is only one parent, the mother is sole or essential family support, or where the health of mother and child is suffering from home conditions) or where children will particularly benefit (where a handicapped child needs to mix with normal children).

To regulate, and where appropriate support, child-minders and private nurseries and play groups serving a similar function.

(*d*) *Housing Assistance*

To assist families unable to afford a fair rent to live in satisfactory accommodation through the operation of a rent rebate scheme or other measures.

(*e*) *Homeless families*

To find or make available temporary accommodation for families in Islington without a home.

(*f*) *Unmarried mothers and motherless families*

To provide help to unmarried mothers through advice, guidance and the provision of suitable accommodation and assistance where necessary; to prevent the breakdown of motherless families by the provision of home helps and other assistance.

(*g*) *Children in care*

To provide for the welfare of children who remain in the care of the Council and their return to their families wherever possible, by the provision of suitable accommodation (including accommodation and treatment on a less-than-full-time basis) situated in or very near the Borough.

(i) *Homes and hostels in the Borough*
(ii) *Homes outside the Borough*
(iii) *Remand homes and approved schools (Community Homes)*
(iv) *Foster Parents*
(v) *Administration and general*

2. *Services for the Elderly*

(*a*) *Home care*

To assist elderly persons wishing to live at home to maintain their health and live full lives within the community, by the provision of meals on wheels and luncheon clubs, rent rebates, equipment for the home and other regular visiting of all types.

(i) *Visiting*
(ii) *Meals on Wheels*

(iii) *Day centres and luncheon clubs*
(iv) *Home bathing*
(v) *Provision of aids*
(vi) *Geriatric health clinics*
(vii) *Economic assistance*

(*b*) *Residential care*

To provide for the residential care of elderly persons unable or unwilling to continue living at home through the provision of suitable accommodation enabling them to live as full and active lives as possible.

(i) *Sheltered accommodation*
(ii) *Hillside*
(iii) *Other residential homes*
(iv) *Non-council homes*
(v) *Admissions*

(*c*) *Other Services*

To give all elderly persons the opportunity to live full lives by the provision of opportunities for continued employment, outings and holidays.

(i) *Workshops for the elderly*
(ii) *Holidays and outings*

3. *Services for the Handicapped*

(*a*) *Home assistance*

To assist physically handicapped persons to live satisfactory lives within the community by visits and guidance, and the provision of aids or adaptations to the home.

(*b*) *Residential care*

To provide for the residential care of the physically handicapped or blind unable to continue living at home through the provision of suitable accommodation enabling them to live as full and active lives as possible.

(*c*) *Other assistance*

To give the physically handicapped the opportunity to live normal lives within the community through their gradual introduction to full-time employment and through the provision of special holidays.

(i) *Social rehabilitation centres*
(ii) *Sheltered workshops*
(iii) *Holidays*

4. Unassigned Administration and General

Figure 4.4 *PROGRAMME STRUCTURE EXAMPLES: Coventry City Council**
The following is a list of major objectives.

EDUCATION

Prime Objective:

To enrich the lives of the people by the optimum personal development of each individual in the community.

COMMUNITY HEALTH AND WELL-BEING

Prime Objective:

To assist in achieving and maintaining the optimum standard of community health and well-being for people in Coventry.

PUBLIC PROTECTION

Prime Objective:

To promote consumer services, environmental hygiene and public safety.

THE PROVISION OF HOUSING ACCOMMODATION

Prime Objective:

To secure an adequate and proper distribution of satisfactory housing accommodation to meet the social and economic needs of the City.

TRANSPORTATION

Prime Objective:

To ensure the existence of facilities for the movement of persons and goods.

LEISURE OPPORTUNITIES

Prime Objective:

To ensure appropriate provision of facilities for the whole community to enjoy their free time and in particular to encourage those pursuits which contribute to the development of the individual and family life and to voluntary participation in the life of the community.

THE PROMOTION OF COMMERCIAL AND INDUSTRIAL DEVELOPMENT

Prime Objective:

The promotion of commercial and industrial development of the City and of the region to meet the optimum employment and social needs of the City, consonant nevertheless with the needs of industrial and commercial concerns which may be involved.

* Position as at Autumn 1971. Again Coventry's system is developing.

THE PROVISION OF A SATISFACTORY PHYSICAL ENVIRONMENT

Prime Objective:

The achievement of a satisfactory physical environment for the community in all its activities. (A satisfactory physical environment can be expressed in two principal forms: 'Sensory Aspects' and 'Functional Aspects'. The objectives should, therefore, be tested to see if they satisfy the various elements of the physical environment which can be generally grouped under these headings. Sensory aspects include visual elements, noise, smell and other aspects of comfort. Functional aspects examine if the environment is functioning satisfactorily or provides a convenient framework for living.)

GENERAL SUPPORT

Prime Objective:

To provide general support and to deal with other unassignable functions.

The Education and Housing objectives are broken down further:

EDUCATION

Objective 1

To ensure in the light of parental wishes adequate educational provision appropriate to the needs of infants below the age of five years.

Sub-objectives	*Activities*
1.1 To ensure the provision of an appropriate pattern of nursery facilities	1.1.1 The provision and maintenance of nursery schools and units
1.2 In association with parents, managers and teachers and, where applicable, in accordance with the Rules of Management, to ensure an appropriate standard and variety of instruction, social training and care for nursery pupils	1.2.1 The provision of teaching and other staff for nursery schools and units
	1.2.2 The provision of educational materials to aid instruction and training
	1.2.3 The provision of inspection and advice
	1.2.4 The improvement in the quality of the teaching force through in service training and teachers' centres
	1.2.5 The encouragement of the development of educational thinking and practice through support for educational research generally and curriculum development in particular
	1.2.6 The provision of medical and other care
1.3 To promote the development of nursery age children by the provision of appropriate assistance and advice to voluntary bodies, parents and others	1.3.1 Assistance to voluntary bodies providing nursery facilities
	1.3.2 The provision of assistance to pre-school play groups

Objective 2

In association with parents and voluntary bodies to ensure the provision for all children other than handicapped children and aged between five and eleven years of full-time education appropriate to their different ages, abilities, and aptitudes and to their particular needs and to secure their participation therein.

Sub-objectives	*Activities*
2.1 To provide and maintain, with other bodies, a sufficient pattern of primary schools appropriate in number, character and location	2.1.1 The provision and maintenance of primary schools
2.2 In association with parents, managers and teachers and in accordance with the Rules of Management to ensure an appropriate standard and variety of instruction and training for all primary pupils	2.2.1 The provision of teaching staff for schools
	2.2.2 The provision of educational materials to aid instruction and training
	2.2.3 The provision of inspection and advice to schools
	2.2.4 The improvement of the quality of the teaching force through in-service training and teachers' centres
	2.2.5 The encouragement of the development of educational thinking and practice through support for educational research generally and curriculum development in particular
2.3 With parents to secure the regular attendance of pupils at school and to ensure they are in a fit condition to benefit from the education provided	2.3.1 The provision of facilities to improve the mental and physical health of all pupils
	2.3.2 Assistance in the transport of pupils to and from schools
	2.3.3 The provision of facilities to improve the standard of nutrition of all pupils
	2.3.4 The provision of assistance so that no child is withdrawn from school because of financial hardship
	2.3.5 Improvement in the attendance of children at school
2.4 With parents, managers, teachers and voluntary bodies to ensure appropriate provision for extramural activities to promote the social and other development of children	2.4.1 The provision of facilities for cultural development, outdoor pursuits, and school journeys and outings
	2.4.2 The provision of assistance to voluntary bodies

Objective 3

In association with parents and voluntary bodies to ensure the provision for all children other than handicapped children and aged between twelve and sixteen years of full-time education appropriate to their different ages, abilities, aptitudes and other needs and to secure their participation therein.

Sub-objectives	*Activities*
3.1 To provide and maintain, with other bodies, a sufficient pattern of secondary schools appropriate in numbers, character and location	3.1.1 The provision and maintenance of secondary schools
3.2 In association with parents, governors and teachers and in accordance with the Articles of Government to ensure an appropriate standard and variety of instruction and training for all secondary pupils	3.2.1 The provision of teaching staff for secondary schools 3.2.2 The provision of educational materials to aid instruction and training 3.2.3 The provision of inspection and advice to schools 3.2.4 The improvement in the quality of the teaching force through in-service training and teachers' centres 3.2.5 The encouragement of the development of educational thinking and practice through support for educational research generally and curriculum development in particular
3.3 With parents to secure the regular attendance of pupils at school and to ensure that they are in a fit condition to benefit from the education provided	3.3.1 The provision of facilities to improve the mental and physical health of all pupils 3.3.2 Assistance in the transport of pupils to and from schools 3.3.3 The provision of facilities to improve the standard of nutrition of all pupils 3.3.4 The provision of assistance so that no child is withdrawn from school because of financial difficulties 3.3.5 Improvement in the attendance of children at school 3.3.6 Enforcement of the regulations governing the employment of juveniles
3.4 With parents, governors, teachers and voluntary bodies to ensure appropriate provision for extra-mural activities to promote the social and other development of children	3.4.1 The provision of facilities for cultural development, outdoor pursuits and school journeys and outings 3.4.2 The provision of facilities for school clubs, hobbies, and out-of-school sports activities

Sub-objectives	*Activities*
	3.4.3 The provision of youth clubs and assistance to voluntary youth organisations
3.5 To ensure that appropriate guidance is available to pupils concerning opportunities in further education and careers	3.5.1 The provision of careers and educational advisory services

Objective 4

In association with other bodies (local, regional and national) to secure the provision of facilities for students over sixteen years of age to develop further their interests, skills and intellectual attainments to achieve the highest possible degree of competence and satisfaction in their vocation and in their personal life.

Sub-objectives	*Activities*
4.1 In association with voluntary bodies to ensure the provision of a sufficient pattern of accommodation to mount courses suitable in number, standard and variety to meet the needs of those students wishing to continue their education full-time before entering employment or wishing to enter higher education	4.1.1 The provision and maintenance of sixth form accommodation in secondary schools 4.1.2 The provision and maintenance of accommodation for full-time post-16 education in colleges of further education
4.2 In association with governors and teachers, and in accordance with the Articles of Government to ensure an appropriate standard and variety of instruction for those students wishing to continue their education full-time before entering employment or wishing to enter higher education	4.2.1 The provision of teaching staff for sixth forms in secondary schools 4.2.2 The provision of educational materials to aid instruction and training in sixth forms 4.2.3 The provision of teaching staff for full-time post-16 courses in colleges of further education 4.2.4 The provision of educational materials to aid instruction and training in full-time post-16 courses in colleges of further education 4.2.5 The provision of instruction and advice 4.2.6 The improvement in the quality of the teaching force through in-service training and teachers' centres

Sub-objectives	*Activities*
	4.2.7 The encouragement of the development of educational thinking and practice through support for educational research generally and curriculum development in particular
	4.2.8 Support for students attending full-time post-16 courses below the level of higher education
4.3 In association, where appropriate with employers and others to ensure the provision of a sufficient pattern of accommodation to mount courses suitable in number, standard and variety to meet the needs of students for instruction and training arising from their employment	4.3.1 The provision and maintenance of accommodation for part-time post-16 courses below the level of higher education
4.4 In association with governors and teachers and in accordance with the Articles of Government to ensure an appropriate standard and variety of instruction for those students in need of instruction and training arising from their employment	4.4.1 The provision of teaching staff for part-time post-16 courses below the level of higher education
	4.4.2 The provision of educational materials to aid instruction and training in part-time post-16 courses below the level of higher education
	4.4.3 The provision of inspection and advice
	4.4.4 The improvement in the quality of the teaching force through in-service training and teachers' centres
	4.4.5 The encouragement of the developments of educational thinking and practice through support for educational research generally and curriculum development in particular
	4.4.6 Support for students attending part-time post-16 courses below the level of higher education
4.5 To ensure the provision either directly or in association with other bodies of an appropriate pattern in number and character of higher education institutions	4.5.1 The provision and maintenance of accommodation for polytechnics
	4.5.2 The provision and maintenance of accommodation for colleges of education
	4.5.3 The provision of facilities for research
4.6 In association with governors and teachers, and in accordance	4.6.1 The provision of teaching staff for polytechnics

Sub-objectives	*Activities*
with the Articles of Government, to ensure an appropriate standard and variety of instruction in higher education courses	4.6.2 The provision of educational material, to aid instruction and training in polytechnics
	4.6.3 The provision of teaching staff for colleges of education
	4.6.4 The provision of educational material to aid instruction and training in colleges of education
	4.6.5 Direct support for universities
	4.6.6 Awards and support to students on higher education courses
4.7 To ensure that appropriate guidance and assistance is available to students in regard to their careers and future employment	4.7.1 The provision of careers and educational advisory services
4.8 To promote the personal development by the promotion, either directly or with bodies of adequate facilities for youth and adult education	4.8.1 The provision of a Youth Service
	4.8.2 The provision of accommodation
	4.8.3 The provision of teaching staff
	4.8.4 The provision of educational materials
	4.8.5 Assistance to other bodies providing adult education
	4.8.6 The provision of support for conferences, exhibitions and similar activities

Objective 5

In association with parents and voluntary bodies to ensure the provision for handicapped children up to sixteen years of age of full-time education appropriate to their different ages, abilities and aptitudes to their particular needs and to secure their participation therein.

Sub-objectives	*Activities*
5.1 To assess the special educational needs of handicapped children	5.1.1 The assessment of the requirements of handicapped children
5.2 To provide and maintain, with other authorities and voluntary bodies, a sufficient pattern of accommodation for special education appropriate in capacity, character and location	5.2.1 The provision and maintenance of special schools and units and boarding schools
5.3 In association with parents, governors, teachers and medical staff and in accordance with the Articles of Government, to	5.3.1 The provision of teaching and other staff for special schools and units, boarding schools, home and hospital tuition

Sub-objectives	*Activities*
ensure an appropriate standard and variety of instruction, training and care for all handicapped pupils	5.3.2 The provision of educational materials to aid instruction and training 5.3.3 The provision of inspection and advice to special schools 5.3.4 The improvement of the quality of the teaching force through in-service training and teachers' centres 5.3.5 The encouragement of the development of educational thinking and practice through support for educational research generally and curriculum development in particular 5.3.6 The provision of medical and social care for children in special schools and units and boarding schools
5.4 With parents, to secure the regular participation of handicapped children in the special education provided and to ensure they are in a fit condition to benefit from it	5.4.1 Assistance in the transport of children to and from special schools and units and boarding schools 5.4.2 The provision of facilities to improve the standard of nutrition of all handicapped children 5.4.3 The provision of assistance so that no handicapped child is prevented from participating in the special education provided because of financial hardship 5.4.4 The provision of careers and educational advisory services

Objective 6

To secure the progressive development of the education service; to identify the changing needs by the initiation and support of research; and to secure an effective consultative partnership of all participants within the service.

Sub-objectives	*Activities*
	6.1.1 The provision of advice 6.1.2 The undertaking of research 6.1.3 Support for research undertaken by other bodies 6.1.4 The provision of consultative machinery

THE PROVISION OF HOUSING ACCOMMODATION

Objective 1
Provision of New Housing

To ensure that there is a sufficiency of new dwelling units and associated facilities to meet the changing needs of the City.

Sub-objectives		*Activities*
		Corporation
	1.0.1	Direct provision of new dwellings (*a*) for old people (*b*) for handicapped persons (*c*) for other needs
	1.0.2	Direct provision of hostels
	1.0.3	Direct provision of caravan sites
		Non-Corporation
	1.0.4	Mortgage loans to individuals for the acquisition or building of new dwellings
	1.0.5	Guarantees to Building Societies
	1.0.6	Loans and grants to housing associations and societies to enable them to provide new dwellings (*a*) for old people (*b*) for handicapped persons (*c*) for other needs
	1.0.7	Sale of land for new private residential development
	1.0.8	Lease of land for new private residential development
	1.0.9	Sale of land for private hostel accommodation
	1.0.10	Lease of land for private hostel accommodation
	1.0.11	Loans and grants to voluntary bodies and housing associations for new hostel accommodation

Objective 2
Improvement and Repair of Existing Dwellings

To ensure that, where appropriate, dwellings are maintained in a good state of repair and condition with satisfactory accommodation, amenities and environment.

Sub-objectives	*Activities*
	Improvement to Residential Areas
	2.1.1 Direct improvement by Corporation of residential areas
	2.1.2 Loans, grants and assistance, voluntary groups and housing associations
	2.1.3 Development control
	2.1.4 Designation and implementation of General Improvement Areas
	2.1.5 Elimination of non-conforming uses
	Repairs to dwellings
	2.2.1 Repair of Corporation dwellings
	2.2.2 Enforcement of repairs to non--Corporation dwellings
	2.2.3 Loans and grants to housing associations
	2.2.4 Repair of non-Corporation dwellings in default
	2.2.5 Loans to private householders and landlords
	2.2.6 Acquisition and repair of unfit dwellings required to protect adjoining fit property
	Improvement to buildings
	2.3.1 Improvement to Corporation dwellings
	2.3.2 Grants to private householders and landlords
	2.3.3 Grants and loans to housing associations
	2.3.4 Loans to private householders and landlords

Objective 3
Elimination of Housing Incapable of Being Made Fit

To ensure that all dwellings which are incapable of being made fit or are otherwise unsuitable for human habitation were withdrawn from residential occupation.

Sub-objectives	*Activities*
	3.0.1 Declaration of Clearance Areas
	3.0.2 Making Closing Orders
	3.0.3 Making Demolition Orders
	3.0.4 Compulsory Purchase of unfit houses

Objective 4
The Securing of the Satisfactory Use of Dwellings

To encourage and, where appropriate, to secure the satisfactory use of dwellings.

Sub-objectives		*Activities*
4.1 To promote and protect occupiers' rights and amenities	4.1.1	Protection of tenants in cases of harassment and unlawful eviction
	4.1.2	Inspection of properties (*a*) For overcrowded conditions (*b*) For enforcement of statutory provisions of Housing Acts in relation to dwelling houses, houses let as lodgings and houses in multi-occupation
	4.1.3	Implementation of Housing Acts to prevent overcrowding and over-occupation
	4.1.4	Protection of tenants by securing provision of rent books
	4.1.5	Planning consent to avoid non-conforming use
4.2 The control of existing and potential housing stock	4.2.1	Direct conversion of Corporation dwellings into flats or other house types
	4.2.2	Grants and loans to housing associations for conversion of dwellings
	4.2.3	Grants and loans to private householders and landlords for conversion
	4.2.4	Inspection of dwellings for detection of multiple occupation
	4.2.5	Implementation of Housing Acts in relation to the control of overcrowding
	4.2.6	Planning control over change of user and overcrowding
	4.2.7	Mortgage loans to private individuals for the purchase of second-hand houses
	4.2.8	Guarantees to Building Societies
	4.2.9	Control of caravan sites
	4.2.10	Transfers of tenants between Corporation dwellings
	4.2.11	Rebates to Council tenants

Objective 5
General Support of Housing Accommodation

To ensure an adequate and efficient administrative and advisory service to undertake research to identify the changing needs for housing accommodation in the City and to carry out support activities for other objectives of the Programme Area.

Sub-objectives	*Activities*
5.1 Research	5.1.1 Research and identification of changing needs
5.2 Other support	5.2.1 Survey, planning and control of development
	5.2.2 Professional and consultancy services
	5.2.3 Inspection and survey of dwellings
	5.2.4 Management of Corporation dwellings
	5.2.5 The provision of an advisory service

Analysing these structures along the dimensions suggested by the IMTA illustrates the usefulness of programme structures themselves. The ultimate test can possibly be best summed up by asking the simple question, 'Does the structure present a useful framework for the exercise of choice?' If it does it is good, if it does not then it needs changing! Both these structures give a basis for choice. The Islington structure, especially, translates its goals and its objectives into activities. It also gives clear expression to the political attitude of the authority, e.g. in respect of the sale of council houses.

GENERAL GUIDELINES, PROBLEMS AND POINTS FOR CONSIDERATION

"Because of the many options open for program structure classifications, it would be unwise to expend too much time and effort in perfecting the design of the initial program structure. After trial, the design can be revised as best suits the requirements of the particular jurisdiction and the needs of its policy decision-makers. The program structure is only one of the several parts of the PPB system. If the fundamental objectives have been sufficiently identified, even a rough-cut program structure should be sufficient for forming the framework for the subsequent analytical efforts that are the essence of a PPB system. The test of a satisfactory program structure will be its usefulness for the on-going processes of choice and decision." (4.5)

There are three basic approaches to drawing up a programme structure. One is to establish a set of goals and related objectives for an authority and then to work down the hierarchy grouping activities which might contribute towards the immediately superior objective. The difficulty here is the tendency to become bogged down in what is a very complex process and at the end of the day to finish up with a structure which is difficult to make operational. It does, on the other hand, force an inquiry into what needs to be done, into where there are gaps in the work of the authority.

The second approach is to begin with a complete list of activities which the authority carries out and to construct the programme structure from these, grouping together activities which contribute towards a higher objective. Here the programme structure is constrained by the scope of the authority's present activities and enshrines these whereas the whole idea of the structure is to present choices outside as well as within what happens at present. This leaves the third approach which combines the two.

As the IMTA tests imply it is plainly essential for any programme structure to be flexible. This is true particularly in the sense that when new problems emerge or different policy issues come up for consideration, the structure can be readily adapted to throw up information relevant to these issues. At some point, for example, information may be required on an areal basis or by client groups (age, sex, etc.). Perhaps more important, when there is a change in policy, e.g. after a change in political control, as was the case in Islington, the programme structure needs to be capable of adapting to new priorities. In the Islington case, the new, incoming political party used the programme structure to give expression to its policies and priorities as distinct from its opponents. The housing programme structure, for example, gives a clear 'Conservative' expression of policy on the sale of council houses as we have noted already.

The question is often raised whether in beginning to explore PPBS an authority should confine its attention to one area, e.g. Transportation, rather than attempting an 'across the board' approach. The evidence suggests that the 'across the board' approach is better for several reasons. The first is that the very nature of PPBS relates activities and objectives rather than separates them. Coventry Corporation in its earlier attempts at PPBS started with Health but soon came to the conclusion that the implications over the whole range of the Corporation's activities were too important to ignore. In reality programme areas (i.e. the group of objectives, sub-objectives and activities contributing to a fundamental objective) have blurred edges. There are always going to be overlapping activities, activities which contribute in some way to more than one programme area. A programme area is best seen as a major focus of attention with fuzzy limits rather than a self-contained set of objectives and activities. In order to arrive at useful programme areas therefore it is important to study them together at the outset.

Another reason for the 'across the board' approach is that of securing commitment and understanding of the different departments. PPBS is clearly of corporate interest and it is as well to generate active participation in the process as the best means of learning right at the outset. It will be viewed with suspicion and scepticism in any event. There is no point in generating more than is necessary.

A further question which is raised is whether the drawing up of a programme structure is not simply a sterile academic exercise. The answer is that it need not be and in practice there is ample evidence both from the United States and this country that the opposite is the case.

"Twenty-six agencies have developed program structures. These differ widely in quality and utility. Generally, they *do* represent helpful ways of looking at agency activities for analytical purposes, involvement in their preparation has been educational, and they do tend to highlight programs which should be considered together. In some cases, they have had impact on officials who had not realised the breadth or triviality of agency efforts in particular fields and in pursuit of particular objectives." (4.6)

The experience in the City of Coventry and the London Borough of Islington has been similar. This does not mean automatically that the exercise is useful. Plainly the degree of commitment and involvement, the extent to which a deliberate effort is made to make the exercise helpful will condition any judgement of the usefulness of drawing up programme structures. The instrument itself cannot be categorised as academic or of practical value (if they are opposites), it depends on how that instrument is used.

There is a temptation or a danger of judging the effectiveness of a programme structure too soon. The cynics will very early on point out that budget decisions are still made in the way they have always been made, that structures still reflect existing organisational designs. If that situation persists for a long time then the critics have valid points. What is more likely to happen is that the framing of information on programme structure lines will develop and increasingly influence decision making. It will not be a process which will be switched on at some appointed day. Similarly programme structures may well be inadequate in several ways including bearing too strong a relationship with existing organisations. Anyone who has worked in local government will know that compromise is, indeed *has* to be, part of the way of life and if compromise is the price to pay for improvement, it is probably worthwhile.

Controversy sometimes arises over the issue of whether or not activities of bodies *outside* the local authority should be included in a programme structure. If the working context set in Chaper 1 is accepted as a starting point for corporate planning in local government then clearly the activities of other bodies must at least be considered. It is a point taken up again in considering the organisation implications for corporate planning in Chapter 7. The degree of influence a local authority can have varies enormously and statutorily speaking it may have no power whatever outside the local government field. Practice varies. Many local authorities seek to influence the location of employment within their areas. They do it in several ways, e.g. by building factories for lease themselves, by pressuring central government to implement different policies, policies which will affect favourably the situation in a particular area. The Rolls Royce collapse in Derby is a good example of this kind of action by a local authority. Liverpool acts similarly:

"*Unemployment*

The rise in unemployment on Merseyside, although part of a national pattern, underlines the City Council's decision of a year ago to express its strategy partly in economic terms. In the new situation the City Council arranged a Seminar on the subject of Unemployment, and, subsequently, a meeting of Merseyside Local Authorities. Arising from these actions, two projects are now being pursued in consultation with local authorities and a number of organisations on Merseyside, namely, (*a*) the establishment of a compact but representative Committee to consider unemployment problems and monitor progress in finding solutions, and (*b*) the establishment of a Merseyside Office in London." (4.7)

Perhaps a more important area for concern is the relationship between the tiers of local government. This will be especially pertinent in Great Britain when local government is re-organised. To sharpen up the point it is interesting to see that Gloucestershire County Council has ignored the functions of the county district councils within Gloucestershire in drawing up its programme structures. But clearly there are distinct overlaps. The transportation, health, and family life programme areas are obvious examples where the activities of both tiers of government overlap in that they both contribute towards the same community objective. What decides whether the activities of both tiers of local government should be included is really whether or not by so doing the community is likely to benefit by having its resources allocated more effectively. The answer is bound to be that it is. The criticism can be levelled against a number of authorities, e.g. Islington for not considering the overlap with the education service, administered by a separate authority i.e. the Inner London Education Authority. The principle can be applied especially between local government, the health services, statutory undertakers and British Rail. In all these fields there is considerable scope for creating new frameworks for consultation and joint working between these bodies. The way in which programme structures and indeed PPBS itself may be adapted to aid decision making between tiers is taken up in Chapter 7.

PROGRAMME ANALYSIS

The purpose of programme analysis is to "provide the best possible information on the cost and effectiveness implications of program alternatives in satisfying the purposes sought in order to aid government decision makers in making their choices. If *improved* insight *useful* to government decision makers is provided by analysis, then it will presumably lead to improved program decisions". (4.8)

The concern in corporate planning in local government is to derive objectives from needs existing and perceived in the community, and then to decide on how to deploy limited resources to meet those objectives most effectively. The relationship is between needs, objectives, inputs (the variety of resources available) and outputs (the effectiveness of action relative to the resources used).

"To perform its key tasks of allocating resources between services and getting the best value for money in each of them, the Corporation requires an organisation in which, as far as possible, a single committee and departments:

> Decide on the priorities within groups of services with similar objectives, e.g. priorities for education or for personal services to the disadvantaged.
>
> Consider all the feasible alternative ways of performing services so as to select the method giving the best value for money." (4.9)

We have already seen the dangers of standards if they become static, too formalised or remain unchallenged. Clearly however, to identify needs or to set operational objectives, standards will be required. Objectives do not stand naked—they have underpinning them some standard or yardstick as a basis both for establishing needs in the first instance and later for evaluating progress. 'Need' itself is a vague concept and plainly varies with the particular value sets of the observer. Notwithstanding the difficulties, some authorities have attempted to map out needs in their areas. The London Borough of Southwark is one such authority which has begun to do this. Figure 4.5 is an extract of the kind of data mapped out.

The whole business of measures of effectiveness or of output measures as they are frequently called is in a state of rapid development and change (4.10). New areas are being probed, surrogate measures and indicators are being devised, areas which were previously thought to be incapable of measurement or evaluation are being explored. It is a very difficult area and often gives rise to violent controversy—fears that measurable factors

Figure 4.5

CENSUS DATA*

Immigrants from India, Pakistan, the West Indies

Low income families

Number of families with more than two children

Number of old people and number of under 5's as a percentage of the population

Single-person households

Number of single-parent households

Amount of overcrowding

Lack of facilities such as hot water, w.c's etc.

Amount of multi-occupation

Household tenure

LOCAL AUTHORITY SOURCES

Families requesting transfer out of local authority housing areas (This might indicate areas which are regarded by residents as low-status areas)

The housing waiting-list distribution

Condition of tenement blocks

Applications for local authority homeless family accommodation

Rent tribunal cases

Some measures of mobility (we thought that the electoral registers might give a rough estimate, or that we might look at the records of Health Visitors or G.P.'s to give us some idea of turnover of known residents)

The distribution of play-space

Number of children receiving free dinners

Distribution of children in care

The distribution of day-care facilities

Distribution of ill-health

Causes of death

Infant mortality rate

Distribution of suicides

GOVERNMENT SOURCES

Families on supplementary benefits

Distribution of unemployed

* Extract from Working Paper on Methods of Analysing Need, Southwark Community Project, National Institute for Social Work Training and London Borough of Southwark Planning Division (1970).

Studies have also been done in Liverpool and Birmingham.

OTHER SOURCES

What 'social servants' say

Numbers without a G.P.

Ratio of families having quarterly electricity and gas accounts to those with slot meters; and those who are cut off

Number of telephone boxes not working

Distribution of criminal offenders

Distribution of known alcoholics and drug addicts

CRITERIA INVESTIGATED

The criteria which we in fact investigated are set out below. These differ in some respects from the original list. In some cases the relevant data did not prove to be available at all, e.g. numbers of families with more than two children, or was confidential, e.g. supplementary benefits, or the amount of work involved in collecting it was recognised to be too great at this stage, e.g. housing waiting list.

DEMOGRAPHIC AND PHYSICAL ENVIRONMENTAL FACTORS

Proportion of immigrants (people born in India, Pakistan, British Caribbean, Africa, Cyprus, Malta)

Proportion of old people

Proportion of children under five

Proportion of single-person households

Proportion of people out of work

Overcrowding

Population density

Lack of open spaces and play-space

Housing tenure

Housing stress

Tenement distribution and condition

Income

SOCIAL FACTORS

Take up of free school meals

Distribution of first offenders

Distribution of Juvenile Bureau cases

High Problem Areas as defined by the social servants

Distribution of applications and admission to homeless family accommodation

Infant mortality and still-birth rates

Incidence of fires

Number of people not on General Practitioners' lists
Turnover of patients from one General Practitioner to another
Size of general practice lists
Educational Priority Areas
Distribution of electricity and gas meters
Incomes (*a*) Take up of supplementary benefits
(*b*) Tax returns
Rent Tribunal Cases
Distribution of Case Work by Ward (Children's and Welfare Departments)
Size of policy beats
Applications to Rent Officer

will prevail over immeasurable ones—that 'quality of life' factors, aesthetics and other similar elements will go to the wall and the technocratic revolution will have destroyed us. These are real fears, not to be dismissed lightly:

(*a*) because the existence of these fears may well block any move at all towards programme evaluation and

(*b*) because they are valid in their own right.

Any move towards evaluation needs to accommodate these fears. To the extent that the expression of these fears is simply a device for avoiding challenge and questioning they are obviously to be resisted. On the other hand, to the extent that they are something much more than this then any evaluation will take analysis to the point where it is valid and beyond that, subjective judgement will rightly take over. In the last resort politicians will certainly apply their value sets to any analysis put before them.

"In discussing output in the public sector one can distinguish between *intermediate output* and *final output*.

Intermediate output is the immediate translation into non-financial terms of what is produced from the money and effort expended on activities. They are the equivalent of the physical products of a manufacturing process. Measures of intermediate output might be in terms of the number of people served, the proportion of people who might require a service who receive it, facilities or capacity provided, and so on according to the type of activity.

However, intermediate output is of interest only in so far as it contributes to the attainment of stated objectives. Assessment should go beyond persons or institutions reached, or facilities provided. One needs to assess the ultimate impact of an activity on its objective(s); that is, its *final output* or *effectiveness*." (4.11)

Examples of output measures in the transportation field are seen in the example from Gloucestershire (4.12) County Council (Figure 4.6).

Figure 4.6 *GLOUCESTERSHIRE COUNTY COUNCIL*

TRANSPORTATION

OUTPUT MEASURES

A. To promote rapid and economic transport of goods and people

	Intermediate	*Final*
		The two major measures of effectiveness of this programme are journey time and vehicle operating costs Comfort is also an output
1. Provision of highways		
1(*a*) Improvement	Capacity	Journey time Vehicle operating cost Comfort
1(*b*) Maintenance	—	ditto
1(*c*) New construction	Capacity	ditto
2. Reducing the effects of bad weather		
2(*a*) Snow clearance	Length of road cleared by class of road Proportion of snow cleared from roads by class of road	Journey time/journeys prevented Accidents due to skidding
2(*b*) Frost and ice treatment	Length of road treated by class of road Proportion of frost occurrences anticipated	Accidents due to skidding
2(*c*) Other	Proportion of snowy or icy days when roads are clear	Accidents on stretches Journey time
3. Other forms of public transport	Modal split in tons/passengers Number of passenger routes maintained Frequency of services Percentage utilisation of facilities	Journey time (*a*) On public transport (*b*) Of other vehicles Comfort
4. Traffic Management Measures		
4(*a*) Temporary re-routing	Frequency of jams and congestion	Journey time Operating costs
4(*b*) Parking control	Frequency of jams and congestion	Journey time Operating costs
4(*c*) Off-street parking	Use of car parks	Journey time Operating costs
4(*d*) Segregation	—	Journey time of favoured vehicles Journey time of restricted vehicles

	Intermediate	*Final*
4(*e*) Control of flow	Road capacity Frequency of jams	Journey time Operating costs
5. Research	—	—

B. To preserve the environment

1. Appearance of *Existing* Roads		
1(*a*) Landscaping	Eyesores concealed Roads concealed from beauty spots Views opened up	Public comment Motorists stopping at view points
1(*b*) Choice of materials	—	Public comment
1(*c*) Prevention of unsightliness		
(i) Litter bins	Amount of litter	Public comment
(ii) Cleansing	Condition of urban roads	ditto
(iii) Abandoned cars	Number of cars removed	ditto
1(*d*) Rehabilitation of run-down areas	Number of areas treated	
1(*e*) Street furniture	Proportion where special care is taken over design or siting	Public comment Landscape architects' judgement
2. Route Selection for *New* Roads		
2(*a*) Alignment	Number of properties affected Noise levels	Property values Cost of noise Public comment
2(*b*) Landscaping	—	—
2(*c*) Materials	—	Landscape architects' judgement
3. Traffic Restriction Measures	Noise Vibration	Property values
3(*a*) Weight restrictions	Violations Noise Vibration	ditto
3(*b*) Control of noise	Noise Violations	ditto

C. To reduce accidents

1. Safety Characteristics of Roads		
1(*a*) Preventing or reducing	—	Accidents rate on new roads Cost of accidents
1(*b*) Measures for temporary hazards	—	Accident rates Cost of accidents
1(*c*) Protection of pedestrians	—	No. of accidents to pedestrians Cost of accidents

	Intermediate	*Final*
1(*d*) Street lighting	—	Accident rates on lit and unlit roads
2. Road Safety education		
2(*a*) School education	Number of children contacted Tests of school children's knowledge of road safety Observation of school children's road behaviour	Accidents to school children
2(*b*) General publicity	Number reached by publicity campaign	Accident rates
3. Road Worthiness of Vehicles		
3(*a*) M.O.T. tests	Failure rate	Accidents per 1000 tested vehicles
3(*b*) Roadside tests	Failure rate	Number of vehicles in accidents that have mechanical faults
3(*c*) Weight testing	Failure rate	Number of accidents involving overloaded vehicles
3(*d*) Tyre pressure gauges	Proportion that are inadequate	
4. Improvement of Driving Standards		
4(*a*) Driver training	Pass rate	
4(*b*) Driver performance	Vehicles stopped by police	Accidents involving driver negligence
5. Research into Accidents		

The distinction between intermediate and final output measures is well illustrated. In many areas we may never move from intermediate measures. It may be that some things remain unevaluated in any but the vaguest terms.

"I can see the education point of view, but nevertheless remain disturbed that, for all the enormous input, educational output is happily (or rather effortlessly) accepted as unmeasurable. We are left with : 'I know an educated child when I hear one !' " (4.13)

Programme Analysis is not merely concerned with output measures. It is concerned also with probing of issues. To this extent it may be said that its concern is not limited to on-going programmes and issues but also with specific *ad hoc* issues which will arise from time to time.

The *issue paper* is a fairly simple approach to analysis and this is probably where it derives its strength. Too often the very complexity of some analysis exercises defeats the object. An issue paper addresses itself to fairly common sense questions but in a systematic manner :

"A. *What is the Problem?*

1. What seems to be the real problem?
2. What appears to be the causes of the problem? To what extent are they currently known?
3. Who are the specific population (i.e. clientele) groups affected? (If other than the general public, identify their special characteristics such as: age, group, race, income class, special needs, geographical location, etc.)
4. What is the magnitude of the problem? How widespread is it now? How large is it likely to be in future years?

B. *Objectives and Evaluation Criteria*

1. Toward what public objectives should programs for meeting the problem be directed? Sought here are the *fundamental* purposes, not the immediate physical outputs.
2. How can estimates of progress against these objectives be made? Identify the appropriate evaluation criteria (i.e. measures of effectiveness). If these do not seem directly measurable, indicate the 'proxies' that might be used.

C. *Current Activities and Who's Involved*

1. What other agencies of the government, what other sectors of the community, or other levels of government, in addition to this government, are involved in attempting to meet the problem?
2. What specific activities are currently being undertaken by this government that are relevant to the problem? Identify each such current program and, to the extent possible, provide current costs and their current estimated impact relative to the criteria in B.2. Indicate the number in each beneficiary group identified in A.3. and those currently being served. If possible, project these into the future based upon current planning.

D. *Political and Other Significant Factors*

1. Are there major political factors that seem to affect the problem?
2. Are there any unusual resource or timing limitation problems of special significance?

E. *Alternatives*

1. What alternative programs or activities should be considered for meeting the problem? Describe the major characteristics of each.

F. *Recommendations for Follow-Up*

1. What is recommended as the next step? The Issue Paper should not normally contain *program* recommendations as to choices among alternatives. But it should indicate what next should be done about the issue. Recommendations as to the timing and scope of needed follow-up analysis should

be made, whether the analysis is to be of the 'quick-response' or 'in-depth' type.
2. What are the major data problems likely to be associated with undertaking an in-depth analysis? How might these problems be met in the short run? The long run?" (4.14)

An issue paper can possibly be best described as a systematic attack on a problem. Take, for example, the problem of vandalism in a particular area. This is a common problem, to which local authorities tend to respond in fairly predictable and conventional ways—and vandalism still goes on. To expose this problem to the issue paper is to probe the problem deeply perhaps to reshape it, to expose different approaches or at the very least to highlight a significant lack of data.

The issue paper is only one approach to analysis but a useful one. The analysis may be rigorous, it may only be exploratory, or as rigorous as scarce manpower resources will allow. There is a case for two stage analyses, an exploratory exercise first followed by a deeper study if it is felt to be justified. In the realities of everyday practice what is likely to happen is that major issues will be selected for analyses or those which happen to be politically significant. Gradually, however, the information base within an authority, the analytical skills and approaches will grow and develop to a point when continuous analysis may be possible or when *ad hoc* pieces of analysis can be tackled relatively easily, rather than to assume giant proportions as they do at present, simply because we lack skills, approaches and data.

Analysis was not invented with PPBS. Analysis is old enough. The PPB system presents a framework for it, gives it a focus, so that it can be brought to bear on the decision-making process in a helpful way.

THE CORPORATE PLAN

After what has been said in Chapter 2 it would be invidious to put too much emphasis on the corporate plan, i.e. on a plan as such. The corporate plan is not a monolithic document containing blueprints for the next twenty years. It is much more closely related to the notion of an on-going, changing picture of the longer term aspirations of a local authority, the shorter term actions and policies it is committing itself to in order to achieve its longer term goals and objectives, and an information indicator to demonstrate the position at intervals.

It is much more a working context for short term action planning. The emphasis will be much more on monitoring and adaptation but as time moves on specific commitments will be made and implemented. As we saw in Chapter 2, these commitments will often be made on inadequate data. That is the reality of life. But data derives also from the learning process and this is where a new emphasis will be placed. Other areas of concern for the corporate plan will be the anticipation of problems, their changing nature and intensity, the anticipation of opportunities.

In practice there will be some tangible form to the corporate plan. It may be a programme budget. Whatever name is given to it, it will be a formal presentation of information about objectives, policies and proposals to achieve those objectives, an elaboration of resource allocation (manpower finance and other) relative to the objectives, targets to be achieved. In particular it will reflect not just capital expenditure but the revenue implications in resource terms over a period, possibly of 5 years—any longer is for most purposes unrealistic though broad indications, i.e. ranges of estimates may be an advantage. The time limit in reality is imposed by a variety of uncertainties including political uncertainties. The corporate plan will be much more than a list of projects to be completed. Rather it will be a 'pocket' information system for the decision makers.

Attempts have been made to produce output budgets (as distinct from our traditional financial control budgets). Controversy rages about them (4.15); whether to have two sets of budgets, whether to convert to output budgets (or programme budgets) only—whether to have cross-walks between the two. In all probability it seems we shall have both—for a while at least. The two types of budgets are intended for different purposes and as we shall see in Chapter 7, the organisational units most suitable for planning purposes do not necessarily coincide with the ones required for implementation and financial control.

At present we do not have anything like adequate data for complete programme budgets and certainly the collection of on-going data relative to outputs, i.e. the traditional practice of monitoring actual expenditure against budgets would be extremely difficult with output budgets. It is probably not necessary to make the effort. Sample monitoring of this kind is probably all that can be justified at the moment.

Accountants tend to fret about the minute details, for example, of what the implications are of output budgeting for computer codings, whether two or three more digits will be required. Of course, details cannot be ignored—they simply have to be overcome if the end product justifies it. (In this respect the Institute of Municipal Treasurers and Accountants has done some very impressive work.)

The following is an extract from Gloucestershire programme plan which is still at the development stage. It well illustrates the emerging form of budget where decision makers can see relationships between expenditure and objectives rather than simply inputs.

GLOUCESTERSHIRE COUNTY COUNCIL | PROGRAMME SUMMARY

PLANNING PROGRAMMING BUDGETING SYSTEM

1971–72 BUDGET | TRANSPORTATION

OVERALL OBJECTIVE: To facilitate the transportation by road of goods and people in the County, to the maximum extent compatible with safety and preservation of the environment, having regard to the existence of other forms of transport.

COST SUMMARY *Capital and Revenue Expenditure (excluding debt charges) and expenditure by other Depts.*	*1970–71 Estimate*	*1971–72 Estimate*	*1972–73 Forecast*	*1973–74 Forecast*
PROGRAMME:				
A. To promote expeditious and economic transport of goods and people	4,337,300	5,924,545		
B. To preserve the environment	82,000	139,340		
C. To reduce accidents	298,850	402,630		
D. General administration and support	355,800	489,195		
Transportation Programme Total £	5,073,950	6,955,710		
Deduct Capital Expenditure £	1,097,400	2,189,800		
Deduct Expenditure by other Departments £	121,305	142,290		
Deduct Income £	1,513,120	1,875,750		
Add Debt Charges £	181,230	254,130		
Net Expenditure to be met from Revenue £	2,523,355	3,002,000	3,092,000	

DESCRIPTION:

A The Highways Department is responsible for the provision of new routes to meet traffic demands and the maintenance and improvement of the existing road system. The free flow of traffic is assisted by control of parking, segregation of road users, provision of direction signs and other aids to movement, aided by police action in enforcement and control.

B The Department assists in preservation of the environment by landscaping of roads, grass cutting and street sweeping. Careful consideration is given to the design and location of new roads or improvements to harmonise with existing features.

C Several sub-programmes are devoted to the reduction of accidents. The Department is responsible for street lighting, providing protection for pedestrians, dealing with temporary hazards and minor improvements aimed at reducing accident blackspots.
The Police are responsible for enforcement of any restrictions imposed, collecting accident data and co-operate with the Education Department's Road Safety Organiser for general road safety publicity, schools, education and training programme.
The Weights and Measures Department carries out tasks to ensure the road-worthiness of vehicles particularly heavy goods vehicles.

D Some expenses cannot readily be allocated under individual activities, for example administrative salaries, central charges and recoverable costs are included on this programme.

GLOUCESTERSHIRE COUNTY COUNCIL PLANNING PROGRAMMING BUDGETING SYSTEM	TRANSPORTATION
1971–72 BUDGET	PROGRAMME C: To reduce accidents

OBJECTIVE: To improve the safety characteristics of the highway system by reducing hazards, providing lighting and facilities for pedestrians, improving driving standards and roadworthiness of vehicles and by education of the public and school children in road safety.

DESCRIPTION: In the last two years the number of accidents in the County in which people are injured has risen sharply to 3211 during 1970 higher than pre-breath test figures. 103 people were fatally injured and 4576 seriously or slightly injured.

Expenditure towards the Objective is incurred by several Departments under the Sub-Programme below and forms a significant proportion of the total sum:

1. The Highways Department seeks to prevent or reduce hazards by:
   (*a*) improvement of blackspots, speed limits, mandatory and advisory signs, control of accesses etc.
   (*b*) dealing with temporary hazards, e.g. floods, fallen trees, etc.
   (*c*) protection of pedestrians by provision of footways, crossings, guard rails, subways etc. and includes expenditure on school crossing wardens by the Education Department.
   (*d*) provision of new street lighting and maintenance of existing lighting.
2. Road Safety Education is undertaken by the Road Safety Organiser and the Police and consists of general publicity and lectures and education in schools.
3. Checks on the roadworthiness of vehicles are not the sole function of any Dept. The Weights and Measures Dept. check goods vehicle weights and tyre pressure gauges and the Police and Department of the Environment carry out random checks.
4. Cycle and motorcycle rider training is arranged by the Road Safety Organiser and Police to improve standards. Heavy goods vehicle driver training for the Authority's own staff is carried out by the Central Repair Depot.
5. Research into the causes of Road Accidents is carried out by the Highways Dept. on data provided by the Police Statistics etc. are issued to Dept. of Environment, other local authorities and various Depts. of the CC.

COST SUMMARY *Capital and Revenue Expenditure (excluding debt charges) and expenditure by other Depts.*	*1970–71 Estimate*	*1971–72 Estimate*	*1972–73 Forecast*	*1973–74 Forecast*
SUB-PROGRAMMES:				
1. Safety characteristics of the highway system	267,050	363,115		
2. Road Safety Education	23,140	26,990		
3. Ensuring roadworthiness of vehicles	650	740		
4. Improvement of driver/rider standards	2,130	2,190		
5. Research into causes of accidents	5,880	9,595		
SUB-PROGRAMME TOTAL £	298,850	402,630		
Deduct Capital Expenditure £	31,200	30,700		
Deduct Expenditure by other Depts. £	51,790	63,120		
Deduct Income £	47,570	63,230		
Add Debt Charges £	5,090	17,900		
Net Expenditure to be met from Revenue £	173,380	263,480		

GLOUCESTERSHIRE COUNTY COUNCIL PLANNING PROGRAMMING BUDGETING SYSTEMS	TRANSPORTATION PROGRAMME C: To reduce accidents through:
1971–72 BUDGET SUB-PROGRAMME C.1:	Safety characteristics of the highway system

DESCRIPTION: The objective of this Sub-Programme is to make road conditions as clear and safe as economically possible, imposing restrictions where necessary. Expenditure is incurred on:

(*a*) 1. Visibility improvements, selected on the basis of accident record and cost.
  2. Adequate signing and road markings within the strict criteria laid down by the D of E.
  3. Speed limits where within the strict criteria laid down by the D of E.
  4. Strict control of vehicular accesses to all classified roads by planning control.
  5. Miscellaneous – e.g. cattle grids.

(*b*) Expenditure on temporary hazards e.g. floods, gales, removing fallen trees, oil spillage etc.

(*c*) Protection of pedestrians:
  1. New footways are generally those adjoining existing roads and are provided only after careful assessment of the need.
  Expenditure on long distance footpaths e.g. Offa's Dyke, is fully reimbursed but since it serves a leisure pursuit is not included in the Transportation Programme.

2. The maintenance of existing footways adjoining roads. Grants are made to Parish Councils for maintenance of cross-country footpaths, generally on the basis of 50%.
3. Pedestrian crossings when authorised by the D of E.
4. Subways and footbridges within strict criteria of the D of E.
5. Guardrails and barriers, provided mainly for pedestrian protection e.g. at schools, junctions etc.
6. The Education Department's expenditure on provision of School Crossing Wardens contributes towards the Sub-Programme and costs £33,200.

(*d*) Street lighting priorities are established by the accident record in darkness, urban conditions etc. Maintenance of old systems forms a major proportion of the expenditure.

MEASUREMENT OF OUTPUT	*Present Position*			*1971–72 Target*		
	M'way & T.R.	*P.R.*	*Non P.R.*	*M'way*	*P.R.*	*Non P.R.*
(*a*) Number of blackspots improved						
(*b*) Number of accidents due to temporary hazards						
(*c*) Number of pedestrian casualties		604				
(*d*) Accident rates on lighted or unlighted roads						

COST SUMMARY: ACTIVITIES Capital and Revenue Expenditure (excluding debt charges) and Expenditure by other depts.		*1970–71 Estimate*	*1971–72 Estimate*	*1971–72 Estimate category of Route*		
				M'way & T.R.	*P.R.*	*Non P.R.*
ACTIVITY:						
(*a*) Preventing or reducing traffic hazards		83,080	117,800	21,500	11,300	85,000
(*b*) Dealing with temporary hazards		710	555	55	80	420
(*c*) Dealing with pedestrians		49,020	97,670	6,000	13,670	78,000
(*d*) Street lighting		134,240	147,090	7,300	30,790	109,000
ACTIVITIES TOTAL	£	267,050	363,115	34,855	55,840	272,420
Deduct Capital Expenditure	£	31,200	30,700			
Deduct Expenditure by other Depts.	£	25,870	33,200			
Deduct Income	£	47,570	63,230			
Add Debt Charges	£	5,090	17,900			
Net Expenditure to be met from Revenue	£	167,500	253,885			

REVIEW

A good deal has been said about feedback and the learning process. As for frequency of review there can be no rules. The approach is likely to be better however the closer review comes to being continuous. This may not be possible. Certainly fixed review periods militate against sensible planning but certain features, such as rate making may need to be fixed although even this is not sacrosanct.

"The overall corporate plan is likely to be reviewed whenever new information about the future environment becomes available which suggests a need for planning action by the local authority. There is no reason to suppose that this will occur at precise annual intervals. However, the shorter-term part of the corporate plan—the programme plan—should be up-dated annually. Each year's revised plan will be built up from assumptions about expenditure on existing programmes, and about the changes likely to be made by Council Estimates of costs and outputs of existing programmes will be assembled for a first draft of the plan, perhaps as early as the autumn of each year. Policy decisions will come available throughout the year as Committees and Council take decisions in principle on the results of individual programme analyses. Both sets of information will be included in the draft programme plan in order to test whether their overall effects produce an acceptable level of expenditure and service to the public. The draft plan should provide a better framework than existing budgetary documents within which to discuss and take decisions on marginal cuts or expansions of programmes in order to reconcile resource requirements and availability." (4.16)

This is a more rigid view than the view set out in this chapter but it probably reflects more accurately the sort of stage the corporate plan will go through in the next few years, but in some ways it stifles the dynamic inherent in the type of planning we have discussed.

REFLECTIONS ON PPBS

Many people are sceptical about PPBS—others have even condemned it as a failure even in *this* country although it is difficult to see how such a judgement can be made when no local authority has yet implemented the system fully nor has had sufficient time to do so. Local government in England did not even hear about PPBS until late in 1967 and early 1968 and therein lies the body blow to its premature critics. Whether PPBS is a success or a failure ultimately depends on what one thinks it is. One view has been presented here—the most important characteristic being that it is not a mechanistic technique or set of procedures but a way of thinking to aid the process of corporate planning. With that as its major characteristic it is difficult to challenge. True, the procedures which have been set up around it, the high expectations unfulfilled can be held up as evidence of something but they do not touch the major part of PPBS.

The United States has had more experience and in an appraisal (4.17) Carlson makes the following observations :

"1. Definition of objectives. During the last 4 years, many agencies have undergone at least a partial reappraisal of their functions and missions. The general result has been an increase in the understanding of programs and in the awareness of possible alternatives and limitations that would not have occurred otherwise.

2. Information. The quality, relevance, and structure of information being developed by the agencies have improved substantially. There is more solid information on program inputs and outputs, related to objectives, than was true a few years ago. The progress in this area includes the all-important element of structuring information into useful form. . . .

3. Use of analysis in decision making. As studies are made, they are used increasingly to assist decision makers. As indicated above, useful analysis in the domestic agencies has increased by about 200% during the last 4 years, and in the Defense Department by a higher per cent during the last 8 years.

4. Evaluation of programs. The federal government traditionally has not obtained sufficient feedback on the results of its programs. But there is now general agreement that it is important to measure the accomplishments of programs and to obtain information on whether the concepts that underlie each program prove to be useful. PPBS has placed emphasis on this, and during the last 4 years the amount and caliber of program evaluation has increased. As more work is done to make the review and evaluation function a routine part of program administration, progress should be faster. It is still true, though, that the evaluation of existing programs is far from complete and receives less emphasis than evaluation of new programs or the redirection of experimental programs.

5. Management efficiency. During the last 4 years in a few agencies and 8 years in parts of the Defense Department, some attempts have been made to trace the use of resources and measure them against predetermined program plans. These steps have been useful in identifying the complexities and difficulties of doing this and also in whetting the appetite to try it on a wider scale.

6. Recognition of the legitimacy and necessity of analytic arguments. When PPBS was initiated, many of the analysts who joined the government were

familiar with quantitative analysis of different types. They were aware of its value and also of its possible abuses and limitations, so many of the problems involved were not entirely unexpected. But they were surprised to find that large numbers of people would deny the relevance of analysis to government activities.

7. Comparisons of related programs in several agencies. Some improvement in ways of displaying related programs in several agencies has occurred. These promise to further the establishment of general priorities by measuring the impact of complementary programs irrespective of organisational lines. For example, the 24 manpower programs found in six agencies, the 21 education programs found in five agencies, and the 16 health programs found in three agencies can be reviewed with related programs irrespective of agency identification."

A comment frequently made in this country is that politicians will not commit themselves publicly to a set of objectives and priorities. As time goes on the comment is increasingly undermined when new authorities turn in their different ways to PPBS. The phenomenon of political exposure in this way is a feature of the Public Expenditure Survey and there is every indication that the kind of approach will spread from central to local government.

It is the framework for thinking inherent in the PPBS concept which is having the biggest impact on corporate planning in local government and it is in *this* area that the greatest advances are likely to be made in urban management.

REFERENCES

4.1 Gloucestershire County Council, Community Care Programme, 1972.

4.2 D. NOVICK, *Program Budgeting,* Chapter 1, p. 12, Harvard University Press, 1965.

4.3 AARON WILDAWSKY and ARTHUR HAMMAN, 'Comprehensive versus Incremental Budgeting in the Department of Agriculture', *Administrative Science Quarterly,* pp. 321–346, Dec., 1965.

4.4 *Programme Budgeting—The Approach,* p. 21, Institute of Municipal Treasurers and Accountants, 1971.

4.5 PPBS Note 5, p. 3, 'State—Local Finances Project', George Washington University, 1967.

4.6 JACK W. CARLSON, 'The Status and Next Steps for PPBS', in *Public Expenditures and Policy Analysis,* p. 374, edited by ROBERT H. HAVENHAM and J. MARGOLIS, Markham Publishing Company, 1970.

4.7 *Strategy, Priorities and Financial Guidelines,* Corporation of Liverpool Report, 1971.

4.8 PPBS Note 11, p. 1, 'State—Local Finances Project', George Washington University, 1968.

4.9 McKinsey and Company Inc., *A New Management System for the Liverpool Corporation,* 1969.

4.10 e.g. (i) J. V. MILLER, 'Output Measurement', in *Programme Budgeting Implementation, some practical problems,* Institute of Municipal Treasurers and Accountants, 1971.
(ii) US Senate, *Criteria for Evaluation in Planning State and Local Programmes,* A study submitted by the sub-committee on Inter-Governmental Relations, 1967.
(iii) HARRY P. HATRY, 'Measuring the Effectiveness of Non-defense public programs', *Operations Research,* 18, 5, Sept./Oct., 1970.
(iv) Urban Institute Washington, *Measuring the Effectiveness of Local Government Services: Solid Waste Collection et al,* 1970 et seq.

4.11 Institute of Municipal Treasurers and Accountants Working Party, Report No. 9, undated.

4.12 *PPBS in Gloucestershire,* Report by the Chairman of the PPBS Working Party, Oct., 1970.

4.13 J. V. MILLER, 'Output Measurement', in *Programme Budgeting Implementation, some Practical Problems,* Institute of Municipal Treasurers and Accountants, 1971.

4.14 PPBS Note 11, pp. 3–4, 'State—Local Finances Project', George Washington University, 1968.

4.15 *Programme Budgeting, The Approach,* p. 17 et seq., Institute of Municipal Treasurers and Accountants, 1971.

4.16 R. B. BUTT, PPBS Note 4, 'The Corporate Plan', INLOGOV, University of Birmingham, 1971.

4.17 J. W. CARLSON, 'The Status and Next Steps for Planning, Programming and Budgeting', in *Public Expenditure and Policy Analysis,* p. 379, ed. by ROBERT H. HAVENHAM and J. MARGOLIS, Markham Publishing Co., 1970.

5
Towards a New Format

ELEMENTS IN CONFUSION

There are several types of plan and planning. They serve, in part, to confuse the situation. They also serve to illustrate the developing nature of planning in which there is cause for a degree of optimism. Many of these different plans and types of planning have emerged only comparatively recently. Some overlap. They are all related but rarely expressly so. There is no commonly understood relationship between types of plan and planning. The catalogue is almost certainly wider than those covered here but the concern is to identify those major areas of planning impinging on corporate planning at the local government level and to map out relationships between them, relationships which, at the end of the road, will assist the processes of planning in local government. Of the elements in this situation, consideration will be given to structure planning, corporate or policy planning, capital plans, revenue plans, regional and local planning, community plans, the notion of social planning and finally the separate service plans for different departments within local government.

The object is not to suggest improved ways of preparing each of these plans, although it will be possible by inference throughout, but rather to approach new forms of planning for urban management, building on the classification of relationships between the various types of planning given both the working context set in Chapter 1 and the notes about the nature of planning in Chapter 2.

STRUCTURE PLANNING

Of all the types of planning considered here, structure planning is the most formal because it is enshrined in legislation (5.1). County planning authorities will, in due course, have a statutory obligation to prepare structure plans for their area. The origins of structure plans are to be found in dissatisfaction with land-use planning as it had developed between 1947 and the mid-1960's. These dissatisfactions were aired in the report of the Planning Advisory Group in 1965 (5.2) and can be summarised thus: (5.3) "(*a*) they (i.e. present land-use development plans) are deficient in policies, particularly those not directly related to land-use, and they are inadequate as guides to developers and as bases for development control;

(*b*) they concentrate on detail and on what are often misleadingly precise boundaries;

(*c*) they try to illustrate in standard forms different kinds of information, much of which is not relevant to positive promotion or control or development;

(*d*) they are ill-equipped to influence the quality of development as distinct from its location;

(*e*) finally, their inflexible form and content are not adaptable to new techniques and concepts, and the centralised procedures required for amendment impose long delays on attempts to deal with rapidly changing circumstances."

Structure plans were conceived in order largely to meet these criticisms but especially (*a*) and (*e*). As it stands at the present in its development it would be difficult to define precisely the area of concern of structure planning.

"The term structure is used here to mean the social, economic and physical systems of an area, so far as they are subject to planning control or influence. The structure is, in effect, the planning framework for an area and includes such matters as the distribution of the population, the activities and the relationships between them, the patterns of land use and the development the activities give rise to, together with the network of communications and the systems of utility services." (5.4)

The main functions of the structure plan are:

"1. Interpreting national and regional policies.

Structure plans must be prepared within the framework set by national and regional policies. They interpret these policies in terms appropriate to the area in question.

2. Establishing aims, policies and general proposals.

The structure plan should contain a statement of the planning authority's aims for the area, and the strategy, policies and general proposals which are designed to achieve these aims.

3. Providing framework for local plans.

Just as structure plans are prepared within the context of national and regional policies, so they set the context within which local plans must be prepared. Thus the broad policies and proposals in the structure plans form a framework for the more detailed policies and proposals in local plans.

4. Indicating action areas.

In particular, the structure plan should indicate the action areas and the nature of their treatment. These are the priority areas for intensive action. Like other local plans, action area plans cannot be put on deposit or adopted, though they can be prepared, before the Minister has approved the structure plan. But the procedure differs from that for other local plans in that the authority's general proposals for comprehensive treatment must have been included in the approved structure plan, or in an approved amendment to it; the preparation of the action area plan is then obligatory.

5. Providing guidance for development control.

Local plans provide detailed guidance on development control. But a universal coverage of local plans is likely to take many years to achieve and may even be unnecessary. In these parts of the area not covered, or not yet covered, by a local plan, the structure plan will provide the basis for development control (in association with the 1962 Act development plan whilst that is continued in force as a transitional measure).

6. Providing basis for co-ordinating decisions.

The preparatory stages of the plan will provide a forum for discussion between the various committees of the planning authority and district councils who deal with, for example, housing, roads and open spaces; they will also offer an opportunity to bring together, through consultation and negotiation, other public bodies such as statutory undertakers, river authorities and regional hospital boards, who are likely to be concerned with important aspects of the plan. Later, the structure plan itself will provide a co-ordinated basis upon which these various interests can develop the individual programmes of work for which they have executive responsibility.

7. Bringing main planning issues and decisions before Minister and public.

The structure plan will be the means of bringing the authority's intentions, and the reasoning behind those intentions, to the attention of the Minister and the public." (5.5)

In essence there are two important features of a structure plan. The first is that it is intended as a policy document focussing on issues in which central government has a legitimate interest for the purposes of exercising control at key points over local government. These issues are mainly distribution of employment and population, major communication networks, major capital investment, and similar strategic subjects. The great desire is to shed the vast burden of irrelevant detail from the central government machine, to avoid the ten-year gestation period common to many development plans. The second feature is that it should represent a broader look at physical planning. It recognises that physical planning cannot be looked at in isolation from social and economic planning. Indeed it is sometimes open to question whether it is helpful to conceive of these three distinct types of planning at all. What structure planning is setting out to achieve is the expression of better based policies for physical development of our cities, the better base deriving from an increased, deeper understanding of the social and economic systems with which it is closely interrelated. The belief is that a set of physical development policies is likely to be better for this improved basis. This can be accepted. What a structure plan cannot become is a *social* plan. A structure plan should be what it was intended to be, nothing more—namely, an expression of policies concerned with the strategic issues pointing the direction in which the particular area might develop in *physical* terms.

In practice a variety of approaches is being adopted towards structure planning and indeed, structure plans themselves appear to be taking differing forms. The West Midlands Conurbation authorities with the Department of the Environment, see structure plans as having the following qualities:

"(*a*) they should attempt to meet social and economic objectives;

(*b*) they are part of a continuous planning process, which informs about the consequences of decisions;

(*c*) they should represent the authority's intentions for an area, in the way in which the authority intends to use its powers or influence to affect the future of that area;

(*d*) they should be as realistic as possible in relation to the available resources. Two additional points can perhaps be added. The first is that early attempts at structure plans, such as this one, will be exploratory. Rather than being viewed as definitive, they should be seen as an initial basis on which to build a continuing and improving planning process. The second is that if plans are to be used with confidence in decision-making, it is important that they should not be firmer than the ability to forecast the future. If they are, then they may well commit resources in directions which will be regretted in the future.

A structure plan is a new form of development plan. It is no longer restricted mainly to the arrangement of land uses. It is concerned with the overall management of investment and land within an authority. This calls for a change in approach to the preparation of development plans. Previously, the approach was directly through survey and analysis to a plan which was a statement of a desirable end-state. A structure plan appears to demand an approach which produces a statement of intended direction, derived from an examination of the various alternative directions an authority could take." (5.6)

The West Midlands approach also embodies the setting of objectives for the conurbation authorities, objectives which go further than traditional land-use planning. To provide the quantity and quality of education, to provide the quantity and quality of health and welfare facilities are examples of the objectives.

As the West Midlands report states, the economic base of development plans is strengthened in the structure plan in that development plans are expected to pay regard to the resources likely to be available for the carrying out of the proposals of the structure plan, ". . . the plan as a whole must pay realistic regard to the likely levels of future investment." (5.7)

". . . because inadequate regard was given to assessing the resources needed to implement the plans, they were often unrealistically optimistic about what could be achieved. This gave them an air of idealism which was not conducive to controlled implementation. Secondly, because there was rarely a systematic and continuous attempt to review and monitor the progress of plans, any proposed phasing of implementation rapidly became out of date as circumstances changed (e.g. Government cutbacks on investment) and so failed to reflect reality." (5.8)

It is encouraging that a variety of forms and approaches is being adopted in the production of structure plans. At the same time there needs to be an awareness of the relationships between these and other forms of planning. The variety needs to be developed with a clearer idea of the direction in which planning should be moving. The relationships are taken up later in this chapter.

POLICY AND CORPORATE PLANNING

The case for corporate planning or local authority policy planning (the terms here are used synonymously) was made in Chapter 1. The movement towards corporate planning has its base in dissatisfaction with the management processes of local government. "It has been a movement to which national action has contributed little, although the Maud Report on Management in Local Government gave an initial impetus to local authorities to appraise their management structure. The roots of that dissatisfaction are probably two-fold although different emphasis may be given in different authorities. The first was an awareness that the tradition of specialist management in local government—the tradition that regarded a local authority as a collection of essentially separate services staffed by separate professions was inappropriate to management of a local authority faced with increasingly complex problems in its environment. The second was an awareness of the need of the authority to review its activities in the light of changing needs and problems. The immediate cause of this growing awareness was the pressure on resources and in particular on financial resources, which meant that in some authorities the movement towards corporate planning has a financial basis. But the long-term need arises not from pressure upon resources alone but from the changing needs and problems faced by the authority" (5.9).

The scope of corporate planning could be defined as being concerned with the 'social, economic and physical systems of an area so far as they are affected or can be affected by the activities of the authority'. This is wider in scope than the definition of structure planning.

Some have argued that corporate planning is necessarily narrower in scope than structure planning since the former is concerned with the activities of the authority, whereas the latter is concerned with a much wider range of activities—activities which affect land-use whether they are carried out by the authority or not. But this ignores the wide-ranging impact and concern of the local authority's activities. These activities are not undertaken for their own sake but for their impact on the environment. The activities of education departments, social services departments, health departments, engineering departments, affect between them virtually all the activities that are affected or are likely to be affected by structure planning—and many more besides. In any event, structure planning is itself an activity of the authority. If corporate planning is concerned with the activities of the authority, it is and must be concerned with structure planning as much as with education or any of the other services. Because the concept of corporate planning hardly exists as yet in any authority, it is perhaps true to say that, at the moment, structure planning is wider ranging as a planning process but in fact the actual impact of other local authority services, is, of course, much wider. Take education—for example, the impact of the output of this service on the wider environment, it can be convincingly argued, is much greater than that of the normal run of land-use planning.

Apart from the area of scope of corporate planning as defined here, implicit in the concept is the requirement that the approach to it should be a corporate one, that is to say that rather than conceiving, in isolation, a series of separate service plans the policies of the local authority should be derived from an integrated approach, should recognise in the planning process itself the interrelated nature of the problems which a local authority seeks to solve.

Corporate planning, of course, embraces the multi-year financial plan (Chapter 4). The traditional separation of capital and revenue budgets, for planning purposes at least comes to an end. Capital expenditure has revenue implications. The two terms simply reflect methods of financing schemes or projects and have little connection with the needs of planning. Local authorities in moving towards corporate planning are moving towards integrating financial planning into the corporate planning process.

COMMUNITY PLANNING

Structure planning focusses on physical development policies. Local authority corporate planning focusses on the expression of the integrated policies of a local authority's various services. Community planning, as yet, does not exist but it is a useful concept to form a background to both structure and corporate planning. Its concern is with setting a community development framework, a background against which not only the local authority but other, both public and private agencies, might operate and plan their own activities (5.10). Much depends, of course, on the degree to which a local authority sees its role as an 'initiative' as distinct from an 'agency' role (see Chapter 1). The purpose of community planning would not be to impose a plan but to provide a means of enabling different organisations to see their part in a complex of interrelationships. At present consultations take place between agencies, often too late to affect decisions fundamentally, but it is possible perhaps to conceive of a situation when the planning process is itself a framework for a more fruitful co-operation. Agencies do not always want to co-operate, indeed they sometimes have conflicting interests. The community planning idea would not impose co-operation, it would facilitate it and maybe even assist in giving focus to issues of basic conflict between agencies.

REGIONAL PLANS

This is not the place to argue the case for or against the existence of regional authorities and regional plans (5.11). That there are issues which transcend local authority boundaries to a greater or lesser degree cannot be denied. There will *always* be considerations which are regional or sub-regional in scale if not of national importance. The machinery necessary or desirable to give expression to them is not our concern. The planning system is conceived, nevertheless, as an hierarchical structure from national to local and a loose, albeit fairly important, system for examining regional considerations has been in existence and is developing on an *ad hoc* basis (5.12). In theory the plans of the 'superior' body should set a framework for the plans of 'subordinate' authorities and indeed this is how the system is expected to work. The Development Plans Manual specifically states that structure plans must be cast in the framework set by regional and national policies (5.13).

It is tempting to imagine the ideal situation as being one in which central and local government in co-operation derive a hierarchy of social and economic objectives for the national, regional, sub-regional and local scales of operation into which the different planning activities could be fitted. This, in the event, would be far removed from the ideal because it would deny the dynamic of the 'real' world situation. It would imply a monopoly of planning wisdom radiating from the top. It would ascribe to the plan a degree of 'rightness' which could not be sustained (see Chapter 2). This is not to say that policies at the local level should not be set in the wider context. Clearly this is right. But, the shaping of policies at all levels is in reality interdependent. Local problems may well be substantial enough to dictate or considerably influence regional policies. The relationship is not a truly hierarchical one, it is much more dynamic than that. What is required are frameworks in which this dynamic may be given expression, where conflict may be made meaningfully explicit. An example of a situation where such a relationship might exist could be found in places like Bournemouth or Hastings where a case can be made for attracting employment sufficient to attract younger people to these towns (or at least to stem the outward migration of young people) when the present situation is one of an ageing population with all its attendant problems. This case can be established despite the fact that regionally speaking the south-east of England needs to curb employment growth especially in relation to other regions.

Whatever form higher plans take, whether they are produced by regional authorities with executive or advisory power, or whether they are simply produced as part of central government's functions, or whether indeed we only have national policies above those of the local authorities, the relationship between them needs to be understood. Granted that the higher level policies or plans will in principle be providing a context for more local policies, a challenging of one by the other will increasingly be the order of the day. Strategic regional type plans are by definition more sketchy, less precise and perhaps even less well founded in data terms. To give them strength, to give them rigour it is of the very essence of planning that within the process they should be challenged. The notions of learning and feedback described in Chapter 2 come to life in this context. The planning process should be one which generates challenge within the on-going system. This challenge will spring more often than not from policies of lower order conflicting with more strategic plans at higher level. One of the richest veins of data in the planning process is at the policy implementation stage. This information needs to be drawn into the policy formulation stages of corporate plans, of sub-regional, regional and national plans which are conceived as changing, as adaptive systems. The relationship therefore should not be, as we have tended to move in the past, an imposition of policies but one of *learning and adaptive guidance*. It will take some time to develop.

The same relationship should exist between structure plans and local plans prepared under the Planning Acts. This presents special problems relating to the split of functions between tiers of government, a problem which is common all over the world, either as such or as between a split of functions between different agencies. The United States suffers especially in this respect (5.14).

RELATIONSHIPS BETWEEN STRUCTURE PLANNING, CORPORATE PLANNING, AND DEPARTMENTAL PLANNING

Earlier, a structure plan was described as being mainly concerned with 'strategic' issues such as the distribution of employment and population, major communications networks and major capital investment. British local government is moving into a period when it is likely that a whole series of so-called 'strategic' plans will be prepared. The Greater London Council's development plan is described as one and no doubt similar ones will be prepared for the other new Metropolitan Authorities when they are established in 1974. There is some disagreement or confusion about the relationship between strategic planning of the Greater London Development Plan type and corporate planning. (The GLC of course has its Development Plan *and* a PPB System.) There are several disturbing features about the relationship between these two as perceived by the GLC (5.15).

Strategic planning and PPBS are seen in Greater London as related in some respects in that there are common elements but fundamentally the two are regarded as separate.

It (PPBS) is concerned with the activities and expenditure of the authority, with the allocation and management of the authority's own resources. When the GLC formally adopted a PPB system in February, 1970, what they adopted was 'a comprehensive and co-ordinated general management process which advances from identifying long-range needs and objectives, planning major strategies, translating these into short-range programmes, and finally into specific budgets, incorporating at all appropriate stages formal procedures for control, monitoring, evaluation and review'. Many of the long-range objectives of a PPB system, expressed in the most general terms (e.g. 'to see that the population is adequately housed'), will coincide with the objectives of an authority's structure plan. But while the emphasis of PPBS is on the management of the authority's own resources, strategic planning is by nature more outward-looking. Its primary emphasis is on the town or county, on the area of the authority, and also on the wider region.

'The second aspect of strategic planning which deserves a mention here is that it is inevitably concerned with the regional scale of activity. Whereas the PPB system must, of necessity, concern itself mainly (though not exclusively) with the resources and tasks of the authority within its boundary, the planner's thinking must give greater emphasis to the framework within which his clients live and work. Thus, London draws half a million workers from beyond its boundaries. It plans to solve its own housing problems in part by the creation of something like a quarter of a million extra dwellings in the rest of the region. London's declining employment has its counterpart in the vigorous upswing of industry and commerce in the ring of new and expanded towns, and other growth zones, elsewhere in the south-east. Recreational needs of Londoners can often be satisfied as easily, and more cheaply, in areas beyond the GLC's boundaries, as within them.

The planner, then, operates on a slightly different plane from his colleagues in the PPB system. First, his spatial horizons are larger. Secondly, he is concerned with objectives which are often only in part, if at all, realisable by his local authority. He may be concerned with creating an environment in which others can make investment decisions, or he may become an advocate—making proposals for action and expenditure to regional or national authorities. He is concerned with the total resources available to a region, and with what can be done with those resources by all agencies—not his own authority alone.'

It may be that this view of strategic planning being wider in scope, more 'outward-looking' than corporate planning is a rationalisation of the separateness of the large departments within the Greater London Council. This would be understandable. It is a danger ever present in such large organisations, one which will increase as more larger authorities are created. Ways of overcoming these problems are treated in Chapter 7. The fact remains however that the relationship described by Eversley and Wood does not meet the needs of the situation even though it may exist that way in practice. We require something very different. The common elements between strategic or structure planning give the key to the fundamental relationship needing to be established.

1. *Understanding the environment*

Both structure planning and corporate planning require a background understanding of the social, physical and economic environment in which the authority is set. The roots of both types of planning, their *raisons d'être* lie in the problems in the environment.

2. *Interpreting national and regional policies*

A local authority is set in a wider context; the impact of that wider context must be understood. At times that wider context is expressed as constraints, in other instances as influences upon the authority. In yet further instances national and regional policies will be influenced by feedback from both planning processes.

3. *Problems present and foreseen*

Planning requires problem identification. Plans are not made in the abstract. Objectives are not set without regard to problems.

4. *Setting objectives*

The local authority cannot be pursuing different objectives in structure planning from the objectives it pursues in corporate planning.

5. *Considering alternative ways of achieving the objectives*

Alternative solutions cannot be considered merely in terms of structure planning. We are concerned with solutions to problems in the community, some of which will lie in structure planning or in land-use, many more will not, but all solutions are probably related and must be seen against a set of common objectives. Again, the danger is that any planning procedure based on one approach will inevitably see solutions from a relatively narrow base cutting out of focus many other alternative solutions.

6. *Monitoring*

The continual monitoring of the environment by the authority, that is part of any planning process, must feed both into structure planning and corporate planning.

The most helpful relationship cannot be struck however before the *differences* between the two are exposed, and some are critical.

1. Structure planning has a legislative base. Corporate planning has none. This difference is very important. It surrounds structure planning with formal regulations and procedures with the effect that the whole process inevitably becomes rigid. The degree of rigidity is made manifest by the lengthy procedures being gone through at the Greater London Development Plan Inquiry at the present time. The Statutory Regulations and the *Management Networks* publication (5.16) which, whilst not setting *compulsory* procedures, sets out guide lines. This is an inevitable consequence of any statutory procedure and notwithstanding the attempts to build in flexibility, the law by its very nature, was never intended to be flexible. Corporate planning can take any number of forms—it is completely flexible.

2. Structure planning has a direct relationship to the stated requirements of central government. These requirements are reflected in the Development Plans Manual (5.17) and because they are designed with one set of requirements in view they exclude other needs essential to the process. For example capital budgets are treated (they are of concern to central government) but

revenue is not and as we have seen the two are simply reflections of different methods of financing projects. For planning purposes they should be treated together. When a local authority builds an old-people's home the revenue implications are equally if not more significant than the capital cost of the building. Corporate planning is not related to any direct central government requirements in the same way. Structure planning is conditioned by its origin in land-use planning. Corporate planning is sometimes, although not necessarily, conditioned by an origin in financial planning (5.18).

It is clear that these planning processes are not separate activities to be pursued by separate organisational units. They are activities which have many common elements, pursued by the same organisation. An authority cannot pursue separate policies in structure planning from corporate planning without giving up the claim to be one organisation. An authority cannot pursue separate policies in structure planning from corporate planning if it is in any way concerned with the impact of its activities on the environment. An authority cannot afford to build up two separate planning systems. The real issue is how the relationship should be worked out. Three main possibilities exist:

(*a*) that the structure plan should be developed, adapted and extended so that it could also be the corporate plan. The difficulties about this proposal are, first that the structure plan raises special problems of central control, legislative procedures, appeals. Those developing corporate planning may feel the structure plan to be too restrictive a framework; and, secondly, that the origin of the structure plan in land-use planning may be felt to provide too restrictive a framework;

(*b*) that structure planning and corporate planning be recognised as separate procedures, but that the elements in each one be identified and where common or related elements are found, clear relationships are established. The problem here is to secure that what is wanted is actually achieved. The pattern of interrelationships could be so complex as to be virtually unworkable;

(*c*) The third possibility is the one which is advocated and which binds, not only structure planning and corporate planning but also the separate plans of departments within the local authority. There would be a central planning procedure within the local authority from which a variety of planning procedures would be derived and to which they would contribute. This would be the corporate planning procedure, but it would be freed from a particular background. From this central planning the corporate plan, structure plans, financial plans, manpower plans and departmental plans would be derived. The various skills of the different departments of the authority would contribute to it. This central procedure would be the common base for these specific plans. One of these plans would be the structure plan. In other words, a structure plan needs to be widely based in terms of its information, the insights, the understanding underlying it, but its concern is limited to those strategic elements in which central government has a valid interest. The structure plan far from being a vehicle for all the policies of a local authority should be one of a number of plans and policies emerging from an interdisciplinary planning process within the authority.

THE NOTION OF SOCIAL PLANNING

It is not proposed to define social planning because it is too difficult—the temptation is to say, impossible. The problem is the word, 'social'. In a sense any planning done in the public sector is social planning because the effects of it, the benefits or profits from it however they may be derived are intended for the 'public' good. The distinction however is not precisely between the public and private sector. It is after all only a political chance that the gas and electricity undertakings for example are public bodies in Britain but the fact that they *are* makes their activities more 'social' than would otherwise be the case.

"Social policy is taken to refer to the policy of governments with regard to action having a direct impact on the welfare of citizens, by providing them with services or income. The central core consists, therefore, of social insurance, public (or national) assistance, the health and welfare services and housing policy. Education obviously belongs . . . (as does) the treatment of crime. . . ." (5.18)

Social policy consists of acts of government, undertaken for a variety of political reasons, to provide for a range of needs, material and social, and predominantly dependent needs, what the market does not or cannot satisfy for certain designated sections of the population." (5.19)

The pursuit of a definition is sterile and not very helpful, for it is clear that there cannot be a breed of planning separate from structure planning or corporate planning or separate from the many types of departmental plans within a local authority which is distinct and can be called 'social' planning. They may all be legitimately described as social plans or policies. Indeed the interrelatedness of policy areas discussed in Chapter 1 underlies this point. Roads and urban transportation policies are as validly considered as social policies as are the policies of fostering children, or giving rent rebates. True, urban transportation policies present technical and engineering problems of implementation but the objectives of such policies have social implications. This realisation, i.e. that physical development policies have social implications or, more accurately, are inherently social in nature, has both made an impact on thinking and debate in the town planning field, especially at central government level. Here there is concern to create frameworks for assisting the process of giving expression to these relationships. It is only recently that it has been said that land use development plans acquire their relevance only insofar as they help to achieve the objectives or solve the problems of the communities with which they are concerned. The danger is that simplistic and even naïve conclusions are sometimes drawn about the relationship between physical development and the achievement of some of the important social aims. The physical plan has, for historical and other reasons, become a powerful instrument. When people speak of plans the implication is that it is a physical plan and it becomes an easy step to extend this physical planning instrument to take on the role of giving expression to co-ordinating social policies.

The relationships discussed so far in this chapter have focussed on the need, within a local authority for a central planning procedure which would have at its core the development of understanding, of data, of insights, of policy analysis and out of which would spring a range of policies, all with this common basis of understanding. The co-ordinating device cannot sensibly be a physical development plan (especially a statutory one) any more than it could be a plan for the development of the public safety services, or the plans for culture and recreation.

A physical plan, it is true, needs to be based on an awareness of social systems, on an understanding of the social impact, the real social implications of physical development policies (5.21). Jane Jacobs has levelled, admittedly journalistic, attacks on physical development plans for their slavish adherence to devices, standards and practices which clearly are not based on this understanding (5.22).

Social planning, then, pervades the public planning system. It cannot be defined as a separate entity. What the planning processes we establish need to be sensitive to is the possibility that ramifications, implications, impacts on the social systems of an area can be easily neglected in the wake of other considerations whether they be technical, engineering, financial or some other.

LOCAL PLANS

At the expense of overlabouring the point that physical plans and planning should not be isolated from wider corporate policies and plans it is worthwhile looking at the issues of 'local plans' in the British Development Plan system. Local plan functions are described (5.23):

"1. Applying strategy of structure plan.

Local plans must conform generally to the approved structure plan: they will develop the policies and proposals in it, showing as precisely as possible the changes proposed in the development and other uses of land.

2. Providing detailed basis for development control.

The broad guidance on development control in the structure plan will be refined where local plans have been prepared. These will give more precise information to developers by allocating sites for particular purposes, by defining the areas to which particular development control policies will apply, and by explaining those policies in terms of standards and other criteria.

3. Providing basis for co-ordinating development.

The planning policies and proposals in local plans will be used as a basis for co-ordinating public and private development and expenditure over the areas covered by them.

4. Bringing local and detailed planning issues before public.

While the structure plan is intended to bring before the public matters which affect the structure area as a whole, a local plan will be concerned to draw their attention to more detailed planning issues in parts of that area; it will do so in terms that will inform property owners and developers how their interests will be affected and where the opportunities lie."

These plans are to be statutory plans. They are not subject, in the normal course of events, to central government approval but they are to be prepared under the terms of the Town and Country Planning Act, 1971. Here again is an example of plans being seen as having wholly or predominantly physical implications. In reality, of course, these elements represent an abstraction, leaving behind other aspects of the problem, other implications. Take, for example, an urban rehabilitation project which will frequently be the subject of local plans. It might involve the demolition of a few houses for say open space and/or garage spaces. It might involve the addition of bathrooms, repairs, the closing of streets, the diversion of traffic—in fact an ordinary run-of-the-mill scheme. The question needs to be posed, 'Why should the physical problems be extracted and given prominence in a 'local plan' in this way—a prominence which serves only to obscure, to hide, or to distort other problems?' The plan is based on limited information, i.e. that relevant to physical rehabilitation.

There is a case for local authorities preparing plans outside the provisions of the Planning Acts. For example local plans prepared in Social Services departments, or Education departments, or by inter-departmental groups, plans geared to giving expression to how a local authority proposes to tackle specific *problem sets.* Envisaged is a type of composite policy cum physical plan, i.e. a plan which recognises that some problems can be solved or alleviated in part through physical action but in part also through administrative and other action. The new breed of plans should reflect this. Physical planners will be involved in their preparation but these plans will give expression to a pooling of skills to tackle specific problems.

Again such plans would be related to other forms of planning through the very planning procedures from which they would be derived. The Appendix to this chapter sets out typical raw material for such a local plan. A study of this material throws into stark relief the realities of urban problems and exposes the complete inadequacy, some would say irrelevence, of our planning procedures to meet the needs of this typical situation. Any new format which is not robust enough to take this kind of situation in its stride falls short of what we are seeking.

In this chapter we have explored relationships and made some tentative steps towards a new planning format. The characteristics of this format are set out in Chapter 8 but first other issues need to be considered.

Appendix to Chapter 5

Valley Park, an Area of Problems

The problems of this particular part of the town were placed under close examination after strong pressure from elected members. A Council debate in April of this year sparked off members' interest in the social and environmental features of the Valley Park area, and there were allegations of poor housing standards, of community problems with the large and concentrated population of Asian, African and West Indian immigrants in this part of the city, of overcrowding, of the exploitation of tenants, of public health nuisances, of prostitution, of the fear felt by elderly residents of the area, and of low standards of street lighting, highway cleansing and maintenance.

There is nothing novel about this sort of situation, and a number of large industrial towns have been confronted with it to a greater or lesser degree. What was novel was the way in which it was decided, again by the elected members, to tackle it: the Housing, Health, Public Works and Social Services Committees were given three months in which to study the area and its problems, at the end of which they were to put forward recommendations for dealing with those problems. It was acknowledged that the time specified was short, but the members wanted an initial assessment of the situation so that such remedies as could be implemented in a short time could be put in hand, and need not await the outcome of the longer processes of examination and implementation necessary to deal with other problems. Incidentally, now that those committees have put forward their proposals, the Education Committee has been asked to undertake a similar task.

It will be apparent that the net could and perhaps should have been cast more widely to embrace the Police and Hospital services, the Department of Health and Social Security, and the Department of Employment. It may be that this will follow, but at the moment the exercise is imperfect certainly to that extent and doubtless in other ways too. However, it has certainly brought about the following:

(i) a concentrated study of the area and its problems;
(ii) a statement of the findings of that study in reports to four committees;
(iii) twelve recommendations, now adopted by the Council, for facilities, services, or further examination of the area in certain respects; and
(iv) arrangements to review progress.

There is some physical innovation in these recommendations, in that the Housing Advice Centre, Family Advice Centre, and Community Home for difficult children of a particular neighbourhood, are the first to be set up in the town.

The Reports are these :

1. Report of Borough Planning Officer
2. Report of the Director of Social Services
3. Report of the Medical Officer of Health
4. Report of the Chief Public Health Inspector
5. Report of the Housing Manager
6. Report of the Borough Engineer
7. Report of the Town Clerk
8. Joint Report of Committees to Council

REPORT OF THE PLANNING OFFICER

VALLEY PARK AREA

1. The 'problem area' of Valley Park (as defined on the plan and bounded by Cambridge Road, Albury Road, Woodlands Road, Greenhill Park Road, Knowle Hill Road, Snowhill Road and the railway, is one which reflects two major aspects of the British housing scheme since the war. First, the need on the part of those living in 'twilight' areas and in the adjoining areas of sound terrace housing to bring their dwellings up to an acceptable standard of amenity; and secondly; the effect which shifting patterns of population and social customs have had on the physical conditions in these areas—particularly where there are large terrace dwellings which are no longer suitable for single family occupation. Into this situation of change and deterioration have come the immigrant communities from India, the West Indies and elsewhere. Their different ways of life and their desire to form their own communities allied to the economic pressures which have pushed them into such neighbourhoods have accelerated the natural deterioration of these areas. Thus any improvement scheme must acknowledge the need for not only an improved environment but also the provision of community facilities for the inhabitants' new requirements.

2. It may be possible to distinguish in the Valley Park area under consideration two distinct zones: the so-called 'twilight' zone where physical living conditions are very poor as the result of slum landlordism, multi-occupation of dwellings and overcrowding, and a much larger zone of sounder two storey dwellings which for the most part remain in single family occupation. It is in the first of these zones lying between Cambridge Road and Church Street–Manchester Road and bisected by the line of the proposed Western Motorway that the defects appear to be most apparent although they are present to some degree throughout the whole Valley Park area. In preparing an improvement strategy for Valley Park we must endeavour correctly to identify the causes which lie behind these defects and to put forward proposals which will effectively solve these problems.

3. When the points raised by Councillor J. Smithson are examined it is apparent that a purely planning approach will not encompass them. The aim of any improvement scheme must be to make the area a better place for the inhabitants. This means tackling the social environment as well as the physical environment of streets, houses and homes.

4 It is, therefore, evident that proposals for Valley Park must be based on a combined approach involving social analysis as well as an appraisal of the physical characteristics. The complexity of physical and social factors in a declining area is shown on the attached diagram (Diagram I) which does not set out to be definitive but merely to indicate the network of relationships. Many of the problems which are cited as part of the Valley Park problem are, in fact, capable of rapid solution through social action. I cannot state what the Director of Social Services and the Chief Public Health Inspector will require in the way of information to formulate their proposals to deal with the evident social difficulties but I have set out below from my point of view the planning problem in terms of the scale of Valley Park within an overall improvement programme.

5. *Woodlands District Plan:* Valley Park forms a part of the Woodlands District for which a local plan must eventually be prepared to comply with the 1968 Town and Country Planning Act. Any proposals for Valley Park (estimated population 27,000) must form an integral part of the larger Woodlands District Plan (estimated population 38,000). It is important, therefore, that the local plan proposals be prepared before the formulation of any detailed General Improvement Area proposals.

6. *GIA Programme:* Valley Park as proposed for improvement contains about 6,200 houses (though rather more families). This is approximately one-quarter of all the houses proposed for General Improvement Area treatment in the town. It must, therefore, be expected that the actual process of physical improvement will take about three to

five years following the preparation of agreed plans which will have been the subject of detailed and lengthy public participation.

7. The extensive nature and scope of the survey which will have to be made in the Valley Park area before any sensible plans can be prepared are indicated by the following preliminary list of information:

(*a*) Dwellings: Number, age, condition, size
(*b*) Tenure: Houses owned and rented
(*c*) Population: Composition, length of residence, origin
(*d*) Community Facilities: Demand for existing facilities, demand for new facilities, e.g. schools, clinics, etc.

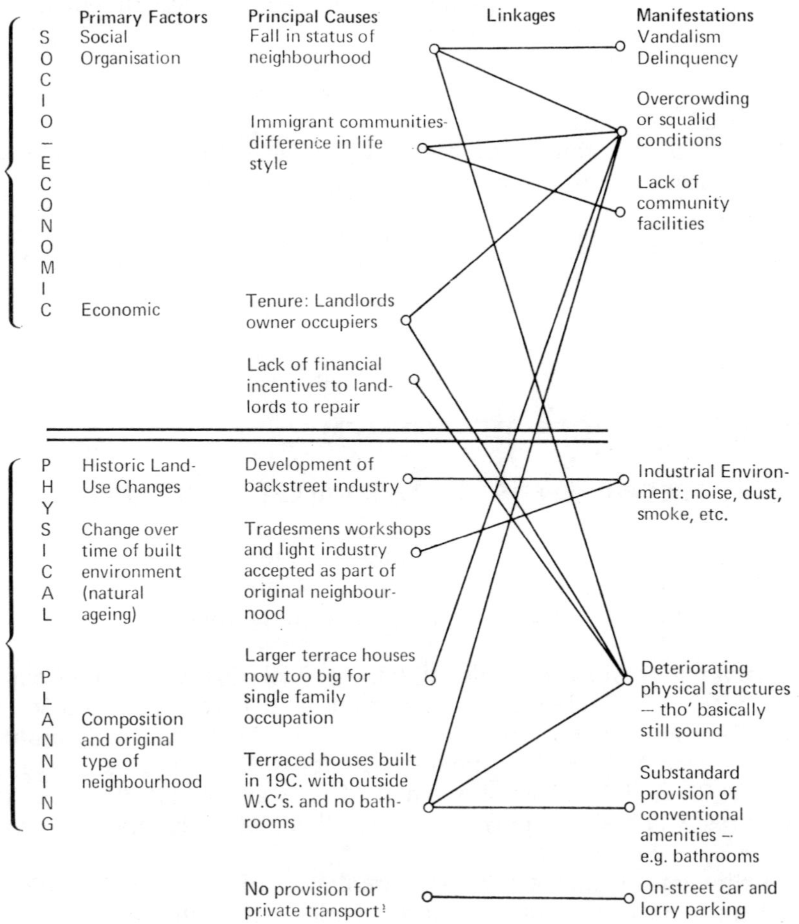

Diagram I: Valley Park area: Linkages between socio-economic and physical planning factors.

(*e*) Social Facilities: Demand for existing facilities, demand for new facilities, e.g. churches and other religious buildings, clubs, etc.
(*f*) Public Services: Telephones, pavements, etc.
(*g*) Land Use: including inventory of non-conforming uses.
(*h*) Car Parking: on and off-street, commercial vehicles
(*i*) Shops: Number and distribution, trades
(*j*) Roads: Through routes, traffic flows, accident statistics, etc.

8. There is nothing in Councillor Smithson's list of matters needing urgent attention for which the remedy would prejudice the subsequent preparation of planning proposals for the Valley Park area. Remedial work on these items can, therefore, from the physical planning point of view, be undertaken by the appropriate agencies now, and at the same time work can be started in the Planning Department on the following sequential programme:

1. Local Plan Proposals: Woodlands District Plan
2. Phased programme for General Improvement Areas in the town (24,000 dwellings)
3. Phased programme of detailed proposals for General Improvement Areas in Valley Park

SOCIAL SERVICES DEPARTMENT

SPECIAL NEEDS OF THE VALLEY PARK AREA

The Director reports, as instructed by the Committee, upon the special needs of the Valley Park area which was the subject of a notice of motion to the Council in the following terms:

"That with a view to maximising the contribution which the Council shall make to alleviating the misfortune and hardship in the Valley Park District and the adjacent area, the Social Services Committee and the Health, Housing and Public Works Committee shall report to this Council by 30th September 1971, at the latest, as to the measures which either individually or collectively they intend to take."

In the time available for the compilation of this report, statistics used must be considered as approximations only and in some cases based upon small sample surveys which have been taken at different times and may not be entirely reliable. A plan of action would first of all include a more careful scrutiny of available information and a survey of problems in the area.

I. SPECIAL PROBLEMS OF THE AREA

In order to examine the special problems of the Valley Park area attention is drawn to the following factors:

1. With the use of the 1966 Census a recently conducted study revealed that the number of old age pensioners living alone in this area is higher than that appertaining elsewhere (25·3% of all pensioners living alone in fact live in Valley Park).
2. The problems of deprived children from this area are greater than in other areas of the city. It should also be noted that the proportion of children in the community is 23·4% compared to 21·1% in other improvement areas of the city.
3. The special needs of physically and/or mentally handicapped persons, whilst not statistically significant at the present time, will no doubt feature prominently after a survey and analysis has taken place.
4. The presence of an advisory and supportive family service available on the spot would clearly indicate the nature of special family social problems.
5. The incidence of homelessness in the area gives concern to social workers although no statistical information is available to show the extent of this problem.
6. Special problems relating to the Immigrant Population which is higher at 21·2% than other areas of the city.
7. There is a shortage of voluntary help from within this area which is to a certain extent due to lack of stimulation and the provision of suitable opportunity.

1. *Elderly Persons*

Statistics shown in appendix I are based on the provision of domiciliary services and the list of those awaiting residential accommodation show the Valley Park district to be higher than other areas. Whilst the settlement of elderly persons in council bungalows on the outlying estates has reduced the number of elderly persons in the Valley Park area many of the remainder feel a sense of isolation. Valley Park as a decaying area presents many problems for the isolated. Attempts are being made to re-create a community spirit but a decline in the material fabric of many of the houses of the area does add to the problems facing old people. Of the 13 names added to the waiting list for residential accommodation in this part of the town from 1st April to 1st August, 1971, 8 persons live in Valley Park. Where houses are to be demolished then a higher number of elderly persons apply for residential accommodation as an alternative to being rehoused. The provision of sheltered accommodation with warden supervision for elderly persons in the Valley Park area would help to maintain a balanced population and sustain those who wish to remain in this part of the town.

2. *Deprived Children*

The statistical information which is contained in appendix I shows clearly that one of the special problems of the Valley Park area is that of deprived children. The statistics show that the number of children in care is three times as many as the Hampton area and four times as many as Mayford Lane the next largest communities. The supervision and preventative work is also higher in the Valley Park area (e.g. the child care caseload in Area I including Valley Park is much greater than the other areas).

Of the 20 families from which children were received into care from this part of the town in the period April to August 1971 18 were from the Valley Park area. Poor environmental conditions by way of inadequate housing were considered to be important factors in leading to the breakdown in family life in a high proportion of cases reported to be needing assessment and help. It is not clear, however, how far inadequate and unstable families moved into the Valley Park area or to what extent the area produced situations causing family breakdown. It is reasonable to assume that overcrowded or inadequate living conditions exacerbate family problems.

3. *Handicapped persons*

As will be seen from the statistics in appendix I, whilst there has been no significant additional demand upon the Mental Health Service and the Services for the Physically Handicapped in the Valley Park area, it is known that many of these problems lie hidden and recent statistics begin to show some marked increase for the first three months of 1971. Further surveys and a social service presence in the area is likely to uncover considerable unmet need. Although there does not seem to be a discernible pattern in the Mental Health referrals from the area, problems can arise and mental health situations are easily triggered by unsatisfactory environmental conditions, e.g. overcrowding and multi-occupancy of houses. The fact that these conditions appertain in parts of Valley Park is known to attract persons who have accommodation difficulties which, sometimes, arise from their own personal problems.

II. OBJECTIVES OF THE COMMITTEE

The foregoing special social needs seem to indicate the main objective as an assault upon these problems *from within the area* of Valley Park, i.e. to establish a presence in the area which would be available for social work advice and support and would be the operational centre for preventative action.

In order to carry out such an assault it would be important to gather much more information and in this connection the Director would recommend the following points:

1. That the assessment of social service need already being arranged by the department during October to December, 1971, should be utilised in assessing need in Valley Park, i.e. a pilot survey in the Valley Park area might be used to test some of the conclusions being made as to the extent of need.
2. That a small team of social work staff be deployed to carry out the project in conjunction with staff of other departments.
3. That a specific plan be operated to involve the community in Valley Park to participate in the proposed assault on social needs.

III. ACHIEVEMENT OF THE OBJECTIVES

To carry out the main objective the department would require:

1. One senior and two additional trained social workers to work full-time in this area—this would effectively establish a presence and would link up with the local community.
2. One additional clerk/typist to give support to the team.
3. The provision of a family advice centre from which the staff can operate and for which assistance would be available—related directly to provision made by other departments and by the local community.
4. The siting of a community home for the care of difficult children from this area—provisionally a request has been included in the Urban Programme.

IV. EXPENDITURE IN ACHIEVING THESE OBJECTIVES

It is not possible to determine the costs of any sheltered housing and in view of the proposal included in Urban Programme, the community home cost is also excluded but as a general guide the other probable costs are as follows:

	Salary £	*Super'n* £	*N.H.* £	*Total* £
1. 1 Senior Social Worker (mid-scale—new scale)	2,055	120	75	2,250
2. 2 AP4 (mid-scale—new scale)	4,110	245	150	4,505
3. 1 Cl.1	985	55	70	1,110
4. Rent of Family Advice Centre and running costs				750
5. Publicity and Miscellaneous Costs				250
			TOTAL	8,865

Family Service Unit

In view of the involvement of the Family Service Unit in this area, the Director requested the unit organiser, Mr A. Mason, for his observations in relation to the problems in this area. The report is attached as appendix 2.

VALLEY PARK

APPENDIX I

1. *Elderly Persons Services*

(*a*) *Mobile Meals*	*No. of cases receiving meals*	*Population of elderly persons*	*Index*
Total town	977	45,800	21·33 per 1,000
Valley Park	68	4,000	17·00 per 1,000
Rest of town	909	41,800	21·75 per 1,000

(*b*) *Luncheon Clubs*	*No. of Clubs*		
Total town	326	45,800	7·12 per 1,000
Valley Park	34	4,000	8·50 per 1,000
Rest of town	292	41,800	6·99 per 1,000

(*c*) *Voluntary Visiting*	*Cases Visited*		
Total town	326	45,800	7·12 per 1,000
Valley Park	37	4,000	9·25 per 1,000
Rest of town	239	41,800	6·91 per 1,000

(*d*) *Home Help Service*	*Caseload*		
Total town	2,142	45,800	46·77 per 1,000
Valley Park	123	4,000	30·75 per 1,000
Rest of town	2,019	41,800	48·30 per 1,000

2. *Deprived Children*

(*a*) Child Care (Caseloads) as at 30.10.70

	In Care	*Supervision*	*Preventive*	*Total*
Valley Park Area	237	67	88	392
Mayford Lane Area	50	39	15	104
Hampton N.-Area	72	28	75	175

(*b*)	*Caseload*	*Child Population*	*Index*
Total town	1,100	65,910	16·69 per 1,000
Valley Park	392	5,290	74·10 per 1,000
Rest of town	708	60,620	10·67 per 1,000

(*c*) *Juvenile Delinquency and Committal to Care*

Fourteen juveniles in Valley Park area appeared before a Juvenile Court in three months April to June 1971 out of a total of 202.

Taking the fit person orders over a 12 months period, 21 cases related to Valley Park of a total of 97 in the town.

	Committals to Care	*Child Population*	*Index*
Total town	97	65,910	1·47 per 1,000
Valley Park	21	5,290	3·97 per 1,000
Rest of town	76	60,620	1·25 per 1,000

3. *Handicapped Persons*

(*a*) *Register of Physically Handicapped Persons*

	Cases Registered	*Total in Population*	*Index*
Total town	2,013	277,000	7·27 per 1,000
Valley Park	139	22,670	6·13 per 1,000
Rest of town	1,874	254,330	7·37 per 1,000

(*b*) *Mental Welfare* (Caseloads)

Statistics for the first three months of 1971 are as follows:

Area 1 (including Valley Park)	31% of the Department's caseload
Area 2	23% of the Department's caseload
Area 3	27% of the Department's caseload
Area 4	19% of the Department's caseload

(*c*) *Mental Welfare—Cases referred for 3 months to March, 1971*

	January	*February*	*March*	*Total*	
Area 1	31	32	24	87	26%
Valley Park	(11)	(15)	(9)	(35)	(11%)
Area 2	27	19	24	70	22%
Area 3	34	25	22	81	25%
Area 4	20	14	22	56	17%
Non town or no fixed abode	7	7	8	22	
Total	119	97	100	316	

Of the 35 cases in the Valley Park area, 22 were considered to be normally resident and 10 were of a transient nature. Three others originated in hospital.

VALLEY PARK AREA

APPENDIX II

REPORT FROM FAMILY SERVICE UNIT

Before commenting on the significance of the problems in the Valley Park area it is perhaps necessary to define the role of the Family Service Unit in relation to the Valley Park area.

The work of the Unit has been primarily concerned with providing an intensive family casework service to those families considered at risk. Because of the intensive nature of the work we have limited the number of families worked with at any one time and the majority of these are referred by other agencies.

In the past twelve months we have in a limited way broadened our base by offering the Unit's play facilities to a small group of eight children from All Saints Primary School. The Unit has also had some association with Brookhill School Summer Project, Knowle Hill Adventure Playground, the Valley Park Neighbourhood Centre, as well as more informal contact with various commonwealth immigrant social and political groups.

(*a*) *Special Problems in the Area for the Unit*

The number of families the Unit has worked with in the Valley Park district during the past 12 months is not significantly greater in number compared with other parts of the town. It can also be said that the problems they have presented, whilst clearly reflecting some of the social characteristics of the area, are, in many respects, no greater than for any other family considered socially deprived or inadequate living in other high need areas of the town.

The nature and type of the problems presented is perhaps significant. Of the 27 families worked with, 61% were single-parent and only three were commonwealth immigrant. The problems facing many of these families could be summarised as follows:

1. The structural conditions of the accommodation and decoration ranges from fair to poor.
2. Some degree of overcrowding is common.
3. The cost of basic amenities: rent, electricity, gas, is generally much higher than compared with council property.
4. Some children eligible for free school meals have not always been able to take advantage of this because of overcrowding in the school.
5. The lack of play space or informal play centres for young children (the number of children living in the area represents 31% of the population).

The very small number of immigrant families the Unit has had contact with might indicate a wider problem of the relationship between the personal social services and immigrant families. There is also clearly a lack of awareness of the range of services and benefits available and associated with this is a reticence to seek help except when there is acute crisis.

In general the less able and poor families are further handicapped by the inadequacy of the social provisions and amenities in the area. The principle problems for the vast majority of the families referred to us were related to this lack of basic social provision.

Comprehensive social change and not casework would seem to be an appropriate way of dealing with these problems.

(*b*) *The Social Service Committee's Objectives in Relation to These Problems*

We are not in a position to answer this question in any detail. However, the manner in which the problems of Valley Park have been tackled to date, by both voluntary and statutory bodies indicates a need for a more comprehensive approach in the future. The redevelopment programme and the setting up of various advice centres and voluntary community based schemes can only be regarded as a partial answer.

Each would appear to be evolving independently of the rest, yet all are converging on the same client population. If this continues the inevitable results will be overlap, discontinuity, confusion and—in consequence—disappointment of the very expectations to which they give rise. It would seem, therefore, important in principle to set up a co-ordinated programme, and a planning process capable of focusing on the total needs of the individual and the family. The development of better community services must be accompanied by a concerned effort to stimulate better co-ordination and communication among them. This must be the primary task for the Local Authority and the independent and voluntary agencies working in the area.

(*c*) *Outline of Unit's Possible Contribution in Conjunction with the Social Services Department*

Essentially one sees the setting up of two Neighbourhood Centres in the area, the primary task of the Centres would be to provide information and advice. There is a good deal of evidence to suggest that in high need areas, locally based social services are more likely to be used by the residents than a centrally based service. Our own experience with the Hampton Neighbourhood Centre would also tend to confirm this. The basis for these two Centres is readily available with the Unit positioned in Valley Park Street and a voluntary Advice Centre based on Elsmore Road.

The Unit will have by the New Year, adequate accommodation for a Neighbourhood Centre and we believe that we have the experience and expertise to develop the Centre in a way that will be meaningful to the local community. The professional staff required for such a scheme would be one worker based in the Centre and a second worker to work in the neighbourhood. The neighbourhood worker would provide a link between the community and the two centres as well as with the statutory services. It is also clearly very important that some significant contact is made at 'grass roots' level with the different community groups living in the area, since very little is known about their needs. The development of the Advice Centre in Elsmore Road would require the direct involvement of area 1 team and it is likely that more satisfactory accommodation would have to be found.

(*d*) *Estimated Cost of a Neighbourhood Centre Based at the Unit is as follows:*

		£
Neighbourhood worker salary	including GNI	2,000
Advice Centre worker salary		2,000
Part-time secretary		750
Capital expenditure for group activities		500
Admin. overheads		200
		5,450

REPORT OF THE MEDICAL OFFICER OF HEALTH ON THE VALLEY PARK AREA

(A) INTRODUCTION

The overall problem of Valley Park (or any similar area) cannot be clearly differentiated into those of environment, social or purely health content, but the summation of a variety of problems in these fields may precipitate a 'medico-social crisis' in the individual or community. This report gives an outline of some of the more critical problems of the area.

(B) POPULATION

The area has a highly concentrated multi-lingual, multi-racial population estimated as 22,670, which is 8·2% of the town population. Special characteristics are as follows:

(i) A very high proportion of immigrants
(ii) A high proportion of children
(iii) Many immigrant families living in multi-occupation
(iv) A disproportionate number of 'poor whites' live in the area
(v) There is considerable movement to and from the area by immigrants and 'poor whites'
(vi) The area is frequented by students
(vii) Unmarried mothers gravitate to the area
(viii) There is evidence of primary poverty amongst the elderly 'poor whites' and unmarried mothers
(ix) There is a high proportion of one-person households amongst the elderly

(C) HEALTH PROBLEMS

(i) *Maternity and mortality*

Although it is believed that the Valley Park population represents 8·2% of the total population, the following above average factors prevail:

(*a*) 17·9% of the sociological maternity bookings for the town come from this area.

(*b*) 18% of all stillbirths in the town occurred to mothers living in the area.

(*c*) 11·8% of all first week deaths occurred in the area.

(*d*) 11% of all violent deaths in the town occurred in this area.

56% of all children born in the area are immigrant births. Many small premature babies are born to immigrant families and these are particularly susceptible to infection. There is some evidence that there is a greater prevalence of congenital abnormalities amongst them.

(ii) *Nutrition*

Under-nutrition and malnutrition is fairly common amongst the elderly. This is frequently associated with anaemia and myxoedema.

In the case of immigrants, although they accept artificial feeding for their children, the onset of mixed feeds presents problems because of religious taboos and the unwillingness to try the range of English foods available. Anaemia is frequently found in the women, and although malnutrition is less common in the children there is evidence of rickets and anaemia.

(iii) *Morbidity*

Hypothermia has been prevalent amongst old people and young babies living in the area.

The area contains a large number of 'old' old people who require prolonged periods of nursing care. Many of these are separated from their relatives who have moved to peripheral estates and other towns.

The incidence of tuberculosis is high amongst immigrants and the elderly. 30% of the total notifications of pulmonary tuberculosis occurred in this area, in which 41% of non-pulmonary tuberculosis was also found. The risk of spread in houses of multiple occupation is obvious, particularly where the standard of hygiene is low. Spitting is common practice.

Similarly, gastro-enteritis is common in the area and should disease be imported from Asia there is no doubt that there is ample opportunity for its wide dissemination.

(D) RELATED PROBLEMS

(i) *Language*

It is estimated that almost 60% of the primary school children in the area are immigrants. 45% of these were, according to the classification of the Education Department, immigrant pupils who by reason of language difficulties are unable to follow a normal school curriculum with profit to themselves.

The increased size of the various sects has encouraged them to become more isolated and this, together with language difficulties, inevitably retards the work of health education which is so essential if standards are to be raised.

(ii) *Housing*

Much of the housing in this area is old with poor internal design by present day standards and showing bad arrangement with a lack of minimal provision of amenities for the number of occupants. These factors, together with a poor standard of repair, dangerous stairways, passageways and yards, frequently constitute a serious hazard to old people. Many of the houses are damp with inadequate means of heating. There is a minimum in the way of amenities for children, e.g. absence of play areas.

(iii) *Child minding*

The Health Department has ceased to be responsible for supervision of this, but experience over many years indicates that frequent movement of these families created a serious risk to the children. The standards of child care were not adequately maintained and parents were willing to accept the minimal provision by child minders responsible for the care of their children. This attitude prevailed amongst whites, Africans and West Indians.

(E) STAFF

Excessive demands are made upon staff working in areas such as Valley Park with a high immigrant population. The caseload of Local Authority nursing staff attached to general practitioners is almost double in a mainly immigrant practice to that in a European practice of comparable size. Because of the high caseload the optimum number of visits to various categories of children is not possible.

Mounting pressures have led to high staff losses. This aggravates the problem and it is impossible to carry out the necessary surveillance and preventative work. These factors must contribute to the high mortality and spread of infection in the area.

(F) RECOMMENDATIONS

(i) A community/neighbourhood/health centre should be established in the vicinity of Woodlands Road.

(ii) A domiciliary Family Planning Service should be provided in the area.

Although additional health visitors are required to work in the area no recommendations are made for additional staff because of the impossibility of recruitment without offering special inducements.

(G) COST

The community/neighbourhood/health centre would cost in the region of £75,000 with annual running costs (excluding loan charges and staff) of £2,000.

The domiciliary Family Planning Service would cost approximately £15 per case. This amount would cover all costs including supervision during the first 2 years.

Medical Officer of Health.

REPORT OF THE CHIEF PUBLIC HEALTH INSPECTOR

VALLEY PARK AREA—SOCIAL PROBLEMS

I have to make the following observations and recommendations on the Valley Park area in relation to the matters specifically referred to by Councillor James Smithson at the Council Meeting, 9 June, 1971.

(*a*) SPECIAL PROBLEMS OF THE AREA

1. General disrepair of tenanted houses.
2 Multi-occupation—lack of amenities, fire escapes, general control as to repair and maintenance, accumulations of rubbish and house refuse, overcrowding.
3. In houses other than those in multi-occupation, absence of amenities (Housing Act, 1969). This applies to both tenanted and owner-occupied houses.

(*b*) OBJECTIVES TO BE PURSUED

1. Increased attention to defects in tenanted houses.
2. Increased control of houses already in multi-occupation.

3. To bring to the notice of owner-occupiers, tenants and landlords yet again the advantages of house improvement under the grant scheme.

PROPOSALS FOR ACHIEVING OBJECTIVES

Disrepair

It is hoped that the Housing Aid Centre will encourage tenants to ask for assistance in keeping their houses in a proper state of repair. Increased pressure on landlords to improve tenanted houses lacking in amenity and drawing attention to the financial assistance available for repairs when coupled with improvements. House to house visitation can be organised with this in mind.

Multi-occupation

Much greater use will be made of the Management Order procedure for the proper repair and maintenance of multi-occupied houses. Accumulations of refuse will be dealt with under this Act and the Public Health Act, subject to the necessary assistance being available from the Borough Engineer's Cleansing Department. The cleaning up of accumulations of rubbish will also have to be pursued in the back entrances to terraced houses as well as in the house yards.

Overcrowding

In an endeavour to prevent overcrowding and to get greater control of houses coming newly into multi-occupation, the declaration of the whole town to be a registration area under the Housing Acts 1961/69.

Improvements of Houses

Further follow-up of tenanted houses dealt with in earlier improvement areas declared under the Housing Act 1964 (this dealt with tenanted houses only) persuasion of tenants to ask for improvement (Section 19, Housing Act 1964) where houses had previously been the subject of suspended notices, general approach to owner-occupiers in these areas and beyond.

General Improvement Area Treatment

Whilst the whole of this area has been accepted for ultimate treatment by area improvement, it presents a great number of problems which require careful examination in the first place. This is essentially a matter for the Planning Officer involving the environmental and other needs of the residents. Open space is sadly lacking and a careful examination by my staff may reveal some small areas of property fit only for clearance which would prove most helpful in the eventual promotion of a general improvement area.

(*c*) EFFECT ON COUNCIL'S EXPENDITURE

Expenditure here will be on new staff appointments, as whilst far more work has been done in the Valley Park area than can ever be apparent, the problem needs even greater attention and particularly continued attention to maintain conditions once they have been improved. This is quite impossible with the present staff.

The additional staff required are two Specialist Public Health Inspectors who will be appointed specifically for this purpose and will have to show evidence that they have an interest in this particular work which can be very frustrating and time consuming.

Chief Public Health Inspector.

HOUSING COMMITTEE

HOUSING MANAGER'S REPORT ON THE NOTICE OF MOTION AT THE CITY COUNCIL 20th JULY, 1971

PROBLEMS OF THE AREA

Valley Park is acknowledged to be an area of housing stress. The statistics available from the local Education Authority of the number of immigrant children in the local schools demonstrates that there is a very heavy concentration of immigrant families living in the area. Information which also becomes available both as a result of departmental investigations and also by contact with other Corporation Departments demonstrates that there must be extensive multi-occupation of dwellings and a high probability that considerable overcrowding exists in many houses.

It is apparent that the immigrants living at Valley Park do not fully avail themselves of the facilities provided by the Housing Department. Many of the families if they had cared to make application for local authority housing would by now have qualified and been rehoused away from the area. There does appear to be some distrust of officialdom in its broadest sense, and every opportunity is taken through contacts with immigrant associations to give assurance and information, but this is proving to be relatively hard going. Over the past year or so increasing numbers of immigrants have added their names to the housing waiting list and increasing numbers are being rehoused, but nothing like so many as might be expected. A high proportion of immigrants are of Asian origin and these people very largely are not interested in renting Council dwellings. The ambition of Asians with regard to housing is to own their own dwellings and many resort to occupying accommodation as lodgers or sub-tenants in order to save money to raise the deposits necessary to purchase.

The types of house normally purchased by immigrants do not usually find favour with Building Societies and private loans at very high rates of interest are resorted to by some purchasers. To help meet high repayments owners are prepared to sublet at very high rents.

A few years ago when the Council's Loan Scheme for house purchase had unrestricted funds, a considerable number of applications were received for the purchase of houses at Valley Park from Asians. This assistance unfortunately became very restricted when finance was subject to quotas. Now that money is again available for purchase of the older type of house, loans can again be made to immigrants in the Valley Park area in order that they may purchase houses either at Valley Park or in other parts of the town.

There has also been a reluctance from immigrants and to some degree from the indigenous residents at Valley Park to make use of the facilities available for house improvement. Here again the maximum amount of publicity has been used and slowly the number of applications is increasing.

ACTION TO OVERCOME PROBLEMS

It is intended to open a Housing Advice Centre at No. 20 Vine Street. This will be staffed on a permanent basis and will give advice and information under the following headings:

- Slum clearance
- Public Authority housing
- Landlord and tenant matters
- Improvement grants and general improvement areas
- Housing controls
- House purchase
- Housing Associations and Societies
- Availability of private rented accommodation

The closest possible links will be maintained between the Department and local immigrant organisations. The promise of full assistance from the local Housing Committee of the Council for Community Relations has been assured and they are prepared to give practical assistance in the running of the Centre.

The prime aim of the Centre will be a dynamic and positive approach to give advice and wherever possible practical assistance with housing to improve living conditions for the maximum number of people in the area.

Every endeavour will be used to improve the Local Atuhority image and no enquirer will be generally referred to another Department for the necessary answers. If information is not available there and then it will either be immediately obtained or person to person appointments made for the enquirer.

COSTS

The initial setting up of the Centre will involve the Council in expenditure of approximately £7,500.

The likely effect otherwise will be on the Council's Loan Scheme and also the cost of improvement grants. This cannot be quantified at the present time.

PUBLIC WORKS COMMITTEE

VALLEY PARK AREA SOCIAL PROBLEMS

The Council at the meeting on the 9th June, 1971, passed the following resolution:

'That with a view to maximising the contribution which this Council shall make to alleviating the misfortune and hardship in the Valley Park district and the adjacent area, the Social Services Committee and the Health, Housing and the Public Works Committees shall report to this Council by 30th September, 1971, at the latest, as to the measures which either individually or collectively they intend to take.'

Various points were raised by Councillor Smithson at the Council meeting and those particularly affecting this Committee are:
(*a*) Rubbish in the streets
(*b*) Broken pavements

(*a*) RUBBISH IN THE STREETS

In common with other densely populated parts of the town, this area has a parking problem which impedes street cleansing. There is, of course, in addition some demolition and new building work going on which causes a considerable amount of dust on some streets.

There is a fair amount of litter and really to cope with the element of nuisance which this introduces it should be dealt with by daily sweeping. This is not feasible for a number of reasons and the target aimed at is twice weekly cleansing.

In addition to this, refuse collection poses something of a problem basically for two reasons, one that with a fair degree of multiple occupation of dwellings there are more than the usual number of dustbins sited in somewhat confined areas, which leads to dirt and spillage. Secondly, reports are received of parcels of various kinds which are deposited in back entries and other passage-ways.

(*b*) BROKEN PAVEMENTS

This problem to some degree does arise from vehicles being parked on the pavements, but the main reason is the amount of demolition work and the age of this area. On the completion of the various building operations taking place in this area, there should be a marked improvement in the pavements fronting these properties and then would be the time to consider possible increased planned maintenance for the remainder.

Until redevelopment has taken place, and especially until the laying of any new Statutory Undertakers' services has been completed it would inevitably make any increased expenditure on such repairs abortive.

I do not consider that there are any other matters in relation to this problem which are the concern of the Public Works Committee and I recommend that the views expressed above be incorporated in the joint report to be made to Council.

REPORT OF TOWN CLERK

RENT ACT EVASION

The Rent Acts are intended to provide a system of security and protection for tenants in private accommodation. The provisions in the Acts against harassment and illegal eviction followed the exposure of the disgraceful methods of managing residential property by Rachman and his colleagues.

The Acts also provide for the reference by a tenant of his rent to an independent arbitrator to establish a fair level of rent which remains in force for these premises even if the tenant changes. This provision is designed to prevent an exploitation of the housing shortage.

The Acts also create other criminal offences to prevent abuses by landlords and generally to regulate the relationship between landlord and tenant.

Power to enforce these provisions has been given to local

authorities, and investigation and prosecution of cases are conducted by the Solicitors in the Town Clerk's Department. At present this is done in response to complaints as received.

THE PRESENT PROBLEM

It has become increasingly apparent that there is wholesale evasion of the Rent Acts by landlords, particularly by those operating in areas of this city where houses in multiple occupation predominate. Evidence of this is provided by the steadily increasing number of complaints. The complaints vary from those of severe intimidation and harassment by physical violence and illegal eviction of families with very young children without any notice to charging rent at almost twice the permitted level.

Prosecutions have been successfully brought and severe penalties often imposed by both the Magistrates' Court and Court of Quarter Sessions. Nevertheless the problem continues unabated and requires action on a larger scale than hitherto. There are numerous instances where tenants through fear or ignorance do not come forward. Complaints by tenants of threat of physical violence or actual violence are quite common.

The Acts are somewhat complicated, and the law relating to landlord and tenant generally gives rise to much difficulty. This results in a reluctance on the part of the police actually to involve themselves in the problem although they are prepared to co-operate when requested specifically to do so, and they have provided invaluable evidence on a number of occasions. Furthermore social workers operating in the areas already referred to, fail to realise the help and the remedies available.

It is apparent that complaints require proper investigation by experienced personnel. Increased use is being made of the services of a reputable Inquiry Agent, although if the problem continues it may be necessary to seek authority to make a full-time appointment. This has been done successfully by other progressive local authorities where the problem was becoming acute.

RECOMMENDATIONS

1. Under the existing legislation local authorities have the power to refer furnished tenancies to the Rent Tribunal in order to settle a fair level of rent. This has the advantage of relieving a tenant of this responsibility which can be particularly important where the landlord is hostile or the tenant is in some way socially inadequate. This procedure can be used to obtain a limited security of tenure (six months) for the tenant. It is recommended, therefore, that the Town Clerk be given the authority to refer any case or number of cases to the Tribunal. By this method it is hoped to extend control over the

problem areas and make both landlord and tenant aware of the role of the local authority.

2. Hand in hand with these other measures there should be a programme of education and information for social workers, which could comprise lectures given by my solicitors.

3. Although it is recognised that the policeman on patrol cannot act as an adjudicator in landlord and tenant disputes, it is recommended that the Police be requested to co-operate fully.

REPORT OF THE HOUSING, SOCIAL SERVICES, HEALTH AND PUBLIC WORKS COMMITTEES

VALLEY PARK AREA

At their June meeting the Council instructed the Health, Housing, Public Works and Social Services Committees to report not later than at this meeting as to the measures which they intend to take to alleviate the misfortune and hardship in the Valley Park district and the adjacent area. The four Committees have agreed to present a joint report.

The time allowed by the Council has not been enough for the preparation of a thorough and co-ordinated report at this stage. The Committees have individually considered reports from their officers and in some cases have been able to approve specific recommendations. In most respects, however, the proposals which have been put before the Committees need further consideration by other Committees or, in some cases, consultation with Government departments, before they can be submitted to the Council for approval. This report is therefore essentially a progress report.

In anticipation of approval obtained at the July meetings of the Committees, when the motion was reported, the Town Clerk asked the officers to prepare reports according to the following outline scheme:

(*a*) What are the special problems of the area for the department?

(*b*) What objectives should the Committees be pursuing in relation to these problems?

(*c*) How was it proposed to achieve the objectives?

(*d*) What was the likely effect on the Council's expenditure of seeking to attain the objectives by those methods?

At the September meetings of the Committee the following proposals for action were considered in relation to the Valley Park area:

1. The staffing and fitting out of the Housing Advice Centre at No. 20 Vine Street. This project was approved by the Council in June.
2. The making of references to the Rent Tribunal in connection with the rents of furnished dwellings.
3. More pressure to secure repair and improvement of houses, and to maintain control of houses in multiple occupation.
4. Subject to the approval of the Secretary of State, the making of a registration scheme for houses in multiple occupation, which would give a measure of control over new proposals for multiple occupation.
5. The possibilities of declaring General Improvement Areas.
6 The allocation of social workers to work full-time in the area.
7. The provision of a family advice centre.
8. The siting of a community home for the care of difficult children from the area.
9. The assessment of need for the personal services.
10. The development of a domiciliary family planning service.
11. The establishment of a health centre in the vicinity of Woodlands Road to supplement those planned for Manchester and Highcross areas.
12. The recruitment of more staff for public health services.

Not all these proposals are necessarily limited to the Valley Park area.

It has been arranged that the Chairmen and Vice-Chairmen of the four Committees will meet again shortly to review progress. The four Committees feel that the Education Committee has a great part to play in improving conditions in the Valley Park area and they recommend that the Council should approve the approach which the four Committees have made to the Education Committee on these lines in order that the Education Committee may join with the other Committees in their further consideration of the Valley Park area problems.

REFERENCES

5.1 Town and Country Planning Act, 1971, HMSO, 1971.

5.2 *The Future of Development Plans*, HMSO, 1965.

5.3 J. R. JAMES, *'Future of Development Plans,'* Town and Country Planning Summer School, 1965.

5.4 *Development Plans—A Manual on Form and Content,* HMSO, 1971. This contains a detailed coverage of the Department of the Environment's interpretation of structure and local plans.

5.5 *op. cit.*

5.6 West Midland Conurbation Authorities Project Report, unpublished report, 1970.

5.7 *Development Plans—A manual of Form and Content,* para 1–7, HMSO, 1970.

5.8 A. MORTON, *Financial Aspects of Structure Planning,* TPI/CES Conference, University of Birmingham, April, 1971.

5.9 J. D. STEWART and TONY EDDISON, 'Structure Planning and Corporate Planning'. *RTPI Journal,* Sept./Oct., 1971.

5.10 TONY EDDISON, 'Wider role of the development plan', *Town Planning Institute Journal,* Dec., 1968.

5.11 The case has been consistently well argued over a period of years by the Town and Country Planning Association—see almost any edition of the *Town and Country Planning Journal.*

5.12 The Burns study team from the South East and more recent similar examples as well as the various standing conferences of local planning authorities. Other regional plans, again *ad hoc,* include the Regional Economic Planning Council's plans, the health plans of the Department of Health and Social Security and other regional plans of central government departments e.g. for the Children's Service by the Children's Regional Planning Committee for the Home Office.

5.13 *Development Plans—A Manual on Form and Content,* para 1–7, HMSO, 1970.

5.14 An extremely illuminating and recent insight into the planning hierarchy and organisation in New York City is given in a case study by BEVERLY MOSS SPATT, *A Proposal to Change the Structure of City Planning,* Praeger, 1971. Many of the problems highlighted in that study would be alleviated by some of the approaches discussed here.

5.15 The relationship was given expression in 'Strategic Planning, and PPBS', DAVID EVERSLEY, Chief Planner (Strategy) and ERIC WOOD, Assistant Treasurer, both of the GLC in *Local Government Finance,* October, 1971.

5.16 *Management Networks. A Study for Structure Plans,* HMSO, 1971.

5.17 *op. cit.*

5.18 It is sometimes argued that because structure planning is subject to statutory public participation this too constitutes a significant difference (see J. M. SHAW, letter to *Royal Town Planning Institute Journal,*

p. 36, Jan., 1972). On the basis of what is said in Chapter 6 on public participation, this cannot be taken as a real difference. It simply reflects the fact that we have chosen to focus on physical planning for public participation. Of course it is crucial to the *whole* public policy-making field.

5.19 T. H. MARSHALL, *Social Policy*, Hutchinson, 1965.

5.20 RICHARD M. TITMUS, *The Role of Redistribution in Social Policy,* 1950.

5.21 R. E. PAHL, 'Poverty and the Urban System', paper read to Teacher's Section of the British Sociological Assoc., 1970—to be published in *Spatial Problems of the British Economy*, Cambridge University Press, 1971/2.

5.22 JANE JACOBS, *The Death and Life of Great American Cities,* Jonathan Cape, 1962.

5.23 *Development Plans—A Manual of Form and Content*, HMSO, 1970.

6
Public Involvement in Local Authority Policy Planning

The concern in this chapter is to explore the issues surrounding the vexed question of public involvement in local authority policy planning. Public participation is a subject which has been written about extensively especially public participation in the physical development field. The intention is to crystallise some important considerations and to point to directions in which policy-making processes might move. Too often the controversy which arises in discussing this topic becomes polarised and the evidence is that despite all the talk, all the writing, little impact has been made on the real solution.

The classical concept of democracy—government of the people, by the people, for the people—does not exist. As we saw in Chapter 3 in discussing problems of goal setting, the unfortunate feature of democracy is that it is very coarsely grained. Politicians cannot represent the multitude of values and preferences of their constituents. It is impossible at an election to vote on separate issues—one opts for a package of policies or a *set* of values. Elections represent a sieving out of values and preferences. The problems the policy-making machine chooses to focus on, those it ignores or those it remains ignorant of altogether, are a reflection of its values and preferences. So too are the solutions and priorities it chooses to adopt relative to those problems. It is not possible to devise a value-free approach to policy making. All groups in the community cannot be satisfied. Public policy making is essentially a conflict situation and the conflict centres on values. The democratic system represents the exercise of power by a few people over the many. This is not to say that this power is maliciously used, that it is corrupt or applied for dubious motives. No doubt this is true in more cases than we might care to imagine but it is not our concern. The system of democracy is broadly accepted* as a basis for our public policy-making processes but a *broad* acceptance is not *total* acceptance. There are many signs of the crudeness of the traditional democratic processes and the need exists for other

* This is an assumption on my part.

devices to secure more useful and relevant inputs into the policy making process, to supplement the normal democratic processes.

"The lack of communication, let alone co-operation, between public authorities and private bodies had to become scandalous before any practical attempts were made to overcome it. There are now some provisions for co-operation and some joint committees. These, for example the Town Centre working party, reveal other interface situations, areas where local authority and Ministry meet, but where from the point of view of the general public, little but friction results. Significant differences have existed between Ministry and City over Lion Yard and between Ministry and County over the Kite area.

Interface areas are no one's responsibility so they are never designed. They are left to take care of themselves : often their existence is not recognised so where there should be rapid communications we find obscure, shifting barriers to understanding. People in one system form a picture in their minds of what the other system is like and proceed to policy decisions relying on their picture without testing it against some measure of objective reality." (6.1)

Before discussing possible devices to increase the degree of public involvement a word needs to be said about the political nature of public policy making. The instruments or channels through which local government will secure any changes in public involvement are the elected representatives and the professional officials. Even action from *outside* the local authority will require a response *by* the local authority unless the action is of a direct or revolutionary kind.

"We are now quickly accumulating the skills for planning and then for engineering social change. This could be a highly felicitous development. But it could also be the basis for a new tyranny of technocrats. Already the specialists operating the simulation systems are finding it difficult, sometimes impossible, even to talk to politicians. The concepts they work with are unfamiliar, and the techniques they use seem mysterious. Decision makers are increasingly forced to accept the conclusions of technical specialists, thus putting the specialists in the role of governors. As the planning technologies grow more complex and as the distribution of information and analytical skills shifts from politicians to technicians, there is likely also to be a redistribution of political power. It now looks as though the post-industrial period will be marked by a new style of government." (6.2)

It is doubtful whether Melvyn Webber is right when he talks about a 'redistribution of political power'. What we are faced with is the increased development of techniques and analysis on the one hand and on the other a growing awareness on the part of the client publics of the impact of public planning decisions on them both in particular and more general ways. The poltician stands somewhere in the middle but there is little doubt where his sympathies will lie if the crunch comes.

Public planning is a political activity, a fact which those involved in it insufficiently recognise. Some would deny it, some pay passing attention to it, some would prefer it if it were not so and a few are trying to adapt the planning process to accommodate the reality. Planning, but especially physical development planning, has its roots in a relatively unsophisticated society and derives its origins from the imagination and vision of a few people who, focussing on and creating interest in problems of the time, gave birth, perhaps unconsciously, to a profession. Professions have their strengths and their great weaknesses not least of which is their strong and inevitable tendency to develop lives of their own, to protect themselves and to suffer from introversion. They also command authority over time. They gain credibility as a body of expertise in a certain field, however ill-defined, and as such become powerful in the decision-making processes of a democracy. The expertise is hired by public authorities ostensibly to aid decision making. In the case of physical planning, what began as a worthy reaction to the conditions of the last century, has developed into a very significant part of the system of intervention we call public planning. In part explicitly, but in some measure implicitly, society has sanctioned the erection of a system of public planning and control to be operated by elected authorities both in Parliament and in local planning authorities. Politicians may talk of modifying the system and frequently do. They rarely talk of abolishing it altogether (although no doubt some would dearly like to do so). What we have, then, is a large complex system of public planning the momentum of which derives from the decisions taken within it. These decisions of course vary in their impact, but essentially they represent the intervention of a public authority in the order of things. Whether it is a decision to adopt a pattern of incentives for industrial location, a decision to adopt a certain strategy for town expansion, a comprehensive education scheme, a system of rent rebates, the approval of a green belt, the adoption of a recreation policy, the refusal of permission to erect a neon sign, or the imposition of planning conditions on a consent, these decisions are taken by public authorities, with the advice of experts in the 'public interest'.

The realisation is slowly dawning on the professionals involved that almost every one of these decisions is value-laden. Over the last 50 years we have moved away from the situation where individuals in society were relatively unsophisticated, many preoccupied with survival or at least with the struggle for an improved standard of living to a state where, for a powerful number, horizons are infinitely wider. Conflicting interests, opposing values and opinions as to what is and what is not in the 'public interest' have emerged. Very few if any decisions can be regarded as *right,* as they were 50 years ago. Many of the beliefs and practices taken for granted for many years now can be seen for what they are, merely expressions of certain sets of values, or instruments to protect certain interests—tree preservation, listed buildings, the many prejudices of the experts and so on.

"*Government of the people, by the people. . . .*

How are we to stop short-changing the people of Cambridge? There is one very simple answer—listen to what they are saying and pay heed to it. Cambridge Planning Interface urges the planners to come out of their hard professional shells and listen to what people living here want their town to be like. If the rest of the world wants Cambridge preserved let it say so—and pay the price, but the planning authority represents each one of us living in the town and the county it does not, as it has so often maintained, hold Cambridge in trust for the rest of the world." (6.3)

The first pre-requisite of any move towards public participation is an understanding by the politicians (6.4) and professional officers of their own power and the political nature of the decision-making system in which they operate, not merely formal politics but other kinds of political processes (6.5).

Sherry R. Arnstein provides an interpretation of the participation spectrum (6.6). It is a useful framework, especially for professionals who tend not to see participation in these terms at all. Figure 6.1 shows the Arnstein 'ladder of participation'. She briefly describes her typology thus :

"The bottom rungs of the ladder are (1) Manipulation and (2) Therapy. These two rungs describe levels of 'non-participation' that have been contrived by some to substitute for genuine participation. Their real objective is not to enable people to participate in planning or conducting programmes, but to enable powerholders to 'educate' or 'cure' the participants. Rungs 3 and 4 progress to levels of 'tokenism' that allow the have-nots to hear and to have a voice : (3) Informing and (4) Consultation. When they are proffered by powerholders as the total extent of participation, citizens may indeed hear and be heard. But under these conditions they lack the power to insure that their views will be heeded by the powerful. When participation is restricted to these levels, there is no follow through, no 'muscle', hence no assurance of changing the status quo. Rung (5) Placation, is simply a higher level tokenism because the ground rules allow have-nots to advise, but retain for the powerholders the continued right to decide.

Further up the ladder are levels of citizen power with increasing degrees

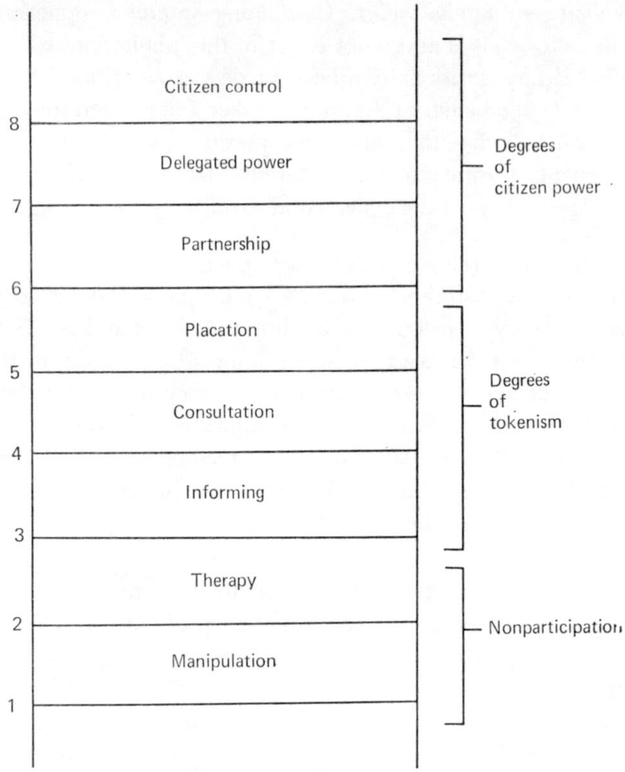

Figure 6.1

of decision-making clout. Citizens can enter into a (6) Partnership that enables them to negotiate and engage in trade-offs with traditional powerholders. At the topmost rungs, (7) Delegated Power and (8) Citizen Control, have-not citizens obtain the majority of decision-making seats, or full managerial power." (6.7)

This ladder is a simplification (Arnstein's own description) but it does provide a framework in which to judge examples from current practice. Any judgement, of course, is best done not here but by the reader himself or, more important, by the policy maker and the client. Appendix 2 to this chapter is a description by a practising town planner, of a few cases in County Durham (6.8). There are many examples from the field of physical development planning (6.9) both here, the United States and elsewhere.

An interesting point is that physical planning should be the area where most effort has been made to increase public involvement. Indeed it is the one field where there has been a Government Committee to look into the issue, and participation in structure planning is now a statutory requirement!

If local planning authorities do not carry out adequate steps of public participation in their structure plan procedures the Secretary of State may, if he wishes, reject a structure plan on those grounds.

The Skeffington Report, *People and Planning* (6.10) made the following recommendations:

"1. People should be kept informed throughout the preparation of a structure or local plan for their area. A variety of methods should be used, and special efforts made to secure the co-operation of the local press and broadcasting.

2. An initial statement should be published when the decision is made that a plan should be prepared. It should state how the authority propose to inform the public, and should contain a time-table showing the main opportunities for participation and the pauses for their consideration. Although there should be full opportunity for public debate, it should not run on endlessly.

3. Representations should be considered continuously as they are made while plans are being prepared; but, in addition, there should be set pauses to give a positive opportunity for public reaction and participation. Local planning authorities should concentrate their efforts to secure participation at two stages. These stages apply to both structure and local plans and are (*a*) the presentation following surveys of the choices which are open to the authority in deciding the main planning issues for the area in question, and (*b*) the presentation of a statement of proposals for the area in question.

Where alternative courses are available, the authority should put them to the public and say which it prefers and why.

4. Local planning authorities should consider convening meetings in their area for the purposes of setting up community forums. These forums would provide local organisations with the opportunity to discuss collectively planning and other issues of importance to the area. Community forums might also have administrative functions, such as receiving and distributing information on planning matters and promoting the formation of neighbourhood groups.

5. Local planning authorities should seek to publicise proposals in a way that informs people living in the area to which the plan relates. These efforts should be directed to organisations and individuals. Publicity should be sufficient to enable those wishing to participate in depth to do so.

6. Community development officers should be appointed to secure the involvement of those people who do not join organisations. Their job would

be to work with people, to stimulate discussion, to inform people and give people's views to the authority.

7. The public should be told what their representations have achieved or why they have not been accepted.

8. People should be encouraged to participate in the preparation of plans by helping with surveys and other activities as well as by making comments.

9. A better knowledge of planning is necessary. Greater efforts should be made to provide more information and better education about planning generally, both through educational establishments and for the public at large. Only if there is a better public understanding of the purpose of planning and the procedures involved will a local planning authority's efforts be fully rewarded when they seek public participation in their own development plans."

Other reports have touched lightly on the subject of public involvement including the Royal Commission on Local Government (6.11) and the Maud Committee on the Management of Local Government (6.12). In *'Management Networks, a study for structure plans'*, (6.13) there is a list of all the activities involved in structure plan preparation. Public participation is mentioned several times but at very specific stages and in fairly specific terms.

Public involvement has not been entirely confined to the processes of physical planning. In the education field there have been a variety of attempts at public involvement (Parent/Teachers Associations are a limited example) but the establishment of various schemes of comprehensive education have involved public participation albeit to a limited degree. A study done in the outer London Boroughs provides interesting comparative data and insights into the degree to which the public was involved (6.14).

"All authorities accepted the Secretary of State's advice to involve bodies very fully in the process of reorganisation. The manner of involvement was, however, varied.

Consultation of Unions (Enfield, Richmond, Barking, Bromley).

Consultation of individual teachers (Ealing, Merton, Barnet, Harrow, Waltham Forest).

Consultation through membership of Joint Consultative Committees (Barnet, Hounslow, Haringey).

Consultation of members of working parties (Bexley, Brent, Hillingdon).

One noted that throughout whatever method was used, and in some areas teachers were given several ways of expressing opinions, the teachers were always given the best chance to express views—usually before anyone else was consulted.

Although the general public was finally consulted by most authorities, few authorities made a point of consulting parents as a separate group. Barking did—after making its decision to adopt a Type I pattern, and Harrow and Richmond alone made a point of consulting PTA's.

Most authorities left themselves open to no criticism, by simply inviting observations from any interested party, but not always at the same stage of negotiations. . . . What perhaps is more noticeable, is that at least two authorities—Redbridge and Newham—showed no evidence of consulting the public at large."

The significant feature about the examples quoted, the position taken by the reports instanced is that, almost without exception (and this is probably true for most other examples too) they rarely come any higher on Arnstein's ladder of participation than the 'consultation' rung. Even at this level there is room for fears and doubts—again they must be resolved in the conscience of the policy makers themselves. Arnstein says of consultation in relation to the American scene :

"Inviting citizens' opinions, like informing them, can be a legitimate step toward their full participation. But if consulting them is not combined with other modes of participation, this rung of the ladder is still a sham since it offers no assurance that citizen concerns and ideas will be taken into account. The most frequent methods used for consulting people are attitude surveys, neighbourhood meetings, and public hearings.

When powerholders restrict the input of citizens' ideas solely to this level, participation remains just a window-dressing ritual. People are primarily perceived as statistical abstractions, and participation is measured by how many come to meetings, take brochures home or answer a questionnaire. What citizens achieve in all this activity is that they have 'participated in participation'. And what powerholders achieve is the evidence that they have gone through the required motions of involving 'those people'." (6.15)

Put simply the issue seems to be a question of moving the policy-making system's approach to public involvement higher up the ladder. As things are at present the 'planners know what is best' whether they are professional or political men and there is a case for a shift in the emphasis towards a self-help approach. This is obviously an opinion but there are manifestations in society at large that in many fields a new emphasis is required to be placed on 'involvement'.

GENERAL NEEDS

1. In public planning there is rarely a 'right' solution—not a matter of fact but of choice. Choice is opinion. It expresses value and neither the expert

nor the politician has a monopoly of wisdom about values. Our planning processes need to be more politically sensitive. There is a case for the creation within the policy planning processes, frameworks within which politicians and professionals can talk with each other and carry on a helpful dialogue with the different client publics. This implies a framework for choice, a process which exposes objectives and alternatives, which opens up meaningful debates on alternative policies, not simply in physical planning but across the spectrum of the policies of a local authority. Up to now politicians and the public have had very little basis for choice. Even where alternatives are put they are the planners' alternatives. There is no framework of information against which other ideas, different sets of values can be set. It may be that PPBS will assist this kind of process. It is not the complete answer by any means but it tells those who want to know what the purpose of expenditure is, what it is trying to achieve. Given that attention is focussed on objectives, alternative ways of securing objectives come more easily to light. They come up for critical examination, not against professional or political sacred cows, but against a stated objective. Political and professional judgements have to be sharpened up. There is a more helpful basis for choice. There is a system for all to see—a platform for community debate, for political argument, and this is where the public interest can perhaps best be served.

2. There is a need to come to grips with politics—to grasp that there can be no separation of planning from politics.

3. The need is to unhitch our minds from stereotype solutions, it is the stereotype which closes the mind to alternatives—alternatives based possibly on a different perspective for the problem. The concern should be to create opportunities rather than controls, to avoid losing sight of the purpose of planning—the interest in the mechanics of the system is an interest with an end—not an end in itself.

4. The links and differences between public relations and public involvement need to be recognised. It has been rightly argued that public relations and public participation are different—the former is no substitute for the latter. That much can be agreed. But the two are very closely related. A base of much better public relations than we have now needs to be laid before any form of participation has even a chance of success. Local government fails or succeeds at its points of contact with its clients whether this is at an enquiry desk, in the classroom, in the press, the receipt of a letter or of a planning refusal notice or the cheerfulness of a refuse collector. Accessibility, ease of communication in information terms is vital. For this reason there is a great need in local government for completely new public relations devices, e.g.

local authority bureaux to be set up, equipped with sophisticated communications systems, where the public can go and have the majority of their problems dealt with or at least where the relevant contacts can be made. It is worth reflecting about the multitude of barriers there are to securing contact between a local authority and its public (6.16).

ADVOCACY PLANNING

This movement has grown in the United States. It has suffered some setbacks but it has also made a case for an alternative approach to securing involvement in planning. The central argument of the movement is (6.17) that it is humanly impossible for the personnel of a public body to provide an adequate and genuine range of alternative plans and policies. The argument runs that it is inevitable for *conscious* and even more so for *unconscious* evaluation to take place as the attempt to draw up alternatives is pursued. The very act of moving through the process involves a cutting down of options, of narrowing issues to the manageable. It is impossible for the same set of planners meaningfully to produce *different* plans from completely *different* perspectives, different sets of values. The advocacy planners therefore argue that the different groups within the community should advance their *own* plans, employ their *own* experts to advance *their* value sets and policies based on them. Plurality of plans is the case. Their belief is that there should be a genuine set of alternatives and all should benefit from the local authority's pool of information which, after all *is* public information. In other words groups outside the local authority should be able to draw on local authority information.

The argument has been extended to suggest that in the same way that individual's may be entitled to *legal* aid, so community groups should, in certain cases, be eligible for a different kind of aid to advance their own planning policies. Whatever the drawbacks of this idea the advocacy planners claim that if it has no other effect but that of providing a challenge and stimulus to local authority policy makers it will have achieved a great deal. *That* point is difficult to refute.

Insofar as any such movement grows up the essential requirement seems to be that it should be spontaneous. It seems inappropriate for it to be formalised in any way. If it were, it would rapidly become just another kind of authority. The system is not without its difficulties because the problems of representing views and reconciling conflict still exist *within* groups of this kind. The scale is smaller, the problem the same. When one realises that *one* man is himself a collection of interest groups the real problems become clearer. John Smith is a doctor, a parent, a tennis club member, a keen motorist, a member of the Labour Party and black.

COMMUNITY DEVELOPMENT PROJECTS

An encouraging development in this country in the last two years or so has been the setting up jointly by selected local authorities and the Home Office, of community development projects. Among the 12 places finally to try these schemes are Coventry, Liverpool, the West Riding, Southwark, Glamorgan and Birmingham.

"The general objectives of CDP have been formulated in the following terms:

'To find out, through experiments in social action, how to effect a lasting improvement in social situations which display many symptoms of individual, family and community malfunctioning.'

This objective has then been divided into components:

Needs and aspirations

To study the needs and aspirations of people living in neighbourhoods with a high incidence of social deprivation; to help them find ways of meeting their needs, and, wherever possible, their aspirations.

Social Services response

In the light of such study, to increase the capacity of the social services to respond to both needs and aspirations more effectively, by a better understanding of the causation of need and by providing help which is more acceptable, intelligible and lasting in its effect.

Community Development

In these and other ways to help people exercise increased control over their own lives, including enlarging their opportunities in directions which they themselves see as desirable; and to reduce their dependence on the social services, while also enabling them to use them more effectively.

Social Planning

Through descriptive studies of action undertaken in pursuit of these objectives, to develop hypotheses about the causes of, and solutions to, social deprivation in such areas; and through further testing of these hypotheses to develop criteria for allocating resources to meet such needs." (6.18)

'There can be no one model or structure which is applicable to all issues or situations in a deprived neighbourhood, so our aim is to explore detailed concrete ways in which

(*a*) Residents can express their views about the neighbourhood and define in their own terms what they see as problems to be tackled or ideas for improvement.

(*b*) Residents can be engaged from the earliest stages in the planning and design of some of the facilities to be provided after redevelopment.

(*c*) Residents can gain increased constitutional control of, or responsibility for, some of the local institutions. (Too often institutions, e.g. schools, casework agencies, embody and impose values which may be quite foreign and inappropriate to the local culture).' (6.19)

The Project trod very carefully when it established itself in the Hillfields area of Coventry. Rather than latch too closely on to any existing formal organisations in the area, the Project rather focussed on issues of concern in the area and built up relationships with the community around them. An information and opinion centre was set up, staffed at first by the project staff but now primarily run by local people with assistance from project staff. A local newspaper has been established, 'Hillfields Voice' (Figure 6.2). The newspaper extract tells its own story.

TOTAL NUMBER OF ENQUIRIES, COMPLAINTS AND SUGGESTIONS 1ST JUNE 1970 TO 31ST MAY 1971—1,148

1.	Housing problems, i.e. all those problems that a Housing Advice Service might deal with (e.g. evictions, rent levels, repairs)	278	25%
2.	Enquiries, problems or opinions about redevelopment	258	22%
3.	Welfare rights (e.g. supplementary benefits, rebates, etc.)	152	13%
4.	Complaints about other groups or individuals (e.g. kerb-crawlers)	85	7½%
5.	Enquiries re neighbourhood group activities (e.g. pre-school play groups, old people's luncheon clubs, youth clubs, etc.)	62	5½%
6.	Suggestions or complaints re public amenities (e.g. open space, pedestrian crossings)	50	4½%
7.	Legal advice	45	4%
8.	To ask for Social Service help	41	3½%
9.	Complaints re rubbish and environment	35	3%
10.	Applications for nursery places	30	2½%
11.	Consumer problems	29	2½%
12.	Miscellaneous	83	7%
	There were also 72 people in to see the Councillor		

The list above gives a breakdown of the type of enquiries in the first year of operation (6.20). For our purposes what is important is not so much the specific detail as the sharp contrast with traditional views and approaches to participation and involvement. It is unlikely that the project staff in

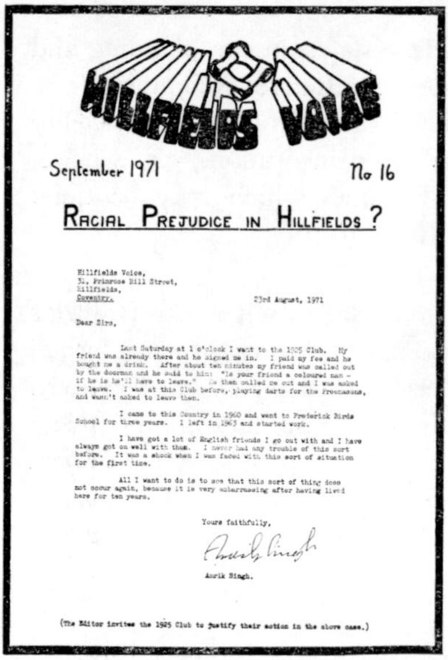

HILLFIELDS VOICE

September 1971 No 16

RACIAL PREJUDICE IN HILLFIELDS ?

Hillfields Voice,
31, Primrose Hill Street,
Hillfields,
Coventry.

23rd August, 1971

Dear Sirs,

Last Saturday at 1 o'clock I went to the 1925 Club. My friend was already there and he signed me in. I paid my fee and he bought me a drink. After about ten minutes my friend was called out by the doorman and he said to him: "Is your friend a coloured man – if he is he'll have to leave." He then called me out and I was asked to leave. I was at this Club before, playing darts for the Freemasons, and wasn't asked to leave then.

I came to this Country in 1960 and went to Frederick Birds School for three years. I left in 1963 and started work.

I have got a lot of English friends I go out with and I have always got on well with them. I never had any trouble of this sort before. It was a shock when I was faced with this sort of situation for the first time.

All I want to do is to see that this sort of thing does not occur again, because it is very embarrassing after having lived here for ten years.

Yours faithfully,

Amrik Singh.

(The Editor invites the 1925 Club to justify their action in the above case.)

HILLFIELDS INFORMATION AND OPINION CENTRE

31 PRIMROSE HILL St. TEL:- 24634 – 28242

OPENING HOURS

MONDAY TO FRIDAY – 9.00 AM TILL 6.00 PM
SATURDAY – 9.00 AM TILL 1.00 PM

FREE SPECIALIST ADVICE AVAILABLE

TUESDAY	CLAIMANTS UNION	9.30 AM – 11.30 AM
"	PLANNER (TELEPHONE LINK)	2.00 PM – 5.00 PM
"	HEALTH VISITORS ADVICE	2.00 PM – 4.00 PM
WEDNESDAY	SOCIAL SERVICES (WELFARE)	10.00 AM – 1.00 PM
"	FREE LEGAL ADVICE	4.30 PM – 7.00 PM
"	COUNCILLORS SURGERY	7.00 PM – 8.00 PM

IF THERE IS ANY URGENCY, PLEASE CALL AT ANY TIME.

WE WANT A DISCO

Why can't Hillfields have a Disco? All the children around here would stop breaking into the shops and could even stop causing fights. The money would come in useful for more stuff for the playgrounds, and it would be great to have a disco because all the kids need a change.

If you give us one to see if it turns out all right we might be able to have one once a week. All the kids are bored of doing nothing.

Come on – give Hillfields a Disco.

Carole Davis and Lynn Westall

WHAT ABOUT US?

I am in agreement with all suggestions for facilities for the young people, also the senior citizens of Hillfields, but nothing seems to be suggested for the people in between. No doubt there is a lot of lonely and possibly shy people in between these ages, who would like to have something for themselves. A community centre, where they could meet in the evenings for entertainment, such as dances, variety evenings, with talent for amongst themselves. Sewing classes, cookery and numerous other things that would interest a vast number of people.

Mrs. Nicholas

HILLFIELDS COMMUNITY ASSOCIATION

ON

WEDNESDAY 29th SEPTEMBER

AT 7.30 PM

IN THE

HOWITZER CLUB

KING WILLIAM STREET

A MEETING WILL BE HELD FOR ALL RESIDENTS OF HILLFIELDS

NOTE: All groups & organizations should make sure they have representatives present

THIS IMPORTANT MEETING WILL ...

1. discuss the need for a Social Centre for Hillfields
2. adopt the Constitution of your Community Association – copies can be obtained from the Information & Opinion Centre

STUDY THE NEXT THREE PAGES CAREFULLY FOR MORE INFORMATION

HILLFIELDS COMMUNITY ASSOCIATION

WHEN DID IT BEGIN?

In January 1967 a small group of people talked about forming a Community Association. Later in the year 30 residents – chiefly from the Stoney Stanton Road side – attended a public meeting. An Association was formed and the old St. Mark's School in Stoney Stanton Road was used as a base.

1968–1969

A few activities were run, and a play group and Youth Club were opened. Local participation was not kept up, and meetings of the Association were attended by 6 – 10 people – mainly professionals.

At the end of 1969, it was decided to withdraw from St. Mark's School because of its derelict state.

1970–1971

Community work started late 1969, and as a result a variety of activities began. Through the Community Development Project, an Information and Opinion Centre was opened in June 1970 and money became available for activities planned by Hillfields' residents.

A number of residents associations came into being, and in January representatives of these met with H.C.A. and decided to form an organisation to act and speak for Hillfields. They kept the name 'Hillfields Community Association', but a new constitution has been prepared. This should be adopted at the meeting on the 29th September.

WHAT IS IT DOING NOW?

It links together more than 20 local groups through monthly meetings and the work of a full time secretary.

It applys for money to support work in Hillfields, and now controls an annual budget of over £9,000.

It employs six full time people and several on a part time basis.

It raises matters of general concern to the people of Hillfields (e.g. problems about the environment, re-development, amenities).

It is responsible for the community newspaper – 'Hillfields Voice'.

THE FUTURE

It is for those of us who are residents of Hillfields to decide what the Association will tackle year by year.

It depends upon YOU.

Wednesday 29th September 7.30 p.m.

Figure 6.2

Coventry and elsewhere regard their approaches as entirely meeting the needs of the situation. Clearly, however, the Community Development Project concept is a good deal closer to what is required. The test will come with the reaction of public authorities. There is a choice between seeing this movement as a valuable input into the planning process, a widening and handing over of decision choices or to put up the defences against it—to crush it. There is little doubt the second is more likely to be the dominant reaction. This whole problem raises for discussion the relationship of professional, politician and public. Very often it is argued that 'participation' in all its forms usurps the function and responsibility of the elected member. The truth is that some politicians dislike participation and community involvement as much as some officers, but there will be no choice, save in deciding which are the most helpful ways of striking up new relationships between these three elements. One thing is sure, it won't happen overnight, but there can be no doubt that it *will* happen. A whole crop of new devices will arrive extending community development projects, green papers, and so on. None of these devices will be adequate in itself nor will they resolve conflict, rather they are likely to heighten it and this is where a new breed of politician and officer will be needed. The distinction to be drawn here is between a situation where public views, objections, comments etc. are treated merely as a piece of data, leaving policy formulation little changed, and a situation where there is continued informal and formal sounding of community reaction through political and pseudo-political activities. The public policy-making system will always fail to accommodate conflict. Outside it spontaneous expression of differences will arise and so they should.

Not all 12 Community Development projects operate in the same way as Coventry's but this example is an important experiment.

The test of these projects will be in the reaction of public authorities.

Appendix to Chapter 6
Experience of Public Participation in County Durham*

SEDGEFIELD

This is a pleasant rural and residential village with a population of about 3,500. It was sufficiently small for us to try to see if we could get maximum public participation in the preparation of a local plan through public consultation techniques.

We prepared three possible plans for the village, setting out the objectives and consequences associated with each. These were *exhibited in the village* for three days. At the same time, we wrote to every householder in the village, inviting them to attend a general meeting to discuss these alternative plans, stressing that there was no question of any predetermined decision and promising continued consultation on the consequences of any decision reached. All clubs and organisations in the village received similar letters.

The public meeting in the village was extremely well attended and, after considerable discussion, a strong preference was expressed for particular objectives and solutions (which we happened to prefer). People living in the village may have adopted this attitude for reasons very different to ours, as it involved preventing further growth of the village beyond existing commitments!

We are now taking this kind of technique a step further by forming village action committees, on which community leaders sit at these public meetings. The Action Committee then initiates and controls improvement work in selected villages. This is now being tried out in large mining villages in East Durham with some success.

SOUTH STANLEY IMPROVEMENT SCHEME

This was a simple landscape scheme to improve a bleak area of inter-war council housing in a mining town, undertaken well before the Housing

*Reproduced with kind permission of R. C. Scarlett, Deputy County Planning Officer, Durham County Council from his paper, 'Objectives and Participation for Structure Planning' presented to CES/TP1 conference, April, 1971.

Act 1969 brought new powers and more financial help from central government.

The scheme involved removal of the major part of large individual gardens which were almost wholly neglected and derelict. The general objectives were to improve the quality of the surroundings, make the area more attractive to visitors and provide better and more convenient living conditions for the tenants.

The wishes of all tenants were first tested through a questionnaire and a preliminary scheme was exhibited locally in a community hall, in which a public meeting with all tenants was then held. A very large proportion of the tenants attended. We tried to have discussion first on the objectives and then on the details of the scheme, but a vociferous small minority of keen gardeners and political opponents of the District Council confined discussion in the meeting almost entirely to argument on the need to take away gardens and again—the cost. Private discussions with other tenants afterwards brought a far better understanding of the general view of those involved!

This meeting certainly improved relations with the general public, and had political repercussions later! It brought small changes in the scheme which has now been carried out and is praised by most of the tenants. I still feel that the formal meeting involved did not permit genuine participation, although it produced better results than the Stanley or Spennymoor efforts, mainly, it seems, because the objectives were limited, local and understandable to the tenants.

This not wholly satisfactory experience then led us to try adding the questionnaire approach to our method in larger urban areas. This was done for example in Bishop Auckland.

BISHOP AUCKLAND

This is a traditional market town which developed into an industrial centre with a total district population of about 35,000. We were moving towards the submission of new town centre proposals involving major highway work and the submission of a town map review, comprehensive development area map, and planning and highway compulsory purchase orders.

The major objective here was to conserve the historic part of the town, create more comfortable and convenient conditions for everyone using it, including better conditions for traders, and to permit a small expansion of the shopping and social facilities. We had gone through the usual exhibition and public meeting processes with much the same sort of limited reactions, when, for various reasons, planning work had to be slowed down, and we decided to use the interval to try out a questionnaire approach to the public.

About 1,680 copies of a questionnaire were sent out by post to one in ten of households in Bishop Auckland and one in twenty in some surrounding areas (enclosing prepaid reply envelopes, of course!). The questions asked covered:

(i) the use people made of the town centre;
(ii) the problems they saw in the centre, and their views on problems we specified;
(iii) what we should seek to do in planning in the town centre, and public attitudes to suggested solutions;
(iv) how they preferred to be given information on problems like this and proposals.

About 50% of the questionnaires were completed and returned, a fair proportion on the basis of previous experience.

The kind of response received showed that the public had understood the issues, and had fairly clear views on which objectives they agreed with and which solution they preferred. By good fortune it was also the solution which we preferred!

Analysis of the questionnaire was followed up by illustrating the preferred solution through the press and an exhibition. A public meeting was then held at which the formal part was kept short intentionally, and the meeting was then developed deliberately into a series of private discussions with a number of officers. This meeting was very well attended and 52 individual interviews followed.

This brought better results than we had achieved in earlier cases, but the efforts required and the time consumed were still pretty considerable when balanced against the gains made!

This technique has been used in other town centre situations, e.g. in Consett, where an 85% response rate was achieved. We also tried out a slightly different form of technique in Durham City.

DURHAM CITY

This is a county town—a cathedral and university city, administrative centre, and shopping and social centre with its historic and magnificent core on a high peninsula formed by a loop in the river. Conservation, redevelopment and traffic management proposals here have, inevitably, aroused keen and widespread interest. At one stage a detailed study was done on conservation and traffic management proposals in this core and we wished to test public reactions to them. In this case we sent out questionnaires to householders on a 10% random basis, but we also distributed questionnaires in car parks, bus queues to university students and even to school children. The results were analysed separately! We were surprised to get only a 50% response in this kind of city.

This was followed through, not at a full public meeting, but at a closed meeting to which we invited representatives of the 'organised public', e.g. the City Trust, the Rotary Club, the University, etc. Separate discussions were held with traders and with several other local societies.

This joint approach of testing general public reaction by questionnaires, while sounding out 'informed' opinion through a series of meetings with invited attendance produced more constructive and understandable reactions. But the objectives here were more local and more easily understandable.

Maybe the success should be measured from the supporting sit-in provoked in the main shopping area by a local group of anarchists.

REFERENCES

6.1 *Cambridge Planning Interface*—the first issue of a local publication published in Cambridge by the Cambridge Planning Interface Trust, —January, 1970. It is typical of many such publications sponsored by pressure groups of one kind or another.

6.2 M. M. WEBBER, 'Planning in an Environment of Change', *Town Planning Review*, Jan., 1969.

6.3 *Cambridge Planning Interface*, No. 3, April, 1971.

6.4 The role of the elected representative in policy formulation is discussed in Chapter 7.

6.5 It is of interest to note that few of the professions in local government include any political science in their examination syllabuses. The professional body I know best, The Royal Town Planning Institute and one which is inextricably bound up in the political process makes no direct reference to politics at all in its Examinations Handbook (*RTPI*, May, 1970).

6.6 SHERRY R. ARNSTEIN, 'A Ladder of Citizen Participation', *Journal of the American Institute of Planners*, July, 1969.

6.7 *op. cit.*

6.8. R. C. SCARLETT, 'Objectives and Participation for Structure Planning' —Paper presented to TPI/CES Conference, University of Birmingham, April, 1971.

6.9 e.g. (i) A. PLUMRIDGE, 'Great Dunmow Town Appraisal—an exercise in Public Participation', *Town Planning Institute Journal*, May, 1969.

(ii) *South Hampshire Plan*, 1972.

(iii) *Public Participation in Regional Planning*—Regional Plan Association, New York, 1967.

(iv) 'History of Public Participation in Coventry'—Appendix 3 to *People and Planning*, HMSO, 1969.

(v) *People, Participation and Government*, Fabian Research Series 293, 1971.

6.10 *People and Planning*, HMSO, 1969.

6.11 Royal Commission on Local Government in England, Vols. I and II. HMSO, 1969.

6.12 Management of Local Government, Vol. 5. HMSO, 1967.

6.13 'Management Networks, a study for structure plans', HMSO, 1971.

6.14 ROBERT LEWIN, from a summary of his M.A. dissertation, University of London.

6.15 SHERRY R. ARNSTEIN, 'A Ladder of Citizen Participation,' *Journal of the American Institute of Planners*, July, 1969.

6.16 For example, (*a*) the signposting system in most local authority offices is based on a language *internal* to the authority and bears little relation to the *reasons* why people go to the offices. Nowhere do you see signposts for 'drains', 'planning applications', 'dustbin complaints', 'smallpox vaccination', or whatever;

(*b*) the written word in letters and other communications is so very often unintelligible, pompous, officious, unsympathetic. Even in documents circulated as part of a participation effort, jargon is frequently used;

(*c*) some people are sometimes excluded by office opening times, physically handicapped people by simple physical barriers like steps, the illiterate by obvious barriers, by arbitrary rules, e.g. rules for inclusion on a housing list;

6.17 'Advocacy and Pluralism in Planning', *Journal of the American Institute of Planners*, November, 1965.

6.18 'Community Development Project', unpublished paper by John Benington, Project leader of the Coventry Project.

6.19 *op. cit.*

6.20 N. A. BOND, Assistant Project Director, Coventry Community Development Project, 'Hillfields Information and Opinion Centre'—Progress in the first year. Report. June, 1971.

7
Organisation for Planning

The fact that within four years of each other three major government committees and two Royal Commissions reported on various aspects of the way local government works (7.1) is evidence enough of a concern over a longer period about the shortcomings in local government's approach to fulfilling its obligations.

Preceding the publication of the Royal Commission reports (7.1 c and d) there had begun a widespread movement to make changes in the management operations in local government, and considerable impetus was given to it by the Maud Committee report on Management of Local Government (7.1b). In practice the greatest interest has centred on the committee structures and to a lesser extent on the departmental structures of local authorities. Indeed there are very few large authorities which, since the report was produced, have not at least reviewed their internal organisation (7.2).

In Chapter 1, one dimension along which the case for corporate planning was considered was that of interaction, i.e. the links between the objectives of different services.

"Many (though certainly not all) policy recommendations presented by scientists, and presuming to rely on science, suffer from a number of serious weaknesses, including the following:

1. A tendency to formulate problems narrowly, to fit into a specialised perception set. Thus, an economist tends to view all problems as economic ones; an engineer, as technological ones; and a depth psychologist, as dominated by personality dynamics.

2. Not only are problems perceived through narrow 'tunnel vision', but the theories (tacit and even explicit) used to analyse the problems are taken from specialised disciplines, with little attention to borders of validity. Thus, life scientists tend toward biological models of all phenomena; the single-minded image of policy issues held by many engineers is clearly related to mechanical models; and economists fondly claim universal applicability for

their sophisticated resources allocation and optimisation models, while implicitly often still holding on to the 'economic man'.

3. In respect to proposals for solutions, scientists tend toward one of two extremes: either they stay within their narrow perspectives and propose as solutions, policy instruments belonging to their specific disciplines, or they freely propose (and with an air of self-assurance) activities going far beyond their areas of competence. It is hard to decide which one of these two evils is worse—the civil engineer proposing new housing technologies as a cure for urban problems or the physical scientist proposing a complex arms limitation treaty. My own feeling is that the narrow specialist who uses his scientific credentials to propose comprehensive policies is more dangerous, because the weaknesses of his position are often not obvious; but narrow proposals for complex issues are also often useless and sometimes dangerous.

A mismatch between the domain of validity of a discipline and the space of a policy issue is the underlying cause of the three above-mentioned weaknesses of many policy recommendations presented by scientists in the name of their expertise. These weaknesses can be summed up as a narrow, mono-disciplinary perspective, which produce single-dimensional images of multispace issues; a distorted perception of problems; careless transgressions beyond one's area of scientific competence; and zero-effective, if not counter-productive, recommendations' (7.3).

Maud saw it in these terms:

"There exists therefore in local authorities in this country an organisation which is based on separate parts in each of which there is gathered the individual service, with its professional departmental hierarchy led by a principal officer and, supervising it, a committee of members. There may be unity in the parts, but there is disunity in the whole" (7.4).

Although the weaknesses in the internal operations of local authorities were not seen quite in Dror's terms, in the late 1960's it is true to say that the organisation structures of local authorities were recognised as being ill-suited to meet the needs of the day. In line with the lead given by the Maud Committee, local authorities sought *structural* remedies to their problems. Maud recommended that local authorities should establish a management board of elected members, that their approach to the management of the affairs of the local authority should be more co-ordinated and that a clerk with higher status and overall responsibility for co-ordination should be appointed (7.5). The way to improvement was thought to be through changes in the structure of committees, of departments and new style leaders in charge of them.

Some changes in the structure of local authority internal organisation are necessary, but there is plainly a relationship between the structure of an organisation and the processes which that structure is expected to sustain (7.6). A change in management structure does not necessarily bring about a change in the management process. It is this relationship between process and structure which needs to be reflected in the new systems of management. The concern so far in this book, has been to explore the planning process, the means by which policies might be formulated in local government. Attention is now shifted to a consideration of possible new structures in relation to the process of corporate planning.

The movement to consider processes and structures in parallel has already begun and several authorities, as will be seen, have implemented or are exploring new structures and processes together. The purpose here is to examine some examples, both theoretical and from practice, to see whether there are any common principles which may assist the convergence of processes and structures.

LIVERPOOL COUNTY BOROUGH

Liverpool Corporation called in McKinsey and Company Inc., who observed,

"the democratic forms of Council and committee and the rigid hierarchical structure of the service have some great strengths, but in many ways they are not geared to the modern task of managing thousands of people and hundreds of millions of pounds of assets, nor to making complex, often technical decisions on the deployment of these assets. The City has neither the organisation structure, nor the planning system, nor the management methods commensurate with the job."

The consultants identified two major limitations to the City's system of administration which were in turn split into specific problems, thus:

(A) The Corporation has difficulty in deciding priorities nationally and planning effectively.

- (i) Committee groupings are not coherently based on common or related objectives of services.
- (ii) No measures of effectiveness exist whereby proposals can be assessed in terms of their contribution to an outstanding need.

(B) The Corporation has little or no control over departmental efficiency and effectiveness.

- (i) Objectives are not clearly established for each service.

(ii) The permanent staff lacks strong direction.

(iii) Administrative and other internal services are fragmented.

The consultants' recommendations can be summarised as follows (7.7):

1. *Assign responsibilities for direct services to the public to seven committees under the Policy and Finance Committee, as follows:*

	Education Committee
	Housing Committee
	Environmental Health and Protection Committee
To have the same membership	Personal Health and Social Services Committee
	Children's Committee
	Transportation and Basic Services Committee
	Recreation and Open Spaces Committee

2. *Group departments into six programme administrations, each under a Programme Director, to match the committee structure*

To perform its key tasks of allocating resources between services and getting the best value for money in each of them, the Corporation requires an organisation in which, as far as possible, a single committee and department:

Decide on the priorities within groups of services with similar objectives, e.g. priorities for education or for personal services to the disadvantaged. Consider all the feasible alternative ways of performing services so as to select the method giving the best value for money.

3. *Appoint a Chief Executive Officer*

Appoint a Chief Executive Officer as head of the permanent staff of the Corporation. The Chief Executive would be responsible for ensuring, through the Programme directors, the efficient running of the administrations, and would co-ordinate the work of the City Planning Officer and Treasurer so as to advise the Policy and Finance Committee on city strategy and allocation of resources.

In order to perform these functions effectively the Chief Executive must be freed from the day-to-day administrative duties that presently burden the Town Clerk. We therefore propose that these duties should be transferred to a Director of Administrative Services. In this section we first describe the responsibilities of the Chief Executive then deal with the functions of the other officers concerned with city strategy, namely the City Treasurer and City Planning Officer, and the proposed new appointment of Director of Programme Planning.

4. *Strengthening the Administrative Machine*

Assign responsibility for all administrative services other than finance and land to a Director of Administrative Services.

Group responsibility for all aspects of land and property management (except direct control of maintenance work) under a Director of Land and Property Services.

Create a General Purposes Committee which, in addition to assuming responsibility for functions not elsewhere allocated such as precepts and cultural activities, will be responsible for monitoring the efficiency of permanent staff operations.

Give the Personnel Committee a more positive role in developing and implementing improved personnel policies.

5. *A new system of planning and control*

Given a structure that makes effective decision making possible, an equally important requirement is to establish an effective system for setting objectives, planning the best ways of achieving them and measuring performance in carrying out these plans.

Diagrams (7.1) and (7.2) show the new structures.

STOCKPORT

Stockport Council employed Booz, Allen and Hamilton to conduct a review of its organisation :

"The purpose was to strengthen management capability in the Borough to meet the responsibilities of the present and future, recognising the considerable growth in services and financial expenditure during the past decade, the growing demands being placed on local government, increasing expectations for management effectiveness and efficiency, and the likelihood of general local government reorganisation. To meet these demands, a new organisation was recommended.

The most important change at committee level is the creation of a Policy Committee to co-ordinate and recommend overall Corporation policy, to allocate resources, and to monitor progress and results in all areas. The membership of this committee will include the chairmen of all other committees as well as minority party representation; two important committees will be responsible for financial and personnel matters respectively. The responsibilities of the other committees, which parallel those of the new divisions, will be for :

Technical Services
Development and Town Planning

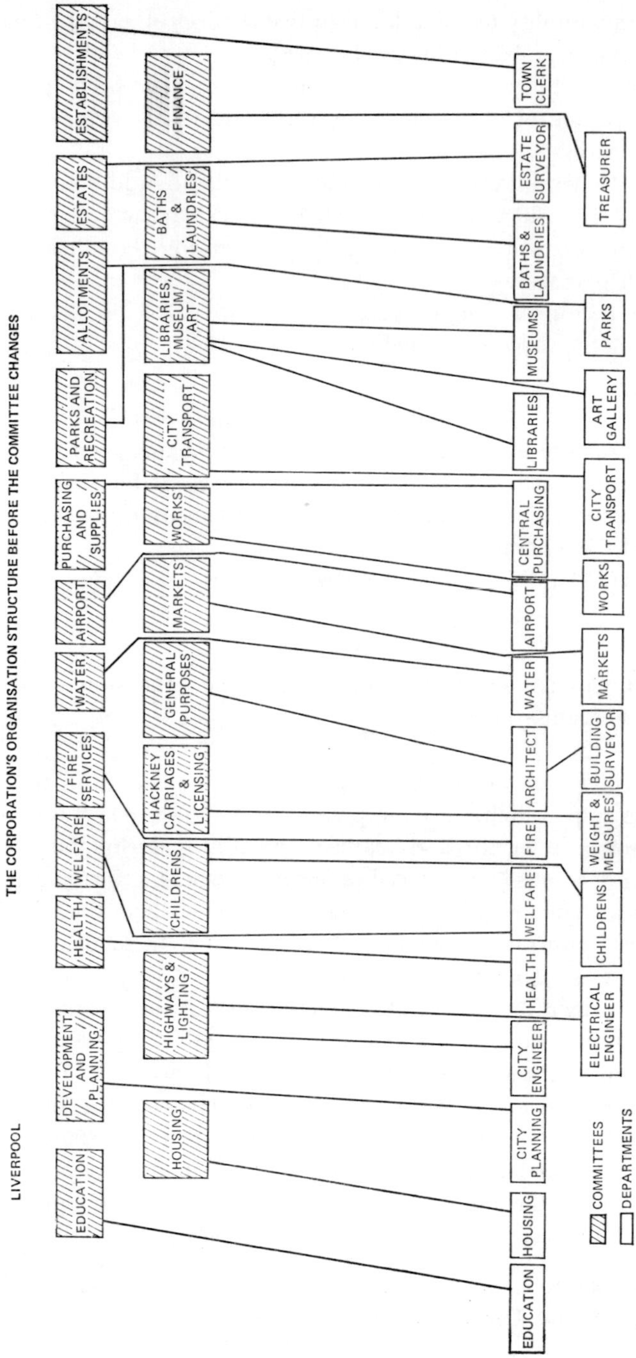
THE CORPORATION'S ORGANISATION STRUCTURE BEFORE THE COMMITTEE CHANGES
LIVERPOOL
EDUCATION
DEVELOPMENT AND PLANNING
HEALTH
WELFARE
FIRE SERVICES
WATER
AIRPORT
PURCHASING AND SUPPLIES
PARKS AND RECREATION
ALLOTMENTS
ESTATES
ESTABLISHMENTS
HOUSING
HIGHWAYS & LIGHTING
CHILDRENS
HACKNEY CARRIAGES & LICENSING
GENERAL PURPOSES
MARKETS
WORKS
CITY TRANSPORT
LIBRARIES, MUSEUM/ ART
BATHS & LAUNDRIES
FINANCE
EDUCATION
HOUSING
CITY PLANNING
CITY ENGINEER
HEALTH
WELFARE
FIRE
ARCHITECT
WATER
AIRPORT
CENTRAL PURCHASING
LIBRARIES
MUSEUMS
BATHS & LAUNDRIES
ESTATE SURVEYOR
TOWN CLERK
ELECTRICAL ENGINEER
CHILDRENS
WEIGHT & MEASURES
BUILDING SURVEYOR
MARKETS
WORKS
CITY TRANSPORT
ART GALLERY
PARKS
TREASURER
COMMITTEES
DEPARTMENTS

Figure 7.1

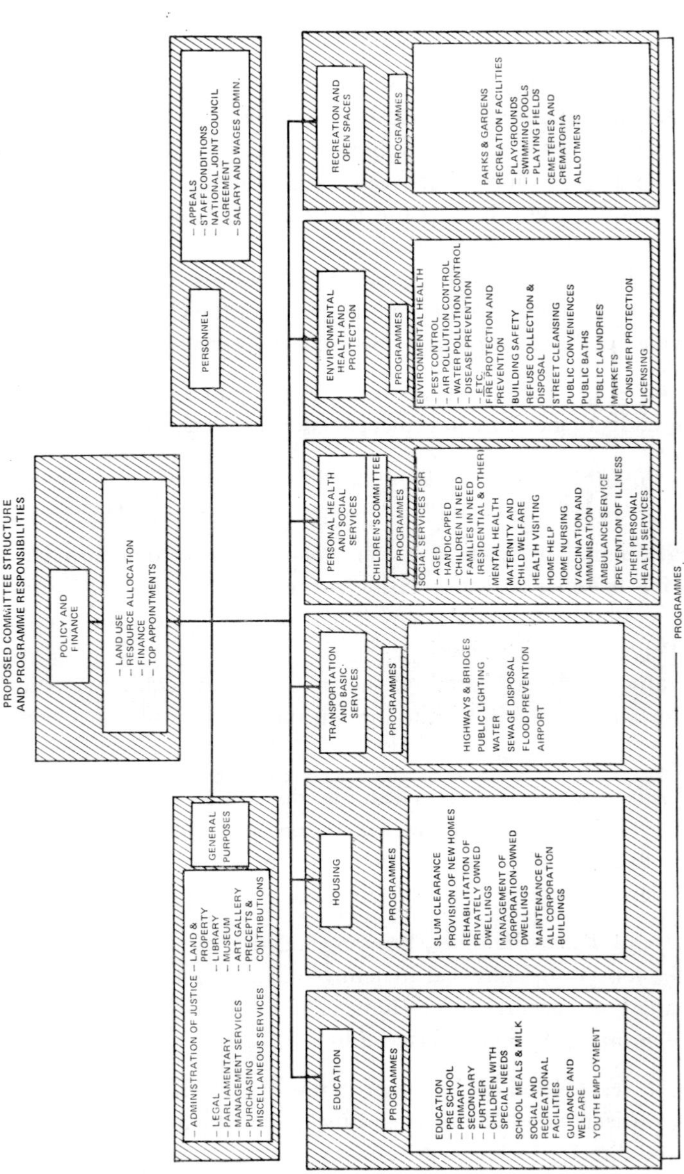
PROPOSED COMMITTEE STRUCTURE
AND PROGRAMME RESPONSIBILITIES
POLICY AND FINANCE
– LAND USE
– RESOURCE ALLOCATION
– FINANCE
– TOP APPOINTMENTS
PERSONNEL
– APPEALS
– STAFF CONDITIONS
– NATIONAL JOINT COUNCIL AGREEMENT
– SALARY AND WAGES ADMIN.
GENERAL PURPOSES
– ADMINISTRATION OF JUSTICE
– LEGAL
– PARLIAMENTARY
– MANAGEMENT SERVICES
– PURCHASING
– MISCELLANEOUS SERVICES
– LAND & PROPERTY
– LIBRARY
– MUSEUM
– ART GALLERY
– PRECEPTS & CONTRIBUTIONS
EDUCATION
PROGRAMMES
EDUCATION
– PRE SCHOOL
– PRIMARY
– SECONDARY
– FURTHER
– CHILDREN WITH SPECIAL NEEDS
SCHOOL MEALS & MILK
SOCIAL AND RECREATIONAL FACILITIES
GUIDANCE AND WELFARE
YOUTH EMPLOYMENT
HOUSING
PROGRAMMES
SLUM CLEARANCE
PROVISION OF NEW HOMES
REHABILITATION OF PRIVATELY OWNED DWELLINGS
MANAGEMENT OF CORPORATION-OWNED DWELLINGS
MAINTENANCE OF ALL CORPORATION BUILDINGS
TRANSPORTATION AND BASIC SERVICES
PROGRAMMES
HIGHWAYS & BRIDGES
PUBLIC LIGHTING
WATER
SEWAGE DISPOSAL
FLOOD PREVENTION
AIRPORT
PERSONAL HEALTH AND SOCIAL SERVICES
CHILDREN'S COMMITTEE
PROGRAMMES
SOCIAL SERVICES FOR
– AGED
– HANDICAPPED
– CHILDREN IN NEED
– FAMILIES IN NEED
(RESIDENTIAL & OTHER)
MENTAL HEALTH
MATERNITY AND CHILD WELFARE
HEALTH VISITING
HOME HELP
HOME NURSING
VACCINATION AND IMMUNISATION
AMBULANCE SERVICE
PREVENTION OF ILLNESS
OTHER PERSONAL HEALTH SERVICES
ENVIRONMENTAL HEALTH AND PROTECTION
PROGRAMMES
ENVIRONMENTAL HEALTH
– PEST CONTROL
– AIR POLLUTION CONTROL
– WATER POLLUTION CONTROL
– DISEASE PREVENTION
– ETC.
FIRE PROTECTION AND PREVENTION
BUILDING SAFETY
REFUSE COLLECTION & DISPOSAL
STREET CLEANSING
PUBLIC CONVENIENCES
PUBLIC BATHS
PUBLIC LAUNDRIES
MARKETS
CONSUMER PROTECTION
LICENSING
RECREATION AND OPEN SPACES
PROGRAMMES
PARKS & GARDENS
RECREATION FACILITIES
– PLAYGROUNDS
– SWIMMING POOLS
– PLAYING FIELDS
CEMETERIES AND CREMATORIA
ALLOTMENTS
PROGRAMMES

Figure 7.2

Housing and Community Services
Education
Social Services
Health

A particularly interesting aspect of the new committee structure is the creation of three sub-committees of the Housing and Community Services Committee, responsible respectively for three geographic areas of Stockport. They will provide a direct linkage between community and neighbourhood groups and the Council itself, in response to growing interest in community development and neighbourhood councils.

At departmental level, the Chief Executive will be responsible for implementation of policy and for performance in all areas of the Council's activity. He will be provided with staff support by two staff divisions :

Finance, responsible for financial accounting, computer services, and development of budgeting and management accounting systems.

Administration, responsible for corporate planning, personnel and management services, and for legal, committee and administrative services.

The corporate planning function in particular is expected to provide a means of bringing together and stimulating planning in all areas of Council service, and providing an essential analytical and factual basis for decision making at the Policy Committee level.

The six operating divisions, based on the management requirements and opportunities for improvement within the various services of the Council are :

Technical Services, which includes cleansing, demolition, vehicle maintenance, building maintenance, highway maintenance and public lighting maintenance, thus bringing together activities of a high labour content requiring efficient management, scheduling and control.

Development and Town Planning, bringing together professional services relating to the long-range physical structure of Stockport, including town planning, valuation, architecture, slum clearance and redevelopment, improvement grants and building inspection.

Engineering, in recognition of the major highway and sewage engineering development projects now underway in Stockport, which require a separate division and director for the near future.

Housing and Community Services, bringing together professional services concerned mainly with managing the present housing and amenity resources of the Borough, including housing, recreation, libraries, museums

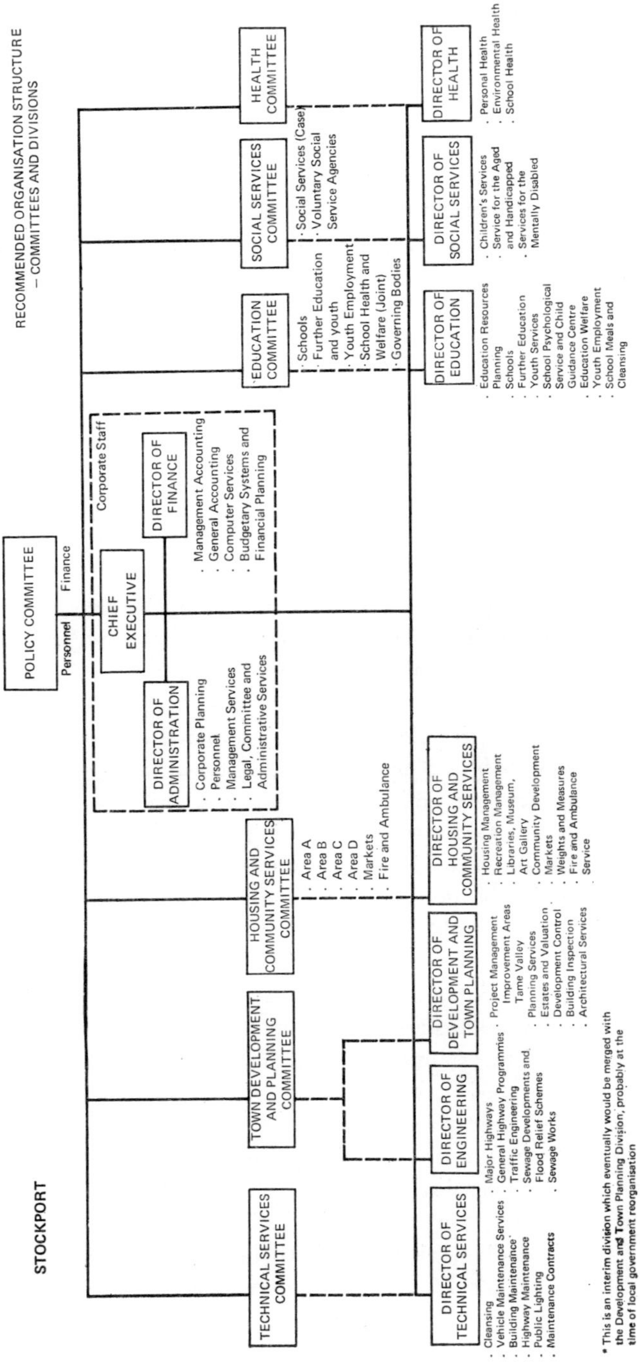
STOCKPORT
RECOMMENDED ORGANISATION STRUCTURE — COMMITTEES AND DIVISIONS
POLICY COMMITTEE
Personnel
Finance
Corporate Staff
CHIEF EXECUTIVE
DIRECTOR OF ADMINISTRATION
. Corporate Planning
. Personnel
. Management Services
. Legal, Committee and Administrative Services
DIRECTOR OF FINANCE
. Management Accounting
. General Accounting
. Computer Services
. Budgetary Systems and Financial Planning
TECHNICAL SERVICES COMMITTEE
TOWN DEVELOPMENT AND PLANNING COMMITTEE
HOUSING AND COMMUNITY SERVICES COMMITTEE
. Area A
. Area B
. Area C
. Area D
. Markets
. Fire and Ambulance
EDUCATION COMMITTEE
. Schools
. Further Education and youth
. Youth Employment
. School Health and Welfare (Joint)
. Governing Bodies
SOCIAL SERVICES COMMITTEE
. Social Services (Case)
. Voluntary Social Service Agencies
HEALTH COMMITTEE
DIRECTOR OF TECHNICAL SERVICES
. Cleansing
. Vehicle Maintenance Services
. Building Maintenance
. Highway Maintenance
. Public Lighting
. Maintenance Contracts
DIRECTOR OF ENGINEERING
. Major Highways
. General Highway Programmes
. Traffic Engineering
. Sewage Developments and Flood Relief Schemes
. Sewage Works
DIRECTOR OF DEVELOPMENT AND TOWN PLANNING
. Project Management Improvement Areas Tame Valley
Planning Services
. Estates and Valuation
. Development Control
. Building Inspection
. Architectural Services
DIRECTOR OF HOUSING AND COMMUNITY SERVICES
. Housing Management
. Recreation Management
. Libraries, Museum, Art Gallery
. Community Development
. Markets
. Weights and Measures
. Fire and Ambulance Service
DIRECTOR OF EDUCATION
. Education Resources Planning
. Schools
. Further Education
. Youth Services
. School Psychological Service and Child Guidance Centre
. Education Welfare
. Youth Employment
. School Meals and Cleansing
DIRECTOR OF SOCIAL SERVICES
. Children's Services
. Service for the Aged and Handicapped
. Services for the Mentally Disabled
DIRECTOR OF HEALTH
. Personal Health
. Environmental Health
. School Health
* This is an interim division which eventually would be merged with the Development and Town Planning Division, probably at the time of local government reorganisation

Figure 7.3

and community development, as well as markets, weights and measures, trading standards and fire and ambulance services.

Education, responsible for all of the Borough's educational programmes.

Social Services, including all social services designated by recent legislation, with an organisation designed to facilitate the transition to multi-discipline social worker teams organised on an area basis.

Health, with continuing responsibility for personal, environmental and school health programmes.

In total, the new organisation is expected to provide significant benefits to the Council and community through improved planning and co-ordination and strengthened management capability. The main benefit will be an improved mechanism and better basis for setting policy, and a more effective management group for implementing it." (7.8)

Diagram (7.3) illustrates the new structure.

COVENTRY CORPORATION

Unlike Stockport and Liverpool, Coventry Corporation has developed, indeed it is *still* developing, its system of organisation which contrasts in many respects with the other two. At the committee level, the organisation looks fairly conventional. There is a Policy Committee with the role of focussing its attention on a study of the physical and social environment of the City as a whole, of assessing its future needs and laying down the major objectives reconciling one with another and determining their priorities. Few policy committees have terms of reference couched in such terms, but the most interesting differences between Coventry's pattern of organisation and most other authorities are in the departmental and offices organisation.

There is a Chief Executive Officer* who has no departmental staff (apart from secretarial services) and a personal assistant of senior rank. The Chief Executive Officer is not isolated however, although this is a potential danger of such an arrangement, and as a result many Chief Executive Officers insist on retaining control of the running and servicing of the committee system arguing that committee clerks are a Chief Executive Officer's eyes and ears! In Coventry the Chief Executive Officer operates through a group of Chief Officers comprising the senior heads of departments (i.e. Treasurer, Associate Town Clerk, Architect/Planning Officer, Directors of Education and Social Services, Engineer, Estates Surveyor and Medical Officer of Health). This group meets formally each week where it treats policy issues both for the policy as well as service committees including recommendations on the capital

* The Chief Executive Officer, unusually for British Local Government, is employed on a contract basis.

and revenue budgets. In addition there are less formal daily meetings (the now almost legendary 8.30 a.m. gatherings) which are open to all heads of departments where officers keep in touch about problems, exchange ideas, spot and deal with troubles as they arise and clear more minor issues quickly.

Of particular interest in Coventry, however, are the three *resource units* for land, manpower, and finance, attached respectively to the Architect/Planning Officer, the Associate Town Clerk and the Treasurer, the *programme area teams* and the *capital programme implementation control groups*. Diagram (7.4) shows the relationships between the groups, departments etc. The programme area teams and the control groups are comprised largely of senior officers drawn from the existing fairly traditional range of departments. Programme area teams are planning teams, each chaired by a Chief Officer whose responsibilities are to look at subject areas coinciding with fundamental objectives of the local authority. There are nine such teams. As their name implies the control groups, of which there are seven, are responsible for co-ordinating implementation of the capital programme.

By local government standards all three reorganisations are fairly radical although there is an increasing number of other examples. A comparison among these three shows that in some crucial respects the Coventry scheme differs from the other two. The guiding principle in them all was the desire to give effect to co-ordination, to cope with integration of services and problems, to create a structure and pattern of organisation which will overcome the 'evils' of departmentalism and separatist management. Liverpool and Stockport have tried to meet the problem by accommodating co-ordination within the formal structure. In both cases boundaries have been cast around related functions. The relation has been determined on the whole by grouping activities which contribute towards the same fundamental objective thus producing some unconventional bed-fellows, e.g. in Liverpool the fire service is now in the same department as refuse-collection and public conveniences —i.e. in the Environmental Health and Protection department. This kind of approach is new and derives from PPBS. By making fundamental objectives the basis for departmental reorganisation the expectation is that the common purpose thereby presented within the structure will itself ensure co-ordination. Unfortunately activities very often contribute to more than one objective. Moreover the needs of planning may be different from the needs of implementation, (the fire service, its personnel and equipment are a good case in point). For corporate planning purposes boundaries present problems. To replace the traditional set with a new, perhaps more powerful set could well be a step backwards. The necessary adaptability cannot be accommodated in a one dimension organisational structure. It is true that in both Stockport and Liverpool there are *other* devices designed to secure co-ordination e.g. the Director of Administration in Stockport and his corporate

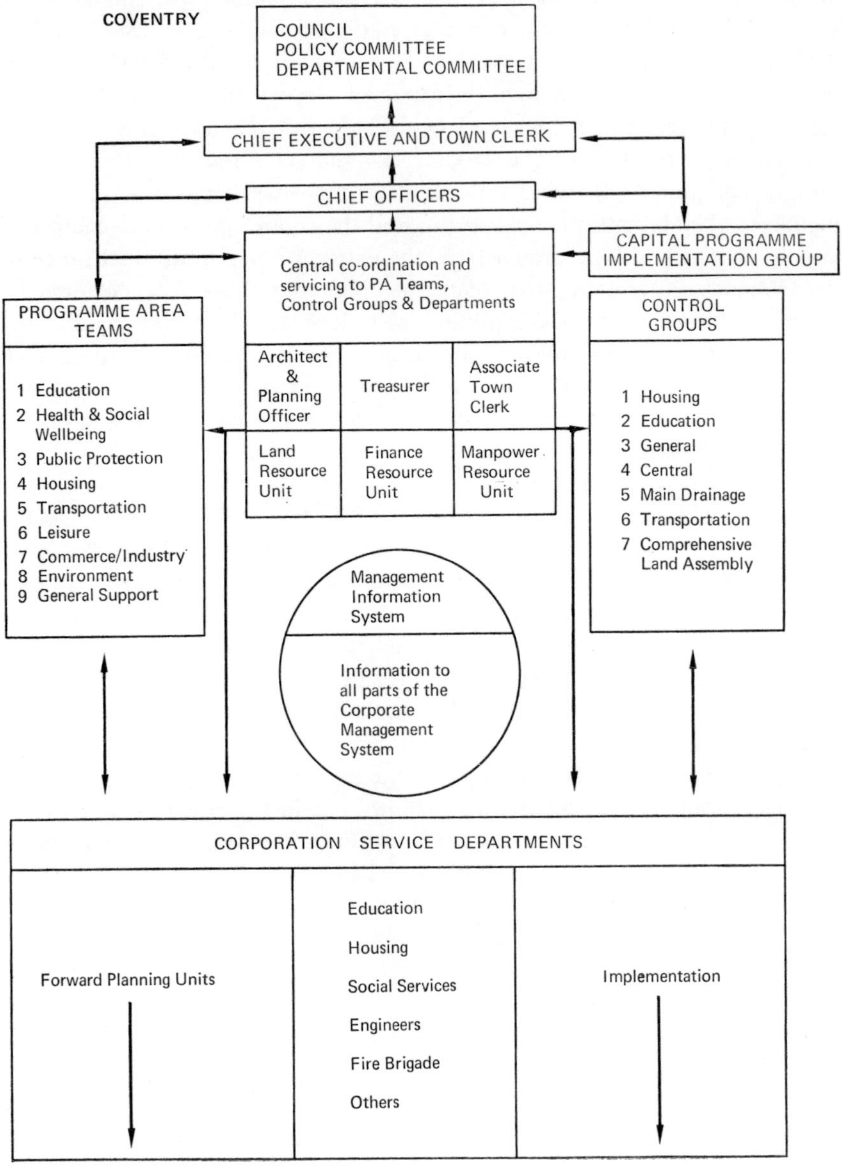
COVENTRY
COUNCIL
POLICY COMMITTEE
DEPARTMENTAL COMMITTEE
CHIEF EXECUTIVE AND TOWN CLERK
CHIEF OFFICERS
CAPITAL PROGRAMME
IMPLEMENTATION GROUP
Central co-ordination and servicing to PA Teams, Control Groups & Departments
Architect & Planning Officer
Treasurer
Associate Town Clerk
Land Resource Unit
Finance Resource Unit
Manpower Resource Unit
PROGRAMME AREA TEAMS
1 Education
2 Health & Social Wellbeing
3 Public Protection
4 Housing
5 Transportation
6 Leisure
7 Commerce/Industry
8 Environment
9 General Support
CONTROL GROUPS
1 Housing
2 Education
3 General
4 Central
5 Main Drainage
6 Transportation
7 Comprehensive Land Assembly
Management Information System
Information to all parts of the Corporate Management System
CORPORATION SERVICE DEPARTMENTS
Forward Planning Units
Education
Housing
Social Services
Engineers
Fire Brigade
Others
Implementation

Figure 7.4

planning function is explicitly charged with the task of co-ordinating planning. Notwithstanding these devices the formal structure is expected to lead in itself to improved co-ordination. The merging of functions in one department, not related by fundamental objectives but by similarity of fields of interest of the professions concerned, is another way of approaching departmental organisation. It was given an impetus by a recommendation of the Maud Committee (7.9).

"We make no recommendations on the way in which departments should be grouped, although, in our view, their number can be reduced to half a dozen or so. This is a matter for local determination having regard to the span of control which can be effectively exerted by any head of a department. Local authorities should consider arrangements on the following lines. . . .

> Grouping certain departments under one senior principal officer, to whom the 'service' principal officers would be responsible, and who would himself be answerable to the Clerk. This arrangement might be particularly suitable for those departments concerned with physical development in authorities faced with problems of urban renewal where there is a need for co-ordination not only at the planning stage but also in the execution of the work 'on the ground'. . . .

This has been implemented in several authorities e.g. Grimsby and Bedford in relation to the Architecture, Planning and Engineering functions—now described as a Technical Services department under a Director. The London Borough of Greenwich tried this scheme and later abandoned it. Perhaps the best known example is in Central Government at the Department of the Environment which combines the former Ministries of Housing and Local Government, Transport and Public Buildings and Works. The belief here again is that by merging departments in the structure, co-ordination is thereby made easy. It is also argued that the umbrella device cuts down the number of Chief Officers requiring to attend a Chief Officers' Group (or the Cabinet) thus having the added benefit of making that group function better by virtue of smaller numbers. It is a point to be returned to later.

The structure of committees both in Liverpool and Stockport mirrors the new departmental structure. Coventry's scheme in contrast, has retained a fairly traditional departmental and committee structure and has set up around it the system of flexible working groups and teams. This approach recognises that problems and issues are mercurial in their origins, that solutions lie in a variety of areas, that problems are ever-changing whereas solutions tend not to be, largely because our organisations constrain thinking and ideas. The structure of organisations, the boundaries cast, are very often hindrances to matching problems with solutions, to recognising new problems and the changing face of old ones. Coventry's system is designed to be flexible—its very structure might almost be described as a changing structure. It is a structure which sets changing tasks against pools of professional skills and which has created interdisciplinary teams of officers suitable to carry out this changing pattern of tasks.

The essential difference between these types of organisation design is the difference between a matrix and a monocratic organisation (7.10), the one emphasising flexibility along more than one dimension, the other laying stress on the hierarchical structure. Other significant examples are Hull CB (monocratic) and Teesside (matrix), although there are differences between the Teesside and Coventry organisations.

PROFESSIONALISM AND ORGANISATION STRUCTURE

There are some important respects in which professionalism influences changes in organisation within local government which require consideration here. 'Departmentalism', 'separatism' and 'professionalism' are often taken to be synonymous. They have all been regarded as weaknesses in the local government system.

"As new needs in the community have been perceived new services have been created to meet them. Frequently the addition of a new service has led to the establishment of a new watertight department responsible to a new committee of members concerned only with the fulfilment of its isolated aim." (7.11)

Professionalism *can* be said to be a hindrance to satisfactory organisation but similarly professional skills are undoubtedly a source of great strength to local government. The problem is to draw on the strengths and reduce the weaknesses. A profession represents status, it is a form of security. Men and women will and do defend their professions. That is one of the functions of professional bodies. When a change in organisation threatens professional status or integrity it is resisted and mightily. There are many examples (7.12).

The Coventry approach does not threaten the profession. Indeed by retaining the professional base within the organisation structure, a sense of security has been engendered which appears to have assisted the process of setting into motion the programme area and control teams. There is every indication in local government that interdisciplinary working is enjoying some success. If this is combined with the retention of professional departments it seems probable that the needs of the situation can be met. In this respect the comments of the Liverpool City Planning Officer are interesting. After some experience of the Liverpool system he writes :

"The essential need is to create a structure in which there can be a high degree of professional competence, coupled with flexibility of operation. Perhaps the best way of achieving these two qualities would be to maintain (or establish as necessary) departments of professional competence, but separately to create programmes and project directorates which would devise and manage programmes to achieve specified objectives. Such directorates would commission services from departments but would themselves be transitory: being formed when an objective was identified and being disbanded when it was achieved or radically changed or if the staff proved to be inadequate. The members of staff involved in directorates would be small and their skills, in addition to planning and management would vary according to the objective. No such structure has so far been attempted, but it is clear that a much more flexible staff management system than is currently practised would be necessary for its success." (7.13)

The comment is particularly significant because the planning department can in no sense have been said to have 'suffered' from the McKinsey reorganisation. Rather it has benefitted in professional status terms and despite this Amos is clearly unhappy with the outcome.

The desire and ability of the professions to protect themselves are forces not to be left out of consideration.

CHIEF OFFICERS' GROUPS

Granted that local government should attempt to achieve integration at the policy formulation stage as distinct from co-ordination in the form of compromises rather late in the planning process, and granted also that the whole policy formulation process is concerned with the affairs of the local authority and maybe the community as a whole, it is clear that the concept of a Chief Officers' Group becomes highly significant.

"Corporate planning is leading to the concept of corporate management in which at least certain chief officers accept responsibility for the affairs of more than their own department. It is expressed through a chief officers' group which differs from the traditional chief officers' meeting in that it concerns itself not with a limited range of issues but with affairs of the authority as a whole. The existence of such a management team which covers the whole range of the authority's affairs may be a good indication of development towards corporate planning. Certainly the existence of an effective management team makes much less important to the development of corporate planning whether particular functions are placed in the principal chief officer's department." (7.14)

Many local authorities have Chief Officers' meetings or groups. Few, however, can be said to be fulfilling the role required of them if corporate planning is to become a reality. Most meet too infrequently (7.15) and their agendas are more often than not *ad hoc.*

Rightly or wrongly the claim is frequently made by officers other than Chiefs that Chief Officers are one of the greatest obstacles to co-ordination, to corporate planning, to innovation generally. That the claim is made is itself significant. It is plainly important for Chief Officers to develop a commitment to corporate planning if it is to come into being. It is probable that this will imply a shift of emphasis in the role of Chief Officers who, at present devote most of their time and commitment to the running of their own departments. The shift will be much more towards the recognition that their most significant role is to corporate planning—to joining with other Chief Officers in the shaping of policy choices for the elected representatives—to provide them with helpful information and alternatives. It would be something more than the more traditional Chief Officers' Group. It would be a group collectively committed to working with the elected members and to drawing out the expertise from within the departments to help to shape these policy choices.

The question arises as to how many and which Chief Officers should serve on this group. The INLOGOV Occasional Paper, No 5 (7.16), shows the following distribution of members.

NUMBER OF AUTHORITIES WITH MANAGEMENT TEAM

Size of Management Team	*Counties*	*County Boroughs*	*London Boroughs*	*Total*
3 members		4	0	4
4 members		1	1	2
5 members		8	3	11
6 members		5	2	7
7 members	5	8	4	17
8 members	4	6	1	11
9 members	3	2	0	5
10 members	3	1	1	5
11 or more	4	5	3	12
No answer	–	1	1	2
Total	19	41	16	76

7 is the most common number but most fall in the 5–8 range.

"There is conflict in setting up the management team between representing all departments and keeping the group small in order to build up its sense of corporate management. Some groups represent all departments, particularly where there has been departmental reorganisation to reduce the number of departments to about ten in number." (7.17)

There can be no magic number for a Chief Officers' Group, but there are compelling arguments for increasing the number rather than decreasing it and certainly not to decrease it to less than 8 or 9. The argument often advanced for smaller management teams is that a smaller group can reach decisions, have more productive discussions than a larger one and up to a point this is probably true. Set against this, however, are the needs of the situation. The object of corporate planning through (amongst other devices) a Chief Officers' team is to secure integration of policy formulation by drawing on the whole range of professional and other skills at the disposal of the local authority. The effect of excluding some of these skills from a powerful policy-making arena and especially some of the major ones, is to secure that the degree of commitment is less than is necessary or desirable for the needs of corporate planning. A City Planning Officer, an Education Officer or a Director of Social Services who is not a member of such a powerful group will at best pay only lip service to the process of corporate planning, to what the Chief Officers' Group demands of him. The necessary commitment will be absent. Granted the inherent weaknesses of professionalism, which require a good deal of personal effort and motivation to overcome, it seems vital to include rather than exclude. Some authorities, for example Leeds and Manchester corporations have a triumvirate of the Clerk, Treasurer and Director of Development (in Manchester, the Planning Officer) as the main Chief Officers' Group but in addition there are other meetings at which a wider range of Chief Officers is brought in. It is highly unlikely that this compromise approach is likely to overcome the difficulties raised. At the very least the situation calls for the inclusion in any Chief Officers' Group of the Chief Executive Officer, the Treasurer, the Planning Officer, Directors of Education and Social Services, Housing Manager, Engineer, Solicitor, Medical Officer (perhaps even after health services go out of local government) and probably the Fire Officer and Chief Constable. The device of calling in Chief Officers 'when required' does not seem to be a way of securing the right degree of commitment.

A further argument sometimes advanced in support of excluding some Chief Officers from a Chief Officers' Group is 'personality'.

From the point of view of making corporate planning relevant it seems that notwithstanding 'personality' difficulties exclusion may well serve only to accentuate them and when a major department is thereby excluded from a Chief Officers' Group, it is a serious matter. Oddly enough the traditionally very powerful departments i.e. the clerks and treasurers, seem never to have these 'personality' problems—or do they?

SERVICING THE CHIEF OFFICERS' GROUPS

Whatever form the Chief Officers' Group takes it clearly needs to be serviced with information. It cannot expect simply to meet and generate policy ideas or shape important policies in any form without a good deal of ground work being done first. In the organisations examined, different methods were used for securing an integration of information, analysis of issues to be fed into the major policy formulation process. In Liverpool, as we have seen, the new structure groups activities into programme areas focussing on fundamental objectives and it is through these new departments that information is fed to the Chief Officers' Groups (comprising the Programme Directors and the Chief Executive, Planning Officer and Treasurer). In Stockport the situation is slightly different in that the onus for drawing information together falls to the Director of Administration who in turn then presents it to the Chief Officers' Group (comprising the Programme Directors, and the Chief Executive, Planning Officer and Treasurer). Coventry has its flexible programme area teams reporting on and analysing issues for the Chief Officers' Group (Chief Executive, Treasurer, Architect, Planning Officer, Directors of Education and Social Services, Estates Surveyor, Associate Town Clerk, Engineer and Medical Officer of Health).

At no point in any of these three organisations is there a widely based inter-disciplinary unit as a group (other than the Chief Officers) looking at the affairs of the local authority as a whole. Liverpool and Coventry have departments and teams based on programme areas. Stockport has its Director of Administration and his corporate planner drawing together the various programme departments. Each one to a greater or lesser degree has boundaries limiting either its area of concern or the width of disciplines integrating the issues. We have seen though, that the nature of problems and the range of solutions to those problems are such that boundaries militate against exposing the widest and most relevant choice. A boundary imposes false and perhaps arbitrary limitations. Of course boundaries cannot be totally eliminated. The question is whether there are ways of reducing to a minimum the adverse effects of these boundaries.

One way would be to have a unit—perhaps called a policy planning unit—comprised of all the disciplines and made up of, say, fairly senior officers (not chiefs). The function of such a unit would be to service the Chief Officers *and* the policy committee (or its equivalent). It would provide information, it would build up gradually a framework for policy making, a framework which would be responsive to changing needs, emergent and sudden problems. A major function would be to generate 'position statements' (see Chapter 9), to keep the members and Chief Officers abreast with the way existing policies are going. There will never be a clean slate for operating on. Policy will have to be formulated very quickly sometimes, we shall have to respond to a variety of pressures requiring new or reshaped policies. What we need is a team within the authority manned by all the disciplines to do some information gathering but more important, some work on it to give new insights, new approaches, new possibilities for action, a wider choice. This team should be seen by the Chief Officers and the elected members as a key point in the policy formulation process and they would draw on it regularly to service both the Chief Officers' Group and the major party policy committee. This team would develop the common basis across the whole authority from which a variety of plans and policies would derive, including the structure plan.

The advantage of such a unit over programme area teams is that it has an unlimited width of focus. It has its dangers, however. It could become isolated, for example. This is the fate of many *ad hoc* units in organisations. They are regarded as 'bands of boffins' by the remainder of the organisation and are effectively ignored. There are ways of overcoming this. Firstly, if Chief Officers and elected members are put in the position by the planning process itself, of recognising their own need for a basis from which to make choices, then the unit cannot fail to be a central part of the process.

Relationships between departments and the unit are important too. In part these will be fashioned by the way the Chief Officers behave, but in addition the practice of making the membership of the policy planning unit flexible and changing, in effect almost to make a period of time serving in the unit a normal part of career progression, would help to secure its complete integration. Moreover the unit would develop close working relationships on specific issues with various departments *and* with interdepartmental working teams which would continue to be necessary but with a somewhat more limited role than in the programme area teams of the Coventry system. In other words, there will remain *outside* the policy planning unit's area of concern, or contracted out from it, issues concerning more than one department. These will be issues tackled by interdepartmental working groups which would take a variety of forms. Some will be temporary but full-time, others will meet part-time only. The Coventry style control groups would still need to exist to cover programme implementation but again there could be a useful relationship between the policy unit and control groups. No set relationship can be prescribed. The principle established is that the organisation is built to form and reform units relevant to the needs of the situation without going through traumatic change. Change becomes a recognised way of operation.

Several authorities have established other *ad hoc* units e.g. management services, establishment, research and intelligence, project co-ordination etc. In any local authority there may be a case for these and similar types of unit. There is no formula for how many, what type, or where they should be situated. Their important characteristic should be that they are relevant to the management process. The research and intelligence function is particularly important and this especially needs to be well-integrated. In the kind of organisation structure described above, the research and intelligence function would be in two parts corresponding to Anthony's split of the planning function between strategic planning, management and operational control (see page 17). In other words there would be a research and intelligence need for strategic purposes and this would be a central part of any policy planning unit. There would remain, however, a strong need for departments to have their own information and research facilities. The linking between the two parts would need to be strong, for much of the 'case' type of information will be required at specific points in strategic planning, but not sufficient to justify cluttering the central unit with substantial extraneous data collecting. The sort of information which might be collected by departments and used additionally by a central policy unit for example, might be policy monitoring data which is very often most conveniently collected by implementing departments.

The case material presented in the Appendix to Chapter 5 is a good example of the isolation of specialist information required both for detailed day to day purposes and collected on that basis but also with an important local authority wide significance. The different 'specialist' profiles revealed of the Valley Park area are an object lesson in themselves.

Given a system comprising Chief Officers' Groups, supporting policy planning unit and patterns of interdisciplinary groups the case exists, for reasons already advanced for retaining professional departments, perhaps not so many as exist in some authorities but certainly for the major professions.

ROLE OF ELECTED REPRESENTATIVES

The elected representative is the decision maker in theory if not always in practice. Local government is likely to become increasingly political, run on political party lines. The practice has grown in the last decade. Many people see it as a retrograde step* but it is a reality. What politicians require is a much better basis for making political choices. At present councillors are on the whole starved of information (7.18), they have little room for manœuvre and their view of the situation in many authorities is that the officers run the show. This situation will not last. The question which remains is how to create a better working relationship in this area, how to create for councillors this basis for choice.

For a long time it has been the tradition in local government that officers shall not become involved with 'politics'. Very few, if any, Chief Officers advise party groups. Indeed, according to the Maud report, some Chief

* It is not a view I personally share.

Officers denied the existence of groups altogether (7.19). The net effect has been that decisions are taken in political party groups without the advice of or a discussion with officers and more often than not with insufficient information about alternative courses of action, information on the nature of the problem, the implications for other services and so on. Members don't like this (7.20). They would prefer to have problems and issues analysed, alternative solutions advanced and generally to debate issues with officers, not at formal committee level but before this stage, perhaps in study groups. In the end they will impose their political values on the situation but not before having had an opportunity to argue the problem through. At present the most politicians can cling to are pet schemes, prejudices and ways of scoring off their opponents. They often have very little time to discuss issues —they are victims of the committee cycle and a lack of debate.

With an officer organisation similar to the one described, it is possible that the elected representative can expect to fulfil this kind of new role. With a PPB system operating also, policy choice becomes much clearer if not easier. Implications and choice are put in a much more helpful framework. No techniques are even likely to be evolved which will tell politicians whether to invest in fire stations or nursery schools—that and similar decisions depend on political values. All PPB offers is a systematic framework within which these political values can be applied.

POLICY AND OTHER COMMITTEES

Committee structures unlike departments are not bedevilled by problems of professionalism but it is clearly important that any committee structure should

(i) be an integrated part of the management process.

and (ii) be meaningful to the elected representatives and their perception of their own role.

The general pattern in local government has been for the departmental structure to be mirrored in the structure of committees but with one or two *ad hoc*, for example 'general purposes' committees, in addition. As far as major policy formulation is concerned it is only recently that corporate or overall policies have been in any way reflected in committee structures. In the 1965 survey carried out for Volume 5 of the Maud Report (7.21) the idea of a policy committee of this nature was shown not to be common and where they *did* exist they were limited in scope :

"Less than a third of the authorities we consulted made any reference to a committee which could be interpreted as in any sense responsible for central policy initiation, and most of those which did mention a committee of this nature expressed some reservation about the extent to which it could be said to exercise this function. One or two Clerks referred to the responsibility of the council as a whole for policy initiation, but comments on these lines seemed to lack conviction that this function could be exercised effectively by a body of that size.

More often than not when authorities did refer to a 'policy' committee they had in mind the finance committee (which in some authorities includes other functions also—for example several are 'finance and general purposes' committees or 'finance and law' committees). These committees usually include influential members of the council and often the chairmen of other major committees.

Several authorities explained that, as most policy involves expenditure, it is at some stage considered by the finance committee, which can in this sense be regarded as a general policy committee. However, a closer examination shows that the finance committee normally considers projects which originate elsewhere (often in the service committee) and, so far from being a positive initiator of policy, it sometimes has a negative function, since in most authorities its approval is necessary before projects are referred for ratification to the council. The function of finance committees (or their sub-committees) in fixing rates and assigning capital priorities includes an element of central policy direction, but here again it is mainly a question of selecting from projects initiated elsewhere. . . .

Some authorities suggested that there was an element of policy initiation in the work of their 'parliamentary' committees; these sometimes include other functions, for example 'general purposes' or 'selection' or, in one case, 'finance'. Again, however, it is doubtful whether these committees are so much initiators as co-ordinators of policy since there are references to their considering matters originally raised in the service committees which are likely to have a wider impact."

Since 1965 the concept has found expression in many more authorities (7.22).

NUMBERS OF AUTHORITIES WITH A POLICY COMMITTEE

	No. of Auth. with a Policy Committee		*No. of Auth. without a Policy Committee*		*Total Replies*
County Councils	20	(47%)	23	(53%)	43
County Boroughs	35	(57%)	26	(43%)	61
London Boroughs	18	(83%)	5	(17%)	23
Total	73	(58%)	54	(42%)	127

DATE OF FORMATION OF POLICY COMMITTEE

	County Councils	*County Boroughs*	*London Boroughs*	*Total*
Before 1965 or date unspecified	5	4	1	10
1965	0	0	1	1
1966	0	5	1	6
1967	1	5	1	7
1968	7	12	8	27
1969	5	9	4	18
1970	2	0	2	4
Total	20	35	18	73

The policy committee, or its equivalent, is now a central feature of local government and although the existence of such organisations can in no way be relied upon as evidence that policy is now formulated more comprehensively, it is certainly evidence of a shift in that direction. The danger is that existing committees will be renamed, given new constitutions, but that they will behave or perform in the same old way. Again the structure has meaning only in terms of the process lying behind it.

If our assumption is correct, that members are anxious and ready to explore policy more frequently and in greater depth it is worth exploring how this might actually occur. Firstly, the existence of Chief Officers' Groups and a supporting pattern of policy planning and programme area units (or their equivalent) requires a relationship with the political machinery. Formally this would be the policy committee but, as we have seen, policy formulation is not a 'clean slate' operation. Policy origins are numerous. Sometimes policies will originate as ideas from any one of these units and will pass through the Chief Officers' Group to the policy committee. Frequently however policies will originate out of issues or from pressure from the community expressing need of some kind. In order that all the policy origin points are equally open there will probably need to be a fairly dynamic and free relationship between the political policy committee, the Chief Officers' Group and the policy planning unit. In other words the policy committee will in practice, *use* the policy planning unit as a test-bed for analysis and data collection—for probing all aspects of the problems raised—in effect for presenting a mapping out of solutions or approaches to problems upon which the members may exercise their political judgements. Obviously any such policy planning unit would work through the Chief Officers' Group and likewise the policy committee would use the policy planning unit through the Chief Officers or the Chief Executive Officer. The important point is that there would slowly develop a recognition of the respective dynamic relationships leading to more relevant and better based policies. 'Better' does not necessarily imply technocratically improved but better *informed* political policy choices.

In addition to a policy committee there will need to be other committees. As we have noted, at present they tend to mirror departments. Even in Stockport and Liverpool the mirror image exists but in those cases reflects the new programme area type of departmental structure. Coventry has retained a traditional departmental *and* committee structure. The question arises as to which structure best meets the needs of the situation. Perhaps the most important consideration is not so much the formal committee structure but the ways in which officers and elected members *combine* to formulate policy. Much of the suspicion which undoubtedly exists between officers and members in some authorities could be removed through the development of such a combined approach to policy formulation.

Given a policy committee, the argument for structuring the other committees around objectives, as in Liverpool and Stockport, is a fairly convincing one. It is particularly important for members to develop an objective orientated approach. Political judgement is probably likely to be much more sharply focussed in such a framework. It does not mean all politicians will become rational animals overnight but it *does* mean more pointed political debate. It could, of course, be politically unpopular as with PPBS in that it tends towards a more explicit policy expression. This is probably a short-term inevitability.

The structure suggested as possibly offering good prospects for giving effect to the kind of planning processes we have discussed is shown in outline in Figure (7.4) (See page 170).

MULTI-AGENCY POLICY PLANNING

Underlying what has been discussed so far has been the notion that all the functions of local government lie in one authority. All three examples quoted are County Boroughs, all-purpose authorities. For corporate planning purposes this is clearly the best system of government. Sadly, however, local government in the United Kingdom is to become entirely two-tier. Even given a one-tier system however, the policies of local government are not the only ones in the public sector to impinge on a community. There are other agencies involved, e.g. the new health authorities, statutory undertakers, British Rail, the proposed new water and drainage authorities. Community planning is a concept, a notion intended to give expression to *community* objectives and policies, to provide a framework for all agencies having an impact on a community to plan their activities (See Chapter 5).

There is therefore a particularly important need for local government as a whole to unite in policy formulation processes for specific areas and to combine with other agencies involved in similar kinds of processes. At present the combination rarely rises above 'consultation'.

A two-tier system of local government is not a happy state to look forward to. Inherent in that kind of system is conflict and strife. No matter how much we pretend that one tier is not subservient to the other, no matter how much we speak about *spheres* of government rather than *tiers* of government, there will be great difficulties of co-operation between the county councils and the district councils. The starting point for co-operation is for local government as a whole to realise that wherever a function is being administered, it is but one part of a combined effort to ensure that certain community objectives are met. We need devices to give some form of basis for co-operation between tiers of government—what better basis than a pattern of objectives, an agreement about what it is local government is trying to achieve in a particular area? Let there be conflict and disagreement but let it be purposeful in the sense that it should be about the different ways of achieving local government's objectives. Let it not simply be controversy because we have two tiers of government. The argument should be whether or not a particular objective is better achieved in one way rather than another, whether it is better achieved through one authority's powers rather than another's. Again, the programme budgeting system offers this kind of framework for co-operation—not just between tiers of local government activities, but also between local government and the health services, between local government and the other agencies. An example between tiers of local government is provided in the present system. A county council as a highway authority might for instance limit itself to a consideration simply of its *own* functions as a means of achieving transportation objectives, but clearly traffic management is a vital area of concern. This is a second tier responsibility however. Some means of co-operation is plainly required and the need extends also to other agencies, in Gloucestershire, British Waterways. Another example is to be found in London. A London borough might well decide that free bus passes for old people were an important element in its care of the aged policies. London Transport is a Greater London Council concern and here again co-operation is called for.

Bringing co-operation about is likely to be difficult. In many places to make the effort will be political anathema—conflict will be a way of life. To those authorities condolences are perhaps the most appropriate offering. The remainder need ways of giving expression to co-operation. The matrix approach to the problem presents a way of approaching co-operation. It contrasts with the more conventional (and not very impressive) methods of inter-agency co-operation. These usually boil down to representation on joint committees (7.23) and other formal arrangements. Again like some of the internal organisations looked at, the belief is that co-ordination derives from

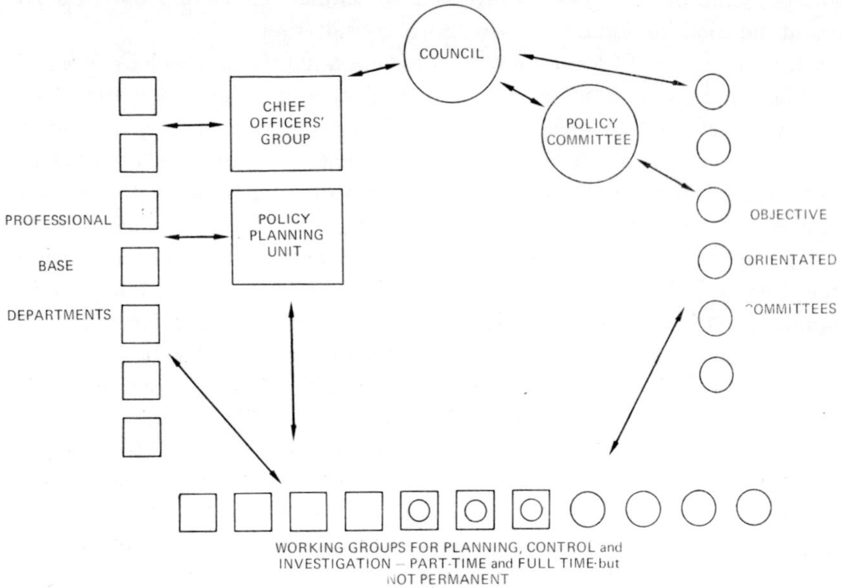

Figure 7.5

such formal arrangements. It is not a very convincing approach. There have been other devices however of which the South East Joint Planning Team is an interesting example (7.24). Here local planning authorities nominated officers to serve full-time on a joint central-local government team. The team reported and their work now forms the framework for regional planning in the south-east.

Clearly joint teams are important but they need to be *seen* politically to be so. Many joint ventures fail at the crunch point when decisions have to be made. The Standing Conference on London and South East Regional Planning was a classic case where very valuable joint team work took place. But, when it came to the point of the formal body taking decisions unpopular with some of its constituent authorities, decisions were avoided.

A possible approach to inter-tier and agency corporate planning would be, as we have suggested here a pattern of joint programme area working teams operating against a PPB background. It may be that such teams would be formed on *geographic* areas so that, for example, in Norfolk there may be inter-authority teams to work on Norwich County District. Any such system would never be ideal, but it would sharpen up issues of differences both for the politicians and the public's benefit. The Stockport reorganisation (see Figure 7.3) in a minor way develops this 'area' base in its 3 area sub-committees of its Housing and Community Services Committee.

It is as the tiers of local government increase, as more closely related functions become hived off in *ad hoc* bodies, that the problems of achieving corporate planning increase enormously and they are complex enough even now. Clearly the principles of organisational adaptability will need to be extended—the concept of community planning explored in this context. Some areas will try—others will not.

REFERENCES

7.1 References:

(*a*) Committee on the Staffing of Local Government Report, HMSO, 1967.

(*b*) Committee on the Management of Local Government Report, HMSO, 1967.

(*c*) Royal Commission on Local Government in England Report, HMSO, 1969.

(*d*) Royal Commission on Local Government in Scotland Report, HMSO, 1969.

(*e*) Review Body on Local Government in Northern Ireland Report, HMSO, 1970.

7.2 R. GREENWOOD, J. D. STEWART, A. D. SMITH, 'New Patterns of Local Government Organisation'—INLOGOV Occasional Paper, No 5, Series A., 1971. Institute of Local Government Studies, University of Birmingham. This continuing series of papers has monitored organisational changes in County Councils, County Boroughs and the London Boroughs.

7.3 D. YEHEZKEL DROR, *Design for Policy Sciences*, Chaper 1, p. 3, Elsevier, 1971.

7.4 Committee on the Management of Local Government Report, Vol. I, p. 26, HMSO, 1967.

7.5 Committee on the Management of Local Government, Vol. I, p. 41 et seq, HMSO, 1967.

7.6 The point is well established by J. D. STEWART in *Management in Local Government: a viewpoint*, Chapter 15, Charles Knight, 1971.

7.7 Structured quotations from the report 'A New Management System for the Liverpool Corporation', McKinsey and Co. Inc., 1969.

7.8 Unpublished reorganisation, May, 1971. I am indebted to the Stockport Council for giving me permission to quote from it.

7.9 Maud Report on Management of Local Government, Vol. I, p. 58, HMSO, 1967.

7.10 I am greatly indebted to my colleague Royston Greenwood who introduced me to these concepts and the following reference. He and Professor J. D. Stewart are to publish a significant article on Corporate Planning and Management Organisation in 1972. See also D. I. CLELAND and W. R. KING, *Systems Analysis and Project Management*, McGraw Hill, 1968.

7.11 R. B. BUTT, 'Planning Programming Budgeting Systems', Introductory Note, INLOGOV, University of Birmingham, 1970.

7.12 In the Local Government Bill (Clause 100 published 1971) there is express provision for the appointment of both an Education Officer and a Director of Social Services, which was entirely due to pressure from the professional bodies concerned and despite an interim recommendation of the Working Group of Management Structure (whose report was commissioned to set guidelines for internal organisation change).

In Liverpool the fire officer was particularly upset by his new position in the reorganised structure.

The Greenwich directorate of technical services collapsed because of resistances from some of the professions concerned and both the RIBA and the RTPI has continually argued against the merging of these two professions with engineering in particular but also with each other.

Yet another area of controversy is the absorption of Libraries in the Education service—a movement violently opposed by professional librarians.

7.13 F. C. AMOS, 'Planning Strategies and Implementation', Report of Proceedings, Town and Country Planning Summer School, 1971.

7.14 R. GREENWOOD, A. D. SMITH and J. D. STEWART, Role of the Chief Executive Officer and the Chief Officers' Group, *Journal of Local Government Studies*, INLOGOV, University of Birmingham, October, 1971.

7.15 Only 10 out of 76 meet at least once a week. Well over half meet only monthly or even less frequently. R. GREENWOOD, A. D. SMITH and J. D. STEWART, Occasional Paper, No. 5, INLOGOV, University of Birmingham, 1971.

7.16 *op. cit.*

7.17 *op. cit.*

7.18 No volume of paper but real information to assist choice and informed discussion of the issues surrounding those choices.

7.19 Management of Local Government Report, Vol. V, HMSO, 1967.

7.20 Evidence for this assertion has been called from a series of talks in several authorities to politicians on the corporate planning issue, but it is only an impression.

7.21 Committee on Management of Local Government Report, Vol. V, HMSO, 1967, pp. 92 et seq, quoted in R. GREENWOOD, J. D. STEWART, A. D. SMITH, 'The Policy Committee in English Local Government,' *Public Administration*, 1972 (to appear).

7.22 R. GREENWOOD, J. D. STEWART, A. D. SMITH 'New Patterns of Local Government Organisation', Occasional Paper No. 5, pp. 22–23, INLOGOV, University of Birmingham, 1971.

7.23 Some of the National Parks Joint Committees are examples and the police authorities.

7.24 Strategic Plan for the south-east, HMSO, 1970.

8
Characteristics of an Emerging Planning Format

What follows is speculative. It stems from an impression that, quite apart from any effects of major local government reform, there is a growing mood of change in the local government air—maybe it pervades the whole public sector. One thing is certain, that these changes are unpredictable in any detail but the fabric of local government seems to be loosening up. We seem to be moving, be it ever so slowly, away from cautious conservative trial and error (and that within our traditional boundaries wherein we feel secure) towards an era of bolder trial, perhaps even greater errors. But they are 'learning' errors, on the periphery of normal patterns of thinking. This is certainly an over optimistic exaggerated description of the tentative moves to change which are taking place but no apology will be forthcoming. The changes in Coventry, in Liverpool and other places, undoubtedly fall within the description—a small sample right enough but pioneers normally travel in ones.

This chapter is a combination of what may happen, what should happen, what will be—it is combination of hopes and some fears about the future. Behind it all is a hope that instead of regarding the future simply as more of the past we shall develop approaches which at the very least move us to plan for future avoidance, but more hopefully to get to the stage where we envisage desirable futures and then work backwards to thread our way through the policymaking systems—to understand them, to redesign them for two purposes. First to try to secure that we reach our desirable futures and secondly to ensure that we don't if those futures turn out to be incompatible with later futures.

After a sentence like that which is bound to irk the man on the job, the Chief Officer with a committee meeting tonight, some explanation is perhaps called for. It concerns the gap, real or imaginary, which exists between the writers on this kind of subject whether they are 'academic' or not and the men and women who are charged with the responsibility of keeping local government going, of coping with an endless list of constraints. Some are men who also have 'flair' and 'inventiveness' which seem to obey no rules of rationality, which would resist to the last ditch any attempt to constrain them. Others are men with little or no imagination, men who do not want to be disturbed from doing competently what they are required to do. There are other variations. The point is that the working situation presents perspectives, constraints, controls, frustrations, which writers can conveniently put on one side even supposing they recognise their existence in the first place. The gap is closing and this is the point at which we can touch on our list of characteristics. The topics are in no special order nor is any attempt made to predict *when* the development will take place, for there can be no way even of telling *whether* they will occur.

1. PURPOSEFUL INTEREST IN POLICY MAKING

The gap is closing. Until recently the writers on urban management, policy making and allied subjects have almost studiously avoided the irritating details (to them) which to the men in practice loom large and constitute the barriers to change, at least in their view. That is their perception of the situation. Thus in local government, there is not much evidence of wide reading in management or political science. This is not a criticism, it simply reflects the gap between the writers and the practitioners. Recently however a common interest has shown signs of developing. It is that of improving policy making. It is an interest in policy making as such, as distinct from intrinsic policy detail. In practice this is reflected especially in the Coventry changes but also in other places. Let it be said however, that the interest is not an interest in policy making as an end in itself. It is to improve policy making as a means of better achieving societal goals through public sector action in combination with action elsewhere. On the writing side Dror's work in particular recognises the realities of the way the machine functions and attempts to embrace these realities in his ideas for improved policy making (8.1). In this country the writing and teaching of Stewart has done much to bridge the gaps (8.2).

The interest is in steering a way through theory and practice to expose the dangers of regarding them as separates. What is likely to develop out of a combination of events are new types of processes and structures within local government and between public agencies. The tendency will be for organisations to develop into changing organisations. The notion of a management consultant coming in, recommending and implementing change only to disappear will decline after a while. Local government will recognise that change is not like a new overcoat—change is a way of life—it reflects the learning organisations. As the needs of the community change so will the policy making organisation need to change also; the one relates to the other. The allegation that change is often advocated for change's sake will secure less of a stronghold, for change will be seen as a common device not only to achieve the intrinsic benefits of a particular change but as a means of preventing an assertion of complacency (8.3). Organisations will be designed to behave in a way which resists the desire to defend the *status quo*. We have seen some approaches in Chapter 7—others will emerge. One type of process development which will arise has been given a foundation in Dror's work when he argues for the strong force of extrarationality to be harnessed on to our understandings of the policy making processes—flair, hunch, intuition, the creative surge forward, vision, are inherent in reality and instead of mapping out rational processes to the exclusion of these vital elements, new processes must be fashioned in which they are an integral part.

It will take time to develop these new processes (8.4). Dominance by some professions at the expense of others—perhaps accountant domination will take a little time to work through but even accountants are developing social consciences!

The whole corporate planning movement will become much more action orientated.

2. LEARNING ORGANISATION

"If government is to learn to solve new public problems, it must also learn to create the systems for doing so and to discard the structure and mechanisms grown up around old problems. The need is not merely to cope with a particular set of new problems, or to discard the organisational vestiges of a particular form of governmental activity which happen at present to be particularly cumbersome. It is to design and bring into being the institutional processes through which new problems can continually be confronted and old structures continually discarded." (8.5)

Stress has been laid several times on the need to increase learning, that policies and plans are likely to fall short of our expectations that action (*a*) may not produce effect (*b*) or if it does it may produce undesirable side-effects (*c*) and (*d*) and a bonus effect (*e*). This kind of monitoring will be extended greatly so that it becomes commonplace—it will have political side effects as we shall discuss below. But it will not stop there. Local government will deliberately set out to invent new solutions. It will try new devices, set up new units to throw up a complete new range of options. Ideas and potential lying latent in the organisation will be allowed to blossom by the processes operating in the local authority (8.6). The new units will represent an interdisciplinary and inter-status breakthrough and problems of 'boundaries' will be greatly reduced if not actually eliminated. The social worker will be able to shed his caseworker's mantle, the engineer will be capable of thinking outside his traditional engineering solutions and so on.

This new learning era will avoid the dangers of research and information gathering for their own sakes. The learning will be relevant to the corporate planning and management processes which in turn will be adaptive and sensitive to changing problems. Limits will be set to analysis. Cut-off points will be determined by the usefulness of particular analyses to the needs of the situation. Research will be part of, not peripheral to the decision-making processes. The policy planning unit described in the last chapter is one possibility. Other examples exist in local government and in central government too, e.g. the Rothschild Policy Analysis and Review Group attached to the British Cabinet Office and the Central Planning Bureau in the Netherlands.

The search for the luxury of certainty (which is expensive and, in view of the obsolescence of plans and policies, of little use) over relatively narrow areas will be replaced with coarser grained and more useful learning over wider areas. This will aid the provision of wider policy choices, it will extend our ability to redefine problems, to plot and understand their relationships with other problem areas, other parts of the system.

Government as a whole will learn in the sense that the hierarchical approach to planning will slowly be abandoned. The belief in the supremacy of national plans over regional plans, of regional over structure plans, of structure over local plans will dissolve on the realisation that planning is more important than plans but also that all planning processes are learning processes. The true *dynamic* between levels of planning up and down will be allowed expression.

It will take some time before this happens. In the recent publications, *Management Networks* and the *Development Plans Manual* (8.7) the prescription is that structure plans will take regional and national policies as their starting point. This lays stress on the *hierarchy* of plans rather than the dynamic of the planning process. It does not correspond to reality or to our needs.

3. SYSTEMATIC PROCESSES

More systematic processes will develop incorporating the learning process. It may be that PPBS will provide the base but whether that is so or not, whether the formal procedures sometimes ascribed to PPBS actually appear, the goal and objective orientation approach will grow. Much more systematic links with the local authority's environment will be struck. Local authorities will become more outward-looking, more sensitive and informed about needs in their area. Area and district profiles will be developed and updated in relation to unfolding policies. The base of understanding and information will increase systematically. The tradition of, for example, planning departments setting up data banks consisting of almost every conceivable piece of information the planners can think of (and which can be related to the National Grid) will decline and be replaced by the collection of relevant information, the richest vein of which lies in mapping out the effects of *current* policies and plans as they are put into effect. This too will have political consequences.

4. EXPERIMENT

More conscious experimenting will go on. This will either continue the lines already begun in experiments between central government and local government, for example the community development projects (see Chapter 6) the experiments with different urban transport schemes. But these will gradually become bolder. There is a case for instance, for adopting different patterns of local government reorganisation in different parts of the country deliberately to monitor the results. The truth is that no one knows that a particular reorganisation scheme is 'good' or 'bad' (8.8) and hence the sequential-decision-making approach should be brought into play (see Chapter 2). The same must be true of many national policies and will apply to policies within a single authority. It is very often impossible to carry out satisfactory market research in order to find out what people want before schemes are put into effect. The leisure field is a good example. Many ingenious market research devices have been tried but at the end of the road we cannot rely on the results. What we can do is to find out as much as we can and then try it out—try different schemes out in different places. Education, transportation, social services, libraries, parks—every service could learn from this approach. There will develop a breed of officer who does not believe in his own unshakeable predilections but who is prepared to experiment. Authorities will grow likewise.

5. POLITICAL CHARACTERISTICS

Myths grow up in political circles as they do anywhere else. One of the greatest is the political price politicians seem to believe is attached to losing face:

"The frightful feeling of being marked out for ridicule came back in all its strength. I don't think I was unduly sensitive; in my experience most people mind being laughed at more than anything else. What causes wars, what makes them drag on so interminably, but the fear of losing face?" (8.9)

Although it will only occur gradually there will be a new breed of political animal to whom losing face will not constitute political suicide. Politicians will become learning leaders, given to experiment. Nailing flags to political masts will become less of a phenomenon but will be replaced with a clearer expression of the values underlying policy experimentation. Politicians will come to rely less on their assertions, and seek much more to probe issues with their advisers *before* they commit themselves to a specific line. They will seek more *relevant* rather than more *voluminous* information to enable them to do this. They will, on occasions, form part of the officer/member working groups within the authority. As far as relations between the public and the local authority is concerned there will be a slow shift up in the ladder of public participation (see Chapter 6). This will probably be reluctant and other devices will become more widespread, devices which will be seen by the politicians as a substitute for yielding to 'citizen power' e.g. the 'green paper' (already a feature of some local authorities), an extension of market research practices (Exeter City Council in 1971 sent out a short questionnaire with the register of electors' forms). Local authorities will very slowly develop their *listening* facilities, they will slowly appreciate that listening is the starting point of understanding.

This will lead to the acceptance that the need exists to recognise and cater for different value sets and that processes need to be established whereby the local authority learns about these value sets, what they are, what implications they hold and what additional policy choices are open in the light of these values.

Public relations will improve (sometimes as a substitute for greater participation) but the needs of the electorate in terms of the points of contact with the local authority will be more closely understood. The break through will probably be made in the social services area but the realisation will dawn that improvements in contact require investment. A new attitude will grow up towards complaints. Complaints will be seen less as anonymous pieces of grit in the machinery but as learning points. More systematic learning from complaints will begin.

Politicians will respond much more quickly to new information and opportunities for probing issues than officers think. Officers will realise how difficult a member's job is. They will slowly understand the nature of the political process, the effect officers' reports have on members, how bad the reporting practice to members really is. They will realise that the member is *not* the obstacle to advance in local government but that it is the gap which exists between officers and members—not necessarily a hostile gap. At least when it is hostile there is an awareness that it exists. But when the gap is benign and perhaps patronising, either one way or the other, the gap is a serious impediment. It will be closed. Awareness will increase on both sides. Political manipulation (by officers or members) will assume a less significant role when the benefits deriving from a recognition and understanding of the complementary nature of the two functions develops.

6. TRAINING

The use of training as an instrument for assisting change is discussed in Chapter 9. It will however, become a feature of local government with more far-reaching implications. The professions of local government will increasingly recognise the importance of the relationship between base skills and supplementary management training. The base training will be adapted to prepare professional men to receive subsequent training in management. In particular, professions will begin to open up their own education requirements to a realisation or an appreciation of how other disciplines relate to their own training subsequent to the basic skills. Professional education will be seen as part of a career pattern with different needs being met at different stages in the career (8.10) right through to a preparation for retirement.

Corporate planning will employ new skills such as operational research, behavioural scientists (see also Chapter 9) as well as economists, sociologists and perhaps skills as yet undeveloped. Some authorities are extending their base of skills, some because it is fashionable. New skills need to be worked—they need to be employed because of their relevance. Professional resistance to new skills will decline and maybe new, super-professions will emerge.

Training will not be confined to officers. There will be an extension of member training.

7. CONSTRAINT EVAPORATION

"What really worries me is a much more fundamental danger, namely, the danger that every political feasibility prediction—and similar analytical endeavours—tends to ignore the capacities of human devotion and human efforts to overcome apparently insurmountable barriers and to achieve not only the improbable but the apparently impossible. A good policy may be worth fighting for, even if its political feasibility seems to be nil, as devotion and skillful efforts may well overcome political barriers and snatch victory out of the mouth of political infeasibility. Any political feasibility estimate, however carefully derived and however correct at its time, must therefore be regarded as provisional, sometimes to be taken up as a challenge, rather than accepted as an absolute constraint. In this respect, political feasibility well illustrates the basic orientation of policy analysis—to serve as an aid in high-level heuristic policy making but not as a decision-determining algoriths or a set of self-fulfilling predictions." (8.11)

There is no disputing that every organisation is constrained in a variety of ways and perhaps local government is constrained in more ways than most. The starting point for corporate planning should be that constraints are to be overcome if the end being sought is worth it. Too often local government moans. It moans that it is constrained by the law, constrained through lack of resources, constrained by the short-sightedness of its members, constrained by the professional narrow-mindedness of its officers, constrained by central government and so on. There *are* constraints, some are real, some are imaginary—they are put up as an excuse for inaction. Local government will become much more adept at overcoming these and other constraints. Analysis of constraints will become a common feature of corporate planning to give clues as to new policy alternatives. The aim will be to challenge obstacles to policy choices. Challenge may be a source of conflict, say between central and local government but it will also develop its own dynamic. That no unit of government has a monopoly of wisdom and challenge will be yet another vital input into the learning process.

Challenge will not only be to an outside body. It is possible that the greatest challenge will be internal—challenge to our own traditional ways of thinking. One area, for instance, which is commonly held up as an obstacle to progress is the constraint imposed by local government's own office accommodation. Apart from new architectural remedies the notion of professional and departmental boundaries being mirrored in accommodation terms will be increasingly challenged. Interdisciplinary working suites will become common, rented accommodation which can be disposed of easily will replace monolithic town halls, more flexible patterns of accommodation will be devised.

We shall not eliminate constraints but the corporate planning process will be designed to evaporate many of them, to skirt them, to probe them. Part of the planning process will be constraint analysis.

8. INTER-AGENCY CO-OPERATION

We have already discussed ways of effecting (Chapter 7) inter-agency co-operation. This will gradually extend and in the long term it is not beyond the bounds of feasibility that perhaps not formal but effective voluntary mergers will take place either for *ad hoc* purposes or even permanent re-shapings. Future legislation about local government will increasingly bestow great room for manœuvre on local authorities in this and other respects.

9. RESOURCES

It is probable that the case for increasing public expenditure, the case for tapping the affluent society will grow in strength and will be heard by even the most right-wing politicians. As the gaps in society grow wider between the haves and the have-nots, as manifestations of maldistribution of resources and opportunities become greater the case will become stronger. But we shall not simply pump more money and manpower into the traditional remedies. We shall first spend resources on developing systems of planning which learn and develop understanding of the problems of our cities, we shall spend resources on experiments and the search for entirely new and more effective solutions.

In many ways the characteristics of the emerging planning format will be influenced by the ways in which we choose to break in to new processes, the devices we invent to introduce change. It is into this related area that we now move.

REFERENCES

8.1 D. YEHEZKEL DROR, *Public Policymaking Re-examined*, Chandler Publishing Company, 1968, and *Design for Policy Sciences*, Elsevier, 1971.

8.2 J. D. STEWART, *Management in Local Government—a viewpoint*, Charles Knight and Co. Ltd., 1971, and many other publications in journals such as *Local Government Finance, Local Government Chronicle, Local Government Studies.*

8.3 Complacency is a subject on its own, but my experience is that officers and members of local government institutions strongly defend the *status quo*. The chaotic system of local government reorganisation which is about to be implemented is perhaps the classic outcome of this kind of complacency. The traditional counties have remained intact to the extent that one of them, Hertfordshire actually boasts about it in an advertisement for a senior post. 'Hertfordshire is unaffected by reform'. Pressure after pressure from groups representing their own corporate interests have rendered 'reform' an inappropriate name for what is going to happen. The characteristic of complacency is a common one—Schon refers to it as 'dynamic conservatism' in *Beyond the Stable State*, Temple Smith, 1970.

8.4 One particularly dynamic, imaginative and dedicated planning officer has argued this point with me several times. His fear is that new integrating patterns of organisation and planning processes will make it more difficult for him to get direct access to the decision-making centre i.e., the politicians. He is concerned lest reactionary forces will prevent him achieving success with his ideas. I have ruled out the possibility that he is just a reactionary himself, resisting change and my answer has been that his inventiveness needs to be let loose on much wider horizons than the ones he happens to have at present. Apply his skills—rational and extrarational to new processes and his sense of achieving will be greatly enhanced.

8.5 DONALD A. SCHON, *Beyond the Stable State*, p. 116, Temple Smith, 1971.

8.6 This is not a new phenomenon but it is by no means widespread. Most local authorities operate on the Henry Ford principle that wisdom is vested in men in direct proportion to their status. One local authority however, recently gave two temporary graduate students the task of compiling a report on evaluation (because they had expertise in the subject) and their report very quickly appeared in the Chief Officers' Group agenda. Few local authorities can make that claim—in most local authorities the problem would be to know how to occupy the students during their stay.

8.7 Management Networks. A study for Structure Plans, HMSO, 1971, Development Plans—of form and content, HMSO, 1971.

8.8 Except that here is an alarming degree of consensus on the point that the present scheme for England and Wales is 'bad'.

8.9 L. P. HARTLEY, *The Go-Between*, p. 42, Penguin, 1958.

8.10 The Royal Town Planning Institute has devised a scheme on these lines for its members.

8.11 D. YEHEZKEL DROR, *Design for Policy Sciences*, p. 60, Elsevier, 1971.

9
Breaking in to Change

There is a great tendency for the innovators to enthuse with other innovators and for the conservatives to buttress each other's resistance to change. Each camp blinds itself to the perspectives, attitudes of the other and the conservatives usually win by default. This book has been about learning, about planning as distinct from plans, about the integration of skills and insights. It has urged the search for new solutions, a deeper analysis of the real nature of problems, an increase in the scope for challenge to established procedures, approaches and methods. The direction has been towards change, not for change's sake but for the more effective impact of local government on the problems apparent and latent in the community. It spells adjustment and change, the abandonment of some practices, the adoption of new ones. It won't happen. It cannot happen, at least not overnight. There will be no flash of lightning, no Aladdin's lamp to bring it about. Any change will have to be heaved into place against the gravitational pull of vested interest, fear, indifference and the pressures of the every day business of carrying out the duties of local government. There is something pressing, something more urgent about teaching 40 children in a primary school class, collecting rents, repairing potholes in the road, controlling traffic, processing planning applications, inspecting meat, taking children into care. These operations are the life-blood of local government and they cannot be switched off until the planners sort themselves out. They will go on.

But change is not best seen as sudden, as a cleaning of the slate. True, on rare occasions it sometimes happens that way, but it is fairly safe to assume that the municipal offices of Britain are not going to be hit by revolution.

In this chapter the intention is to suggest ways in which a local authority interested in change (for the right reasons) might break into it. The intention is not to set out a series of steps to follow but to highlight some dangers, some opportunities, some ways of bringing about change, real change as distinct from illusory change which often manifests itself on formal organisation charts and committee terms of references whilst what is actually happening on the ground remains unchanged.

Any local authority, any chief executive officer, group of chief officers or political party group, anyone interested in effecting change should understand at the outset that it is a complex operation not merely in mechanistic, system terms but much more because it concerns an intervention in very strong, established forces (9.1). The two most obvious are the political machine and professionalism. They both display similar characteristics when it comes to change. They represent status, security, a way of life to their members. Change constitutes a potential threat, it gives rise to fears and suspicion and will result in fairly common, predictable responses. The surprising thing is not the nature of these responses but rather the fact that we continue to approach change in the same old way and each time seem surprised that the same responses occur. These fears and suspicions clearly have to be accommodated, they have to be understood. They may have to be separated out into the ones that are justified and the ones which are ill-founded if such a distinction is valid. It raises the question of perception of change, perception of motives for change. Different officers will have different attitudes towards change, not everyone will share the same commitment to local government or to his profession or department. The *status quo* very often provides a base of security. An officer will defend his section, his post, his field of activity, because it represents his security, his basic orientation. Men only too hastily assume that an imminent change will involve a loss of a role with only a hazy chance of an equally or more attractive one to replace it.

The traditional devices brought into play to soften the anxieties surrounding change can too readily be exposed for a lack of understanding of these factors. Consultative procedures seem, more often than not, designed to heighten anxiety rather than to alleviate it. Superiors are frequently surprised that the main response is suspicion. They seem incapable of grasping that a subordinate is almost bound to see a 'consultative' document setting out changes as the beginning of an imposed change. Even when the document poses alternatives they are too frequently based on only one set of perceptions and perspectives—those of the superior, and the response is bound to be one of suspicion. There can be no easy way round these realities but the starting point must be a recognition that these realities are a part of the environment of change (9.2). Appendix I to this Chapter is an example of one response to proposals for change. It is perhaps atypical because in this case the Union is seeking more radical changes than those proposed!

The greatest impact in bringing about change is likely to be through the processes of management rather than its structures. Changes in the formal structure as we have discussed already, are of little significance in themselves save that they probably cause the greatest reaction and hostile response with the least effects in terms of what is desired as far as change is concerned. It is a lesson which local government will take some time to learn. Changes in the processes can be approaches in a variety of ways.

THE ROLE OF THE TRAINING FUNCTION

An extraordinary feature of British local government are the resources poured into professional education and training compared with the scant attention paid to subsequent management training. In the one case it can be up to seven years. In the other if it is more than nothing it is rarely more than a few weeks. Yet the job of a local government officer at the senior levels requires both *specialist* and *management* skills, and knowledge. The one is weak without the other. This is why a 'lay' administrator is inappropriate as a local government chief officer and why a man who has had nothing but a professional training and only management 'experience' is similarly weak. Two sets of skills are required.

Training is still regarded prevalently as an exercise in itself, as separate from the management processes. Officers are sent on courses quite haphazardly in many authorities with no pre-conceived pattern of training or management development (9.3). Yet training is a vital element in bringing change into effect and indeed as a source of new thinking on what change might comprise.

Training can usefully be seen in two strands, the strategic and operational. Strategic training is concerned with helping the processes of policy making within the authority. It bears a strong relation to Anthony's definition of strategic planning (9.4) in relation to managerial and operational control. It shows a concern for focussing on systems of policy making, of major policy as distinct from planning at a lower level. But, in the present context training can be regarded as an important element in assisting change. It needs to be thought of much more as assisting the development of new patterns of thinking and much less as the cramming in of new management techniques and rules of management. A good deal of the blame can be traced to management education itself which, like the training function, is too often isolated from the needs of management. There is a strong case for a local authority devising strategies of training *in relation* to their management needs. This means considering change in the management processes *in parallel with* a training programme designed to assist that process of change. It could mean striking a dual relationship between a management training institution and a pseudo-consultancy or co-operation about the problems of change. Rather than sending a man or two away for 3 months, the case exists for a local authority or even a *group* of local authorities using training as a base from which change may be derived. It implies selecting, in the first place, key figures, change agents, within the local authority to undergo a programme of training together. It would probably best be designed partly external to the authority but some internal training would also be desirable directly related to the particular environment of the authority. It would probably involve Councillor training also. Training in this sense does not exist because it is fashionable. It can only have meaning if it is consciously used as one break-in point to the generation and implementation of relevant change.

There is a role for training during the process of change also. We have mentioned the crude 'consultation' processes which often go on. These cannot be dismissed entirely. Their failure is often due to the fact that they are seen in isolation. One way of supplementing them is to hold seminars or teach-ins with a wide range of staff, not to 'sell' a particular change but to explore the needs of the organisation at a particular point in time and to set discussion off about possible approaches to meeting those needs (9.5). If at this type of session, the imagination is captured, again, not about a particular change, but about the purposes of changing, then the environment for implementation is improved.

Elected members too would benefit from training. Indeed, the evidence is that their response is often more positive in that they do not share such quite strong defence mechanisms as do professional officers. Many more committee structures have been changed than have departmental structures. Politicians of course have other fields to defend, but training is a tool which members can usefully turn to.

BEGINNINGS OF CORPORATE PLANNING

(i) *Position statements*

The movement towards corporate planning in British local government is taking many forms. Most of them are exploratory and tentative and it will be some time before any local authority can justifiably claim to be operating corporate planning. It is the break in point which is important. Some authorities are using PPBS as a starting point with varying degrees of success.

In other authorities e.g. East Suffolk County Council, Lambeth London Borough and Stockport County Borough, the 'position statement' is being used as a break-in device. This is of great interest because it is new and at once sparks off different avenues of thought about policies both in officers and members but does not constitute a threat in organisational terms. A position statement is (9.6) the bringing together of activities of a local authority related to objectives. It is an attempt at making policies more explicit and to start a process of policy assessment and review.

Figure 9.1 shows an extract from one part of the same East Suffolk statement (9.7).

The surprising thing is that these recent attempts are the first at presenting a local authority's policies as integrated in any way. It is the first real and

CHILDREN

1. Preventive Work

1.1 *By supportive work with families to keep children in their own homes wherever possible rather than admitting them into care.*

This is achieved by

(*a*) *Rent Deficiency Guarantee Scheme.* Housing authorities (County District Councils) are given guarantees when they reach the point of seeking eviction of a family for non-payment of rent or when rehousing families from County Council temporary accommodation. Since October 1966 guarantees of the full amount of rent have been given in respect of 40 families who would otherwise have been rendered homeless. £375 has been paid in honouring guarantees of which £61 has been refunded.

(*b*) *Payment of rent arrears.* These are mainly in the form of loans to prevent eviction from both local authority and private accommodation. Families have been helped as follows 1967–68 7 (£59), 1968–69 8 (£142), 1969–70 8 (£200).

(*c*) *Financial help.* Grants and loans are made to needy families and help is given in providing holiday facilities at Felixstowe and Lowestoft.

(*d*) *Domestic help.* The number of children taken into care for short periods because of the mother's confinement or illness is shown in Table 4.

(*e*) *Accommodation for homeless families.* Since July 1966 an average of 7 houses has been used (out of an authorised provision of 10) to prevent the break-up of 33 families involving 125 children.

(*f*) *Preventive Case Work.* Approximately half of the time of field staff is spent on preventive work as distinct from work with children in care. This is the equivalent of 11 full time staff.

(*g*) *Day Care.* The extent to which Day Nurseries, Nursery Schools and Nursery Classes are available may affect the achievement of this objective. Children under 5 are a high proportion of children taken into care (1966–67 53%, 1967–68 51%, 1968–69 45%, 1969–70 41%). Facilities for day care for 10 children are provided at Sunnyside Nursery. Further reference to the under 5's is made under Education (Pre-School Children) and Health and Welfare (Care of Mothers and Young Children).

CHILDREN—*continued*

1.1.

(*a*)	Provision in 1970–71 estimates for (*a*) (*b*) (*c*) and (*d*) *£525*
(*b*)	
(*c*) ***Financial help.*** Increased provision will be made over the five year period.	
(*d*) *Domestic help.* Action will be taken in conjunction with the Home Help Service to reduce this number. In 1971–72 a mobile home help equipped with a Dormobile for sleeping accommodation will be introduced.	
(*e*) *Accommodation for homeless families.* 10 houses will be used in 1970–71 and it is intended to provide for an additional house in each of the following 3 years.	Provision in 1970–71 estimates for accommodation for homeless families (after deduction of income) *£1,020*
(*f*) *Preventive Case Work.* The addition of the equivalent of a further six full-time staff in 1970–71 will increase the capacity for preventive work.	Proportion of field staff costs in 1970–71 estimates attributable to preventive work. *£18,000*
(*g*) *Day Care.* Further study will be made of the provision for under 5's in conjunction with the other services involved.	

Figure 9.1

simple step towards 'general' as distinct from specialist management of local government.

From the point of view of bringing about change, the advantages of producing this kind of document are fairly self-evident. It presents for the first time a basis for policy development related to objectives. In Stockport the exercise was completed in a few months, albeit crudely, but the real benefit derived from the processes of thought which the preparation of the document evoked. Co-ordination and change of orientation began through a change in process not through a change in formal structure. The position statement can clearly be a vital link in assisting the change process on both the professional and political front. One of the difficulties of implementing PPBS (9.8) is to get departments to identify their objectives in the abstract. The position statement leads into objectives through an *assessment* of present policies.

(ii) Programme Management Systems (PMS)

Granted a desire to implement PPBS as the way to establish corporate planning there are many obstacles to securing implementation.

"Whatever the new system was to be, it had better not be called PPBS. The perception of PPBS in some key quarters included informed knowledge of some of its failures, and ranged all the way to heel-digging resistance to any change in the budget process whatsoever. This circumstance had a most constructive effect, because it forced immediate recognition of the overriding importance of attitudes as against theoretical niceties."

Quite apart from the approaches being adopted, e.g. in Islington and Coventry, there are other ways of capturing the PPB framework without the name and avoiding some of the resistance which has been encountered. It has been described (9.9) as the Programme Management System (PMS) which is being studied in the State of Massachusetts, USA.

"In PMS, the program manager is asked to give his perception of his program (and of the way he thinks it is linked with other programs). Because there is no pre-existing model of program or goal relationships into which his program is to be slotted, top-level decision models have to be arrived at by synthesis (aggregation) when all programs are on PMS." (9.9)

The focal point here is the existing department (i.e. no threat to the existing formal organisation is involved) and basically each Chief Officer would do a position statement for his area of operation but he would also give his ideas of how his department could assist the achievement of another department's objectives (resource 'puts') and also where he thinks other departments could assist, through the medium of *their* activities, the achievement of *his* department's objectives (resource 'calls'). In many respects the approach is very much like the approach to management by objectives (Chapter 10) where the *individual* first sets his own objectives rather than have them dictated to him. There follows a process of reconciliation and integration.

The framework for the presentation of a department's programme would be the same as for a PPB system (needs, objectives, activities, outputs etc.). Where PPB might meet resistance it seems that PMS may meet significantly less. Casselman's evaluation of it says : (9.10)

"Already, though—and increasingly as more program statements are completed—the analytic potential contained in these statements is being utilised. Selection of particular programs for in-depth analysis and evaluation is not only greatly facilitated but becomes most inviting simply through quick review of the condensed summaries. High-cost programs, poorly stated programs, obviously duplicative programs, over or undersupervised programs, underproductive (low performance standards) programs—all reveal themselves for critical analysis. So too do programs which are well-directed, well-managed, highly productive, and this is one large reason why PMS has come as far as it has with the program managers. This is also why one can hope to move into an analytic, evaluative posture without destroying the motivational elements that have brought PMS along this far."

(iii) Issue analysis

In Chapter 4 issue analysis was treated in some detail. As a break-in point to sparking off a move towards corporate planning of course, it has great advantages. It is inhererently attractive (9.11) and presents a valuable framework for problem analysis. Issue analysis can be regarded as another pathway to objective orientation. It is also capable of immediate use with the crudest of data. Again it assists new ways of thinking, opens up new avenues of thought about common problems, but does not constitute an organisational threat—a challenge to present policies maybe, but not a threat to status.

(iv) Use of data and techniques—a caution

In a sense this is not a seperate break-in approach for it is inseparable from some of the others. Essentially the point is this, however, that the ardent advocates of sweeping changes have dreams of sophisticated analysis and vast banks of data. The 'planner's thirst' is the perpetual complaint of lack of data and the persistent search for complete information. This often creates a barrier to change, to innovation. The use of crude information, crude indicators of measures will always be a feature of planning processes. An insistence on the collection of vast amounts of data, whilst ultimately worth aiming for, may well constitute the greatest obstacle to the acceptance of a systematic framework for policy formulation and review.

In devising break-in points the approach is to secure a reorientation of the planning processes. Improvement of data sources will follow and in any event the richest source of data will be the feedback processes of planning itself. First get the process established. A similar warning could be sounded about techniques. Sophisticated techniques, even the word, 'techniques' constitutes a barrier. The break-in will require their discreet use.

CHALLENGE

There is no doubt that the example set by the local authority itself, the example set by the style and approach of a Chief Officer in his department, has a marked effect on the remainder of the organisation. Examples of cheese-paring authorities are common, of authorities who are concerned much more with reducing rates than with meeting needs, the 'cautious authority', the authority which has a reputation for rules and no policies, which lives by using the law as a defence for inaction. Conversely there are authorities or particular parts of authorities which innovate, which lead, which pioneer developments (with or without boasting about them). There are town clerks who *use* the law to achieve things or who promote new private laws where existing ones prevent achievement. Some councils have shown themselves as masters of constraint evaporation (Chapter 8). A leadership, political or professional, which sets a dynamic style will secure the same response. Stolid caution as a style breeds solidity or frustration beneath.

Change is not easy. It demands subtlety and understanding, courage and persistence. There are no rules. It cannot however, spring from one point. Change and innovation cannot be imposed. Change has to spring, and subsequently requires sustenance, from many points. The greatest impetus for securing an easy passage for change will derive from the creation of a situation where change is not exceptional. When it becomes a common feature, when the organisation itself develops into a learning system, then it ceases to talk about change.

The development of such a learning system faces tremendous odds:

"The first crucial fact is the existence of a universal sense of powerlessness. We seem to be living in a society that no one created and that no one wants. The feeling of powerlessness extends even to the inhabitants of executive offices. Yet paradoxically, it is also a fact that we have available to us the means to begin coping with virtually all of the problems that beset us. Most people would initially deny this, but reflection shows how true it is. We know what causes crime and social disorder, and what can be done to eliminate those causes. We know the steps that can be taken to create greater economic equality. We are in possession of techniques to fashion and preserve more inhabitable cities and environments. Our problems are vast, but so is our store of techniques; it is simply not being put to use. . . .

The American crisis, then, seems clearly to be related to an inability to act. But what is the cause of this paralysis? Why, in the face of every warning, have we been unable to act? Why have we not used our resources more wisely and justly? We tell ourselves that social failure comes down to an individual moral failure: we must have the will to act; we must first find concern and compassion in our hearts. But this diagnosis is not good enough. It is contradicted by the experience of powerlessness that is encountered by so many people today. In 1968 a majority of the people certainly wanted peace, but they could not turn their individual wills into action by society. It is not that we do not will action, but that we are unable to act, unable to put existing knowledge to use. Is something wrong with the machinery of society? It apparently no longer works, or we no longer know how to make it work." (9.12)

The same symptoms, the same powerlessness rests in organisations, and local authorities are no exception. The move towards breaking this impotence in local government requires the setting up of 'change-linkages' within the local authority.

The most successful chief executive officer will be the one who captures the imagination of a number of other officers and members throughout the local authority. He will not 'sell' his own solutions, he will seek to spark off a process of learning by the local authority. This in turn will lead to the production of ideas from many points. Through the learning linkages, which will cross formal organisation boundaries, the base will be set for the changing organisation. One great danger of new management processes is that the management or the policy formulation part becomes separated from implementation, from the on-going business of running the service. Our traditional notions of vertical, status boundaries within the local authority will need to be transcended by the change-linkages. An officer's value on the change-linkage system will derive, not from his status, the name of his post, but from his aptitude for contributing to the learning process.

There can be no recipe for creating the learning system but Reich's analysis of societal powerlessness offers a thought-provoking starting point for considering the position local authorities are in at present. Recognising the symptoms, whether they are as Reich suggests, or of some other kind, is the first step towards securing what is required by way of improvement. Boldness, risk, experiment, constraint evaporation will be ingredients of any such improvement but not merely from the top—all these things need encouragement throughout the system.

Appendix to Chapter 9

Figure 9.2 is a facsimile of a National Association of Local Government Officers document circulated to all union members in one authority. The small passages scored out are simply to achieve anonymity. It is worth noting that the outcome of this particular campaign was successful for both sides in that discussions were opened up and change much more openly treated by staff and elected representatives.

"I involved the officers from the start, partly as an educative measure, but chiefly because, if you are going to get their cooperation, you must involve them."

FRANK IRELAND, NEWCASTLE PRINCIPAL CITY OFFICER AND TOWN CLERK.

- WHY IS NALGO WORRIED?
- WHAT IS WRONG WITH THE PRESENT ORGANISATION?
- THE BASIC NEEDS FOR REORGANISATION
- WHAT ABOUT THE CHIEF EXECUTIVE'S PROPOSALS FOR REORGANISATION?
- WHAT NOW? DISCUSSION AND ADVICE

APPENDIX. NOTES ON CORPORATE MANAGEMENT

THE COUNCIL REORGANISATION

A DISCUSSION REPORT

NALGO BRANCH

1

START HERE

Discussions have been taking place for some time about the Chief Executive Officer's proposals for reorganisation.
NALGO is very worried and has, therefore, produced this preliminary discussion report.

WHY IS NALGO WORRIED?

NALGO IS WORRIED because, so far, everyone concerned has not been consulted and NALGO believes that everyone should be involved in formulating the new reorganisation. The idea is to open up the discussion and get everyone thinking and talking about a new streamlined Council.

NALGO IS WORRIED because it has seen the Chief Executive's draft proposals for reorganisation

NALGO IS WORRIED because it believes that only the best organisation is good enough. Good enough for the staff to work in, good enough for the elected Council members to serve in and, most important of all, good enough to give the best possible service to the community.

REORGANISATION PROPOSALS MUST NOT BE BULLDOZED THROUGH WITHOUT YOUR INVOLVEMENT. REORGANISATION PROPOSALS MUST RESULT IN THE BEST ORGANISATION.

BUT WHAT IS WRONG WITH THE PRESENT ORGANISATION?

Maybe you think we are muddling along all right just now - so why change?

Then ask yourself these questions.

If you are an officer: "Are you completely satisfied with your present job?" "Is your time spent in the most valuable and productive way?" "Do you never do something that is just put in the bottom drawer (or just waste time) because the right decision was not made in the first place?" "Do you help give the best value-for-money service to the community?"

If you are a Council member: "Do you spend your valuable time concentrating on the most important issues?" "Have you sat back and decided what these issues are in the first place?" (i.e. established Council's overall objectives and priorities) "Is the ratepayer's money spent in the best way towards solving these problems?" (i.e. resource allocation) "Are you not frustrated at how long it takes to get decisions made and plans carried out?" (poor committee/departmental structure, poor policy making machinery and poor overall co-ordination). "Do you help give the best value-for-money service to the community?"

2

If you were a member of the public: "Would you be satisfied that the Council knows what you really want?" "That you get a quick and efficient service at the Town Hall?" "That your money is being spent in the right way on the right things?" "In fact, would you be satisfied that you get the best possible overall service from Council?"

NALGO believes that at present it would not be possible to say "YES" to any of these questions.
If this is so then something radical must be done and done soon.

THE BASIC NEEDS FOR REORGANISATION

The need is to have a Council organisation that would allow you to answer "YES" to all the above questions. (Check back now).

The first basic need is for the Council to examine and then state clearly what it is really trying to do.
This is a question of setting the Council's objectives. It is most important because: first, the actual process makes everyone sit back and think coolly whether things are being done the right way now; second, it gives all the Council's activities a sense of direction and, thirdly, it establishes a means of measuring the Council's actual performance.

Setting objectives (and then considering alternative programmes for achieving them) is a basic need. Since they should be capable of being achieved, it is clear that all the Council's objectives must be balanced against each other and co-ordinated.

The second basic need is for an overhaul of the Council's policy, decision making and co-ordinating machinery.
In fact, at present, this most important part of a Council organisation hardly exists at all and what is there is inadequate and distinctly creaky. It is here where things often go wrong now (or do not go at all!)

As a result the Council is possibly not getting value for money, not doing the right things in the right places or often not doing anything at all. For there is no point in making plans if decisions are not taken to carry them out and if, subsequently, the overall control is not there to ensure that they are, in fact, carried out according to programme.

Also, at present, various separate and almost unconnected programmes for action are prepared. e.g. road construction, open space, social services and most important of all the Borough Treasurer's 5 year Growth Programme. There is a need for the various physical, social and economic plans to be considered in an overall, or corporate, way.

3

The third basic need is to tidy up the number of different departments and committees.
The present fragmented structure (as shown in Diag. 1) means that the issues with which the Council has to deal (e.g. housing, recreation etc.) cut across many different committees and departments. Therefore, establishing needs, objectives or priorities let alone getting decisions made is a cumbersome, slow and almost impossible business.

THESE THREE BASIC NEEDS ARE INTERDEPENDENT. WHAT IS REQUIRED IS AN OVERALL (OR CORPORATE) VIEW OF WHAT THE COUNCIL IS TRYING TO DO WITH AN ADEQUATE POLICY/CO-ORDINATING MACHINERY AND COMMITTEE/DEPARTMENTAL STRUCTURE THAT SEES THAT IT GETS ON AND DOES IT.

WHAT ABOUT THE CHIEF EXECUTIVE'S PROPOSALS (OR "NOTES") FOR REORGANISATION?

How do the Chief Executive's proposals match up to these basic needs? NALGO hopes that the Chief Executive will soon explain his proposals to you personally. However, in NALGO's opinion these proposals would involve little change from the present unsatisfactory situation (except for changing a few names) and go nowhere towards setting up a structure that could tackle the basic needs outlined above.

The Chief Executive has recently stated that co-ordination cannot be imposed. It is true that no one can force people to co-ordinate or co-operate together. However, NALGO firmly believes that if the proper co-ordinating machinery and Council structure is established, with the wholehearted support and confidence of all those who will be involved in carrying it out, then co-ordination and co-operation will occur naturally.

The nature of the Chief Executive's proposals and the way in which they are being put forward could only mean completely inadequate co-ordination.

THE PRESENT FRUSTRATION FOR STAFF, MEMBERS AND THE PUBLIC WOULD CONTINUE, TOGETHER WITH AN INADEQUATE AND INEFFICIENT SERVICE.

WHAT NOW? DISCUSSION AND ADVICE

Reorganisation should mean better value for money. It should mean that you will have a more responsible and productive rôle to play. It is essential that you have your say, for it is often the person doing the job who knows what is going on, what the real needs are and what may be wrong. It is a question of the involvement of all concerned if the best reorganisation is going to take place. Do not forget that it is you who

Figure 9.2

4

are going to have to carry it out and, therefore, you who should believe in it. Quoting from a recently published article* "The key factor in performance is the attitude of members and officers. Unless they are committed to improved performance nothing will result, however sophisticated the management techniques."

In this country considerable research and experience has gone into thinking about Local Government reorganisation and management techniques - very often borrowing good ideas from the worlds of commerce and industry.

Radical reorganisation has been introduced in various Local Authorities (Liverpool, Hull, Newcastle, Greenwich etc.) It has sometimes met with difficulties (often because individual personalities have not sensibly co-operated together). However, NALGO believes that only the best organisation is good enough for   and that the ideas of Corporate Management should be applied to a new Council structure here.

It must be remembered that the present Council organisation has useful resources of know-how, manpower, land and money. It is a question of adapting these resources and using them more efficiently. As already stressed, the main need is for an overall view of what the Council is trying to do with an adequate policy/co-ordinating group and committee/departmental structure.

Diagram 2 shows what this could look like: the simplicity compared to the existing Borough organisation is obvious. There are two things to look for: first, the emphasis on an adequate policy/co-ordinating group (within the box) and, second, the fewer number of committees and departments (say, five of each) with a direct relationship between them.

It should be noted that an organisation on corporate management lines would not mean an increase of staff numbers. According to the level of service to be provided, it should be possible to reduce the overall number of officers - having the right man in the right place doing the right job. No redundancies, of course, but greater job opportunity and job satisfaction.

It is not considered necessary, at present, to go into detail about the various management techniques available (such as P.P.B.S.[1], MBO[2] and the like). However, if you are interested, a few notes on what corporate management is about are included in our following Appendix.

*"Increased Effectiveness in Local Authorities" Local Government Chronicle, 3 July, 1971.

1. Planning, Programming and Budgeting Systems
2. Management by Objectives.

5

<u>What is necessary is a full, informed and continuing discussion</u> (including working groups, seminars etc.) on what present Council members and officers think the new organisation should be like.

<u>What is necessary is to obtain outside advice on the best tailor-made Council structure to suit   special needs.</u> NALGO believes that   should benefit from the experts on Local Government reorganisation, learning from the good and bad experiences of elsewhere. It is suggested, with the help of an agency such as the Institute of Local Government Studies in Birmingham, that either reliable consultants could set up a broad structure, or that persons experienced in this matter could be brought into the Council's services - either temporarily seconded or on a permanent basis.

This report does not provide the answers. However, it is hoped that it shows you the present deficiencies and the basic needs for reorganisation. It provides some guide lines for a new organisation and it shows the way forward. MOST IMPORTANT OF ALL, IT IS HOPED THAT THIS REPORT WILL, AT LAST, FORCE THE DISCUSSION WIDE OPEN. SO JOIN IN.

6

- PLEASE USE THIS PAGE FOR MAKING DISCUSSION NOTES.

- SOME FURTHER READING:

- Local Government and Strategic Choice: by Friend and Jessop, 1969.
- Corporate Strategy: by Ansoff. Pelican Business Studies.
- New Approaches to Management in Local Government: by Prof. J.D. Stewart (reprint of articles from Local Government Chronicle 1969).
- Increased Effectiveness in Local Authorities: a series of articles by McKinseys, Consultants. Local Government Chronicle, July 1971.
- Organising the New Authorities - Some Pointers for Discussion: by Prof. J.D. Stewart. Article in Local Gov. Chronicle 26, June 1971.
- Economic Progress Report: Planning, Programming, Budgeting. From Information Division of the Treasury, 6th Aug., 1970.

Diagram 1. Diagrammatic representation of present Borough organisation

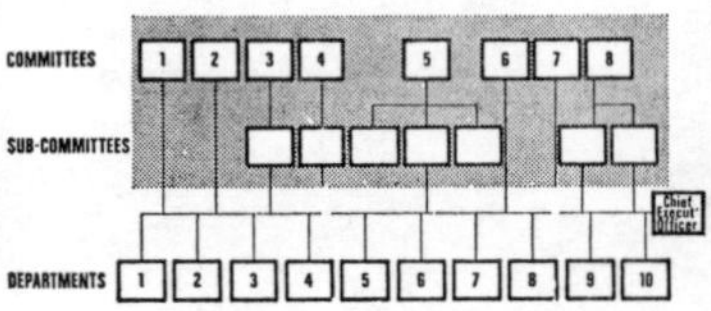

Diagram 2. Possible rationalised committee and departmental organisation

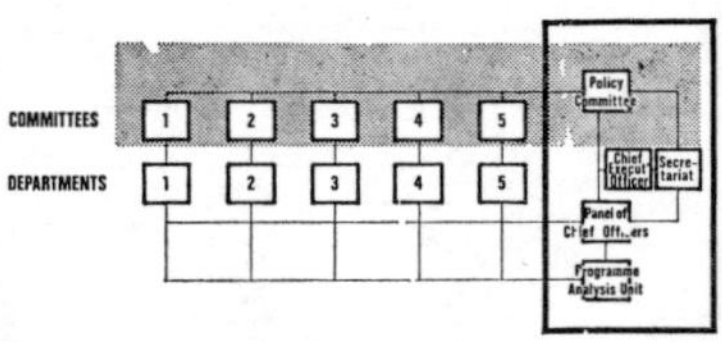

Figure 9.2 (*contd.*)

REFERENCES

9.1 I do not claim to be an expert in human behaviour or indeed to have read extensively in the field. These are observations of phenomena and reflections deriving from extensive contact with local government officers involved, in varying capacities, in change.

9.2 There are those of course who would not regard this as an important factor. The authoritarian leader would override any such considerations and proceed to impose his solution. I cannot say that he would be wrong, although I believe it to be so. The assumption is that participative management is likely to produce better results. (See Chapter 10).

9.3 Many course members on advanced courses at the Institute of Local Government Studies are unaware that other officers from the same authority have preceded them. Most get little opportunity to follow up or to use their training back in the authority. They are expected rather to get back into line as quickly as possible.

9.4 R. N. ANTHONY, *Planning and Control Systems: a framework for analysis*, Harvard University, 1965.

9.5 My colleagues and I have been involved in several such exercises. Our perception has been that in most cases they were valuable exercises for the authorities concerned.

9.6 Cf. TONY EDDISON, 'Local Government in Perspective', *Local Government Finance*, p. 222—a possible new approach, June, 1970.

9.7 From the introduction to Allocation of Resources 1970–1975, East Suffolk County Council. This was probably the first attempt at a position statement of this kind in Britain and represents a significant yet simple advance.

9.8 See Chapter 4—programme structures as academic exercises.

9.9 ROBERT C. CASSELMAN, 'An old state takes a new look at public management', *Public Administration Review*, July/August, 1971.

9.10 *op. cit.*

9.11 A planning officer told me recently that he had structured a committee report on issue analysis lines to the joy of the elected members who found themselves debating policy choices, and to the annoyance of the County Clerk who presumably saw it as a threat.

9.12 CHARLES A. REICH, *The Greening of America*, pp. 16–17, Penguin, 1971.

10
Management by Objectives in Local Government

Much of this book has been concerned with the process of planning, with inducing a learning approach to the planning processes in local government. Inducing a learning system will take many forms. In this chapter we shall discuss management by objectives. Although the approach will be described in detail, the probability is that in few local authorities will it be implemented in the forum set out here. That is not the intention. The concern is to generate interest in another way of inducing the learning approach—this time in the individual. This approach can be derived from management by objectives on any variant of it, and that is what is important. Self appraisal, discussed at the end of the chapter may be the break-in point.

Notwithstanding the considerable difficulties of implementing PPBS there is an undeniable attraction to the almost cold logic which lies behind it as an approach or working framework for planning, implementing, controlling and reviewing the policies of a local authority. The same rationality is to be found in management by objectives—and, as we shall see, many of the same difficulties. The one may be conveniently seen in relation to the objectives of a local authority or agency as a whole, the other is concerned much more with the individual officer in his department or even within a section of a department. It is on the objectives of the individual that management by objectives focuses mostly. It is sometimes known as 'performance planning', 'improving management performance' or simply MBO—here it will be called management by objectives throughout.

Even at the risk of being over-cautious it is important to realise at the outset that management by objectives, like any other approach or technique, is not magic, it is not an instant remedy to management problems. Given reasonable conditions, which will be set out later, it merely creates an improved framework within which departments (or sections of a department) can work. It is an attempt to introduce system into what is often being done already, albeit perhaps in a crude fashion. What will be clear is that there are real or potential pitfalls and difficulties and there could well be disadvantages in introducing it, whether to a local authority as a whole or to one specific part of it. It will be apparent that it is easier to operate in some fields than others, that it relies to a degree, as does PPBS, on measurement, on quantification which is not easy—some would say impossible in many aspects of the public sector's work. But again, as with PPBS, the difficulty of measurement or evaluation is often erected as a reason for not attempting it. This has its dangers and so of course does the converse, i.e. of introducing spurious accuracy in a field which is rightly the field of political values.

Although we shall lay considerable stress on measures and indicators, it is intended to show here that provided there is an awareness of the possible dangers, provided the approach is introduced sensitively, then there are considerable advantages to be reaped from it at all levels and for all sizes of authority or agency. Moreover it need not be introduced as a whole system—some of its more basic approaches may be applied or adopted with little or no trouble and certainly with no added expense.

The purpose here, then, is to explain management by objectives, to expose its limitations and to give some constructive guidance on how it might be applied in local government and the public sector generally.

RELATIONSHIP BETWEEN PPBS AND MANAGEMENT BY OBJECTIVES

As we have seen a Programming Planning Budgeting system casts a framework for policy planning and it has as one of its major elements the programme structure, the hierarchy of objectives of the local authority, beginning with the wide objectives and progressively narrowing on moving down the hierarchy. Often the distinction between 'objectives' and 'means' is a blurred one. Clearly what at one level is an objective can be seen as a means from another point. The usefulness of the objective as a tool in PPBS or in management by objectives is that it relates one activity or operation at one level to a higher level. There can be no hard and fast definition of the relationship between PPBS and management by objectives, nor indeed of the relationship between objectives and activities. There can only be a variety of ways of looking at and using these relationships and, depending on the purpose of the interest, some are more helpful than others. If PPBS is regarded primarily as a thinking framework, for planning and control, then it is perhaps more helpful to see management by objectives as operating more at the implementation end of the scale.

Thus there is a series of different levels:

(*a*) the local authority or agency objectives;
(*b*) the departmental or sectional objectives derived from (*a*);
(*c*) the individual officer's most important tasks in securing or making his contribution to (*b*) (and hence (*a*)).

Perhaps a further stage could usefully be distinguished involving the review and feedback element: clearly all four are related and interdependent. Progress through one affects the others both upwards and downwards and to greater or lesser degrees. Management by objectives, in the model presented here, has its greatest impact in the area of the individual but with ripple effects to other areas. Few of these approaches or techniques have clear boundaries and in fact attempts to erect them will very frequently undermine their value—it is the relationships between them that are often important rather than their separate characteristics. Management by objective *can* be seen as something separate and *can* be treated separately from PPBS but it is much more useful when it is seen as an extension or even a part of PPBS.

THE SPIRIT OF THE APPROACH

The consideration of the relationship between management by objectives and PPBS has concentrated on the two as thinking frameworks. However, there is an important element, particularly in relation to management by objectives, which needs treating with perhaps more care, understanding and attention. A common enough comment from those who are cynical about management teaching, management techniques or innovation in this field generally, is that new approaches, new thinking and so on, are all right but 'people' are more important—'people' have to work the system—'you have to take personalities into account'. The comment appears in a variety of forms. It is a familiar enough comment and of course it is fully justified, but only if the comment is seen as a starting point for understanding people—for understanding human behaviour and the implications, in a behavioural sense, of the new approaches. Too often the comment is made to avoid the issue, as if by recognising in words that people are important that practice automatically embraces and enhances that importance, which is not the case. The whole field of human behaviour in organisations is a vitally important one. We are not pursuing it here except in non-specialist terms and insofar as it relates to management by objectives. One cornerstone of management by objectives is a participative or democratic style of management. This is based on the theory that;

"1. The expenditure of physical and mental effort in work is as natural as play or rest. The average human being does not inherently dislike work. Depending upon controllable conditions, work may be a source of satisfaction (and will be voluntarily performed) or a source of punishment (and will be avoided if possible).

2. External control and the threat of punishment are not the only means for bringing about effort toward organisational objectives. Man will exercise

self-direction and self-control in the service of objectives to which he is committed.

3. Commitment to objectives is a function of the rewards associated with their achievement. The most significant of such rewards, e.g. the satisfaction of ego and self-actualisation needs, can be direct products of effort directed toward organisational objectives.

4. The average human being learns, under proper conditions, not only to accept but to seek responsibility. Avoidance of responsibility, lack of ambition and emphasis on security, are generally consequences of experience, not inherent human characteristics.

5. The capacity to exercise a relatively high degree of imagination, ingenuity, and creativity in the solution of organisational problems is widely, not narrowly, distributed in the population.

6. Under the conditions of modern industrial life, the intellectual potentialities of the average human being are only partially utilised." (10.1)

A system of management by objectives, as well as resting heavily on this theory, also relies on a freeing up of relationships between subordinate and superior. It demands a frank, critical dialogue between individuals in this relationship and also generally throughout the department or organisation in which it is being applied. The object behind this is to produce constructive information which in turn goes towards the improvement of performance, of individual officers, of groups of officers and even the whole department. So often in any organisation peers will raise, discuss, and complain to one another about the shortcomings of the organisation but all too often the complaints are never put to anyone who is in a position to take action to alleviate the problem. Conversely, an officer may be conscious of, even worried about, some weakness or failing in one of his subordinates but avoids discussing it with him when in practice this may well be the opening up of the way to a remedy. Is it kinder to leave a man ignorant of his weaknesses in his job or to tell him about them? There can be no rule laid down—it will vary, but if the atmosphere is created where criticism, both up and down, is commonplace, is not the exception, then the task is easier—it has a meaningful framework. The system, of course, cannot, or at least should not be imposed without some appreciation or awareness of the problems which are likely to arise in this area. Everyone involved in the system will adopt his own approach—some exchanges will indeed be frank and free—others will stop short at points, determined in the privacy of the minds of the individuals concerned—others will be very restrained. The important point about the frank exchanges is that they are purposive and systematic. One-off frank exchanges are of very doubtful value and it is questionable whether they are very frank. Many officers convince themselves that theirs is an 'ever open door'—the comment that 'people can come to see me any time' is common enough and belies the true state of affairs. Other officers convince themselves that by building up a sense of camaraderie they effectively construct frank communication channels. Perhaps communication is improved but it is unsystematic and hence biased and unreliable. But in any event almost all communication is sieved either by the 'transmitter' or by the 'receiver'.

Criticism in these exchanges is not the complaining kind, it is not punitive, but the kind which examines critically the work of each individual and the conditions and environment in which he has to do it. The spirit is more easily talked about than captured, but its importance for the success of management by objectives will become increasingly apparent as we move on. The relationship, however, can be seen as a dynamic one—that is to say, management by objectives requires the participative management style as a basis but itself may well induce it.

KEY TASKS

Despite the classic jokes about the tea-drinking public servant, it is mostly true to say that he is an extremely busy man, often overwhelmed day to day by a host of time-consuming, sometimes unpredictable activities, many of which cannot really be said to be central to his job. Perhaps only about one-fifth of a manager's activities are crucial to the achievement of his main work. The rest of the activities may be essential in the sense that they have to be done by someone, but they are only peripheral to the particular manager's job. In other words, if the object is to improve the performance of the department through improvements in the individual's performance, then it is on these *key* activities that attention should be focussed. The first step clearly is to identify these *key tasks*—perhaps five or six of them, are those tasks upon which his contribution towards departmental objective depends most. For the officer concerned, and of course for the department as a whole, it is more important that he achieves reasonable standards of performance in these areas, rather than excel in those activities which are purely marginal. The identification and subsequent analysis of these key tasks is one of the important features of management by objectives.

A helpful way of arriving at key tasks is for the officer to list his activities or jobs, and subsequently group them into five or six key tasks. It should not stop here, however. Merely considering present activities is insufficient—it spells stagnation. The key tasks must be looking to what should be rather than what is.

KEY TASKS ANALYSIS

The identification of an officer's key tasks is not necessarily simple, but even when it has been done it is of limited value in isolation from the key tasks of other officers in the same department or section. Clearly there is a relationship between the key tasks of all personnel within the department—their key tasks should interlock and the relationship should be explicit. The aim should be to achieve a fully integrated set of tasks compatible with those of departments as a whole. The importance of relating the tasks of one officer with those of his superior and his subordinate is perhaps self-evident but it can be thrown into sharper relief when one compares the view of what, for example, a Chief Officer regards as his own and his deputy's key tasks with what the deputy sees as *his* own and his chief's key tasks. The results of the comparison can be revealing (and embarrassing!). Only when tasks throughout a department are integrated can the system begin to be useful.

In the first instance the process of key tasks analysis is undertaken by the individual officer himself by defining his own key tasks. Having established to his own satisfaction what are his key tasks the officer himself then attempts to identify or suggest his *results to be achieved* or the *standard of performance* in relation to each key task. What we are seeking here is some indicator by which an officer can judge to what extent he has been successful in achieving or completing his key tasks. These will take a variety of forms. The standard will sometimes be a continuing one. For example a treasurer responsible for payment of wages and salaries may be expected to have inaccuracy in no more than one payment in five hundred. This type contrasts with the target where an officer establishes a time within which some particular project shall be completed—a project which is distinctive and not likely to be a regular feature of his job, at least not in the same form. An example might be an architect required to complete designs for a particular project by a certain date. Wherever possible the results should be quantifiable. This is easy to say and not so easy to achieve. It should be possible however, to give a conveyancing solicitor, for example, some guidelines as to what is a reasonable turnover of conveyances. True, there will always be the awkward case which may take many weeks or months but this does not deny the underlying pattern of turnover. If the task is to deal with conveyances speedily then a guideline can be acceptably set. On the other hand, speed is not always the most crucial factor with conveyancing—there are many occasions when it is irrelevant. Obviously each task has to be probed in this way to uncover *useful* standards. There are obvious dangers in striking false measurable standards. An absolute measure is more often than not impossible—spurious measures may be invented which in the event are possibly counter-productive. As much as anything else the individual officer needs some helpful indication which *he himself* may use to judge his performance against the tasks he has identified. Any measure which fulfils this function is a good one. In most cases there will not be one single measure but a range of measures or indicators related to each key task. It is the combination of measures which will most frequently give the officer the information he requires to judge his own performance.

Speaking in general terms about measurement, e.g. identifying pitfalls, sounding notes of caution is relatively easy but in practice not much has been done in the public sector and certainly nothing that is entirely satisfactory. In Figure 10.1 an attempt has been made to draw up a model of a Chief Officer's key tasks performance indicators. They are discussed in more detail later but are perhaps a useful reference point at this stage. It is important to realise that these are a Chief Officer's key tasks which differ in the degree of specificity from an example at a lower level.

Apart from the test of usefulness which we have mentioned, there is another crucial factor which may determine the validity of a standard of performance and this is the availability of control information. Obviously if there is no way of telling how long individual conveyances take to complete, there is little point in adopting a turnover standard for the conveyancing solicitor—he has no information. The question has to be asked, 'If the information is not available, can it be made available and if so, at what cost or trouble?' In doing his own key tasks analysis the officer must specify whether the control information he requires is available and in what form, or if it is not available, what he requires, how he sees it being collected and so on.

The final component of the key tasks analysis is a statement of what action he, the individual, can take to improve his performance, the action he thinks his superior should take and what other steps he feels might be taken possibly at a higher officer or member level towards the same end. Some examples of the sort of action involved here may help to illustrate the point. The development control planning assistant may agree or reorganise a whole series of procedures in his office to speed up part of his work. This he can can do himself. He may also, however, want to reallocate work such as the plotting of planning applications or the answering of land charges as between members of staff in the same section or he may want to have better or different typing arrangements, all of which may require action by his superior. The sort of thing which would require action at a higher level than his immediate superior might be the appointment of additional staff, the purchasing of new equipment or the adjustment of his area for development control purposes. Other factors which might appear here, the exposure of which, like all the rest, should be encouraged, are things like an expression of the need for some form of additional training or guidance. For example, some officers have difficulty with report writing. Another possibility is inadequate authority or some other limitation or problem which affects the officer's performance.

Each authority and department will have its own ideas and needs in this respect—the examples are given as guides. The important thing is that the system actively induces officers at whatever level to give consideration to their working environment in a wide sense and to suggest ways of improving it relative to the achievement of his key tasks. In practice it may be helpful to use a standard form to assist the officer in undertaking his own analysis.

So far the analysis has been carried out by the individual officer himself. It now needs to be discussed between him and his superior who will have been analysing his own tasks. Their discussion will be structured under various heads and making mutually agreed changes, they will eventually establish for the subordinate:

(*a*) The key tasks.

(*b*) The results to be achieved.

(*c*) The control information which it is reasonable for the officer to have.

(*d*) (i) The suggestions the officer has made for action he can take.
(ii) That which the superior might take.
(iii) The items for action at a higher level.

At the end of this process of analysis each individual officer has his plan of action for the period ahead, usually about six months or so—it is known sometimes as a Job Improvement Plan—complete with the agreed supporting action of his superior.

THE MANAGEMENT OR STAFF ADVISOR

At this stage it is appropriate to introduce the concept of the management or staff advisor. Most people need some help to define their own key tasks. For some officers the process of defining key tasks can be disturbing—some begin to wonder whether theirs is a job at all—others see their job as a meaningless collection of odds and ends, and the thought of having to distil their work into five or six key tasks is a frightening one. What is required is a person trained in this area, who is able to ask helpful, pertinent questions about an officer's work, to give some leads to assist the definition. Similarly the discussions between subordinate and superior in agreeing the job improvement plan may need a catalyst, someone to prompt or ask relevant questions, indeed to just get a flow of conversation going. This is the management advisor's role; he assists the individual in drawing up his own key tasks and

Key task	*Performance indicators*	*(Notes)*
1. *Relationships with Councillors/politicians* Establishment of such relationships with elected Members as will create a situation in which they will become informed and respond appropriately to professional advice.	*Examples* Level of confidence in professional advice and action—grapevine reports useful here. Self-assessment in retrospect of advice given on major items. Level at which resources are provided to meet established need. Intensity of communications with elected Members.	*Relative* performance is useful here, i.e. the pattern of *change* from one period to the next.
	Number of direct conflicts (absence of disagreement on major issues?) Whether in self-assessment integrity maintained.	
2. *Staff Relations in his Department* Establishment and maintenance of good working relationships between staff at all levels, both vertically and horizontally. (This task differs in type from (1) in that here the C.O. is less *directly* involved but would nevertheless pay attention to it through his senior staff especially. It may involve the C.O. in appointing major posts, perhaps laying down guidelines for training policy etc.)	Nature and frequency of referring up of differences (absence of buck-passing). Turnover of staff compared with similar size authorities. Length of time vacancies unfilled compared with similar neighbouring authorities. Quality of staff attracted. New schemes initiated, i.e. relative level of ideas being discussed. Case with which C.O. fits into M.B.O. operation. Training record (this function would probably be someone else's major responsibility).	

3. *Relations with other Departments* Maintenance and promotion of co-operative relationship with other departments to achieve the objectives of the authority as a whole. Making available professional advice and help and seeking it where necessary.	Absence of departmental *bickering* (N.B. not differences of opinion, which may be healthy). Type and frequency of communication with other Departments (communication could be ranked on a scale as to its nature and frequency). Pattern of advice sought of and by department. Ease with which disagreements can be expressed. Grapevine or other complaints from other C.O's of performance of his staff.	(Involvement of his staff in working parties.) (Looked at in this kind of framework remedial measures come more readily to mind.)
4. *Relations with the public* To promote and maintain a well-informed public about the service and to retain confidence in it.	Nature and frequency of public contacts—complaints and other. *Nature* of press coverage. Pattern of requests for outside talks. No. of times consumers *insist* on seeing Chief Officers.	(Relative changes over time here—will vary from department to department.)
5. *Development of the service as such*	Performance standards here would in part at least be specific to objectives of service concerned. Relative level of resources devoted to service. Some indicators from other areas would be useful—public relations, recruitment levels etc.	

Figure 10.1 *Management by Objectives*

Specimen Key Tasks and standards of performance for Chief Officers

This is intended mainly as a framework within which a Chief Officer may reflect systematically about his own performance and by definition of course, that of his department. Many of the standards—indeed most of them—are mere indicators—aids for reflection. The model is incomplete—groups should look at it critically and add to it.

the analysis, and would figure in the subsequent discussions. Over time the presence of a third party at these discussions may not be necessary but in some cases it will always be required. The sooner the system operates without the advisor the better, provided of course the exchanges are as productive without him. The advisor's role is important but it must not dominate the superior / subordinate relationship.

The skills and qualities required for the post are many—they are of the kind which many of us think we possess but in practice don't. It is not a post which any officer can be slotted into and at the end of the road will probably turn out to be the man the department can least afford to release, that is, if he is taken from within the authority. The post is a difficult and often a controversial one and perhaps his most important attribute should be that he is highly acceptable to his seniors, his peers and his subordinates. There is obviously a lot to be said for appointing someone from within the authority or department as has happened in the West Riding of Yorkshire County Architect's Department and the Somerset County Treasurer's Department. Other authorities have turned to industry for help and experience. The post in itself will form a powerful training medium in general management for the man appointed and this fact has possibilities in the form of seconding a series of key officers to this post for a period specifically to supplement their own training.

JOB REVIEW

A pre-requisite of any system such as management by objectives is a review procedure. This takes place after about six months from the operation of the first Job Improvement Plans. There is nothing magic about six months—in practice this is a convenient period and may be varied either way. The review comprises a discussion between the subordinate and superior with the management advisor in attendance and possibly the Chief Officer at a sample of interviews. The results or standards of performance set in the plan are discussed in relation to the control information. If the results set have been achieved the question of whether the standard should be set higher is discussed. If the results have not been achieved there is no recrimination or blame—rather it is used as an opportunity to find out why. In many cases, particularly at the first review cycle, it will result from an over estimate on the part of the individual as to what was a realistic target for him to achieve. There is a tendency always to over stretch. The approach, having discovered shortfalls in performance, is jointly to decide on remedial action.

The review stage is not only directed at the subordinate from superior level. It will be remembered that at the analysis stage, and subsequently in the Job Improvement Plan, action of varying kinds was agreed by the superior himself. In other words, to assist the subordinates in the achievement of his performance standards, the superior undertook certain supportive action. The review period examines his performance in respect of these.

Out of the discussion at the review stage will emerge

(*a*) A revised set of results or standards of performance, some of which will remain, some stepped up, some revised downwards or even eliminated. In the first review period and maybe at subsequent reviews the key tasks themselves may be seen to be ill-defined and they will be re-formulated.

(*b*) Action to be taken in the next period to improve performance or assist improvement by
  (i) the individual officer;
  (ii) the superior;
  (iii) a higher level.

(*c*) Some indication of appropriate training if this is necessary—e.g. report writing, project control, or perhaps some specialist technique related to the post in question.

From these results the revised job improvement will be compiled and the cycle repeated.

DEPARTMENTAL IMPROVEMENT PLAN

It should be clear now how each officer's key tasks are closely integrated with those of his peers, his superiors and his subordinates and how these combine together to achieve the department's objectives. During the whole of this process will have emerged a range of items which seem to require action at a fairly high level, perhaps for the Chief Officer himself or maybe a committee or even the Council. Any Chief Officer who is anxious to keep his department's performance will show close interest in these trouble-spots. These are the items which have been identified by his staff as impeding the work of the department. Some the Chief Officer will already know about, perhaps not in detail, but there will be a large number about which he is totally ignorant. Some will come as a shock. His reaction is extremely important. Many Chief Officers will instinctively blame the management by objectives system, others will try to rationalise the trouble and will choose to ignore what they have been told. The Chief Officer who regards it as important new information bearing heavily on the efficiency or effectiveness of his department will look at it critically. It should prompt in him questions which he will ask and will then result in his agreeing to take action on some of the points if not all of them. He will discuss this with the management advisor and out of these discussions will be produced the Departmental Improvement Plan. It will relate closely to the separate job improvement plans and will similarly have results to be achieved attached to it. Moreover it will also be subject to review.

Some management by objectives exercises begin with a Departmental Improvement Plan or at least begin by looking at objectives of the department and sections of it which results in this list of topics being put to the Departmental head. It is the way some parts of the Greater London Council have operated. Its attraction is that in the first instance it does not focus on individuals but on groups or sections and insofar as it is impersonal it perhaps is more likely to command support and attention. On the other hand it can be seen as a way of avoiding the issue of the individual in his job which sooner or later has to be faced.

IMPLEMENTATION AND ITS PROBLEMS

At first thought it is tempting to write an instruction manual as to how to go about implementing management by objectives but this would clearly be a waste of time. There are no 'off-the-peg' answers. What is useful, however, is to be aware of the many pitfalls and to understand some of the disadvantages and dangers.

The most obvious danger, and despite this the most commonly experienced one, is when the staff involved do not know what is happening, when they have no basis for understanding the system. Particularly for an approach like management by objectives, which has at its centre a strong participative element, it is vital that the staff know what it is all about. There are a variety of ways of doing this—films, lectures, case study exercises and so on. Whatever method is chosen all too often the explanation is too slick, too glib. It is presented as magic when it is not—the weaknesses are understressed and expectations are raised too high or the converse is the case, that resistance is high. A frank exposure of the difficulties likely to be encountered as well as the bald explanation of the system and its merits is much more useful to intelligent people than the 'hard sell'.

One of the most difficult aspects to explain, to justify and subsequently use is, not surprisingly, the measurement of performance. Performance standards will cause trouble not only because they *are* troublesome and difficult to establish but because some officers will stubbornly insist that their job does not lend itself to measurement. The warning to the management by objectives addict is that they are probably right. Advocators of management by objectives who press hard for precise, numerical measurement are probably doing a good deal of harm. We can only stress again here that a performance standard or a combination of standards, in whatever form, precise or a vague indicator, which enables an officer to judge his performance againt his key tasks is a good one. This is one of the aspects which are most usefully stressed in the very early stages.

Because management by objectives relies on participation, on critical self-examination, on appraisal by working associates and on a free exchange, a large part of the staff must be committed to it and especially at the top. The potential strains here are enormous. There are possible strains associated with the role of the management advisor if one is involved, especially at the point of the superior/subordinate relationship.

It is at this point too that another danger may be present. The whole system is participative and 'democratic' but at the same time, of course, it throws into stark relief the hierarchical nature of the organisation.

There are many situations, certainly in local government, where, although a formal hierarchy exists, it is rarely at the forefront in the working situation. For example, in many architects' departments or in the social work field, in some planning offices, the *group* is the significant unit and to impose or make persistently explicit the underlying formal hierarchy may be a disadvantage. Here the system needs to be modified and attention perhaps focussed on the group rather than the individual.

It is so easy to become obsessed by the system itself that it escapes our notice that what we have done is no more than introduce a sledgehammer to crack a nut (and sledgehammers don't even do that very well!) Clearly the degree of sophistication, the effort and resources devoted to it must bear a sensible relationship to the likely results to be achieved. The people to consult about management by objectives are the consumers not the ardent advocates. The system can so easily become the cuckoo in the nest. For example, it is quite easy to generate a form-filling-in procedure which is time-consuming and counter-productive in that the officers filling them in may become blasé, derisive or even bent on sabotage. The amount of control information and form-filling should be kept to a minimum. The system should ideally be set up to encourage the individual himself to want information for him to judge his own performance and to want to discuss it with his superior. Seen in this light, the system is much more likely to be a success but again, success can only be judged insofar as those involved see it has been helpful to them. If they do not, then it needs looking at afresh.

SOME ADVANTAGES OF MANAGEMENT BY OBJECTIVES

We have mostly stressed the dangers, pitfalls and disadvantages so far; it is perhaps time now to look at where the benefits lie in management by objectives.

"Management by objectives . . . substitutes for control from outside the stricter, more exacting and more effective control from the inside. It motivates the manager to action not because somebody tells him to do something or talks him into doing it, but because the objective needs of his task demand it. He acts not because somebody wants him to but because he himself decides that he has to—he acts, in other words, as a free man."(10.2)

This is the strength of management by objectives and from it flow a series of other benefits.

(*a*) It clearly concentrates an officer's attention systematically on his important tasks and thus forces him away from the unimportant, the trivial, perhaps those jobs which he enjoys doing which he has brought with him from his previous post. As a corollary it almost inevitably improves delegation to his subordinates or it may result in the discontinuance of some practices either because they are no longer relevant and necessary or because better ways can be envisaged of achieving the same end.

(*b*) The system focusses attention and often forces action on problem areas which previously may not have been known of at the level where action can be taken. Where action is not taken, explanation and justification is called for.

(*c*) It leads to *relevant* training through the identification of areas of weakness in the officers' performance. Where training cannot help it perhaps points up the need to transfer an officer to another post where his skills are more closely related to the tasks involved.

(*d*) It highlights wasted talent and forms an essential key to promotion by results *over a period of time*. Too often promotion is based on an isolated piece of 'good performance' at the right time rather than a consistently good standard over a period. There is a point here. Some schemes of management by objectives are linked to payment by results. Quite apart from the difficulties of application in the public sector, the question is worth raising as to whether such a link would be counter-productive. With a wide range of performance standards, some more readily measured than others, there is ground for doubting whether payment by results could really be operated equitably and with no ill-effects on the more fundemental advantages of the system.

SELF APPRAISAL

It will be self-evident that a full management by objectives system is likely to be difficult to implement satisfactorily. It has to face all the problems of change. A useful break-in point is self appraisal. Even if self appraisal is not followed by a variant of management by objectives it has obvious advantages in itself. The view is that the most valuable approach to establish a learning organisation is to secure that it comprises learning individuals.

Figure 10.1 advances an outline of a Chief Officer's key tasks and some examples of possible appraisal indicators. Whether the Chief Officer is an engineer or a social services director will not substantially change the nature of the key tasks except possibly task 5. Many of the indicators (and the list is incomplete) are vague and could not be taken in isolation as a reliable guide to performance. It is the *combination* of indicators which gives the clue to a deteriorating or improving performance. More important than the imprecision of the indicators shown, however, is the way in which self appraisal is approached by the officer himself. We have all at some time or another completed one of those questionnaires in the Sunday newspapers on 'How successful are you as a husband?' or 'Are you a high-flyer?' and perhaps we have cheated. Self appraisal can be approached in this way. The individual can delude himself. He can approach self appraisal in this way in which case he is probably wasting his time. None of us of course can be completely objective. Delusion is not necessarily concious. The belief however is that if an officer (in this case a Chief Officer) uses this set of key tasks and performance indicators as a *framework for reflection* and reflects honestly then he is genuinely learning. Of course he may rationalise, he may fail to take remedial steps, he may lay blame anywhere but on himself. This of course he should try to avoid, but even if he does not he is a step ahead of the man who *never* reflects on his own performance in a critical way. The object is to spark off self criticism and the desire to seek self improvement.

Taking one key task, relationships with councillors, this is clearly a very important area, most would argue the most important key task of any Chief Officer. If he fails or performs badly here he is not likely to perform well in the other areas. The first point to be noted is the key task definition, which comprises two elements. 'Informing' members implies building a base of understanding in members of the nature and problems of the particular service or problem area. This then relates to the way members respond. Members do not have to agree but the nature of their response can give a Chief Officer an indication of whether he and his staff are approaching members in the right way. The note 'integrity' is important and is an element which can probably only be assessed by the individual himself. Clearly it is relatively easy for an officer to tell members what they want to hear—some Chief Officers do it frequently. It is for example, quite a common occurrence for young professional men to despair at their chief's lack of integrity when he appears not to have stood up to members. The young professional men are not necessarily correct of course—politics is a difficult game, but undoubtedly they are not always wrong. A Chief Officer can usefully reflect upon his own integrity in this respect.

A general point about performance indicators is that many of them will not reveal much in themselves over one period of time. Much more revealing are changing patterns of performance. How does performance seem on reflection, to be different in a particular area than from what it was a year ago? Do staff relations seem to be the same, better, or worse than before? Why is this? Can it be traced to a particular source? A whole series of questions will spring into focus once a framework for reflection like the one presented here is used.

REFERENCES

10.1 PETER DRUCKER, *The Practice of Management*, Pan Books, 1968.
10.2 *op. cit.*

Epilogue

Caminante, no hay camino;
se hace camino al andar

Antonio Machado.
"Proverbios y Cantares"*

(To the walker there is no pathway
save the one he creates for himself)

* I am indebted to Sr Javier Canelles for drawing my attention to this collection.

Index